With all
our love to
Daddy
"Happy Valentine
Day"
2-14-74
Shirley, Tommy & Eric

HORSES
IN
AMERICA

(Courtesy, The New-York Historical Society, New York City)

HORSES IN AMERICA

Francis Haines

ILLUSTRATED

Thomas Y. Crowell Company

NEW YORK

ESTABLISHED 1834

Manufactured in the United States of America

L.C. Card 74–139096
ISBN 0–690–40253–8

1 2 3 4 5 6 7 8 9 10

To Plesah

Contents

The cowboy became an American legend in the space of twenty-five years, from the end of the Civil War to the closing of the range by barbed wire. Here, cow horses graze in foreground; cattle in background. (Huffman Pictures, Miles City, Montana)

1

The Horse in American History

MOST FAMOUS IN OUR Western annals and Indian traditions is that of the White Steed of the Prairies; a magnificent milk-white charger, large-eyed, small-headed, bluff-chested, and with the dignity of a thousand monarchs in his lofty, over-scorning carriage. He was the elected Xerxes of vast herds of wild horses, whose pastures in those days were only fenced by the Rocky Mountains and the Alleghenies. At their flaming head he westward trooped it like the chosen star which each evening leads on the hosts of light. The flashing cascade of his mane, the curving comet of his tail, invested him with housings more resplendent than gold- and silver-beaters could have furnished him. A most imperial and archangelical apparition of that unfallen, western world, which to the eyes of the old trappers and hunters revived the glories of . . . primeval times. . . . Whether marching amid his aides and marshals in the van of countless cohorts that endlessly streamed over the plain, like an Ohio; or whether with his subjects browsing all around the horizon, the White Steed gallopingly reviewed them with warm nostrils reddening through his cool milkiness; in whatever aspect he presented himself, always to the bravest Indians he was the object of trembling reverence and awe.

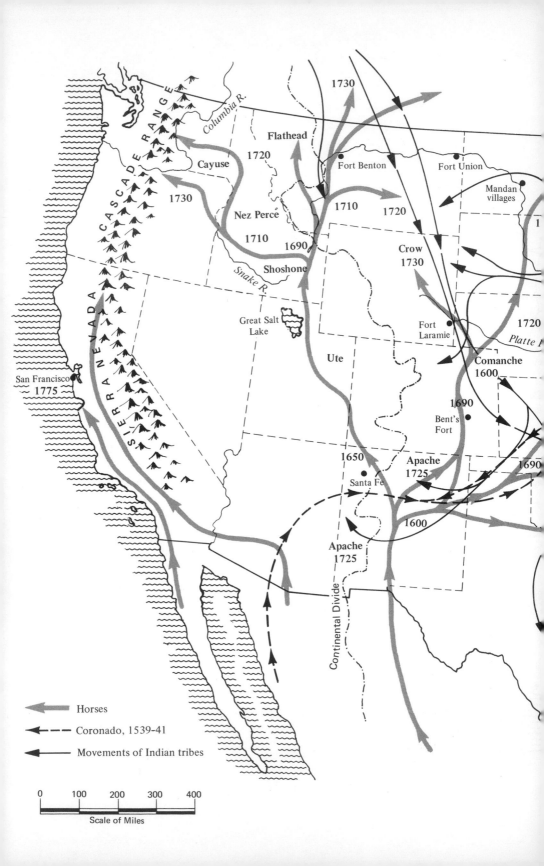

1730

Flathead

Cayuse

1720

Fort Benton

Fort Union

Mandan villages

1

Nez Percé

1710

1730

1710

1720

Shoshone

1690

Crow
1730

Great Salt
Lake

Fort
Laramie

1720

Platte R.

Ute

Comanche
1600

San Francisco
1775

1690

Bent's
Fort

1650

Apache
1725

Santa Fe

1690

1600

Apache
1725

Continental Divide

Horses

Coronado, 1539–41

Movements of Indian tribes

0   100   200   300   400

Scale of Miles

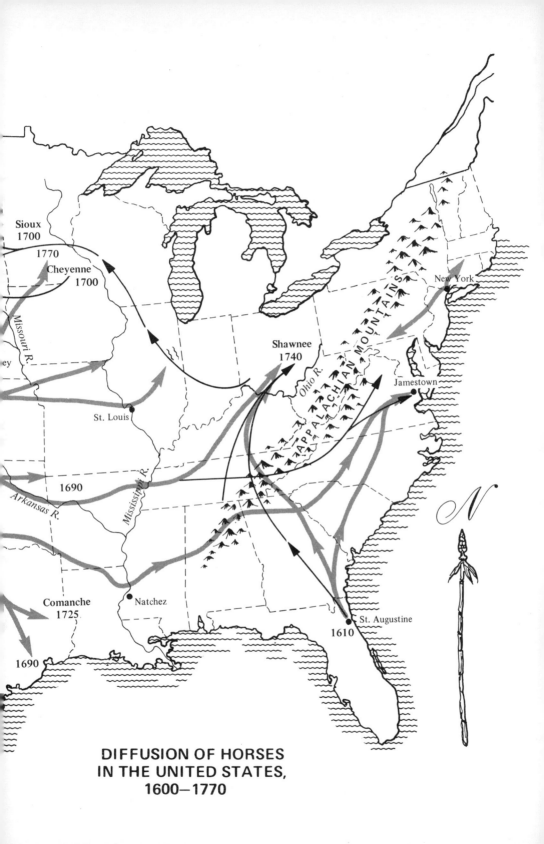

Sioux
1700

1770

Cheyenne
1700

Missouri R.

ey

St. Louis

1690

Arkansas R.

Mississippi R.

Comanche
1725

Natchez

1690

Shawnee
1740

Ohio R.

APPALACHIAN MOUNTAINS

New York

Jamestown

St. Augustine
1610

N

**DIFFUSION OF HORSES
IN THE UNITED STATES,
1600–1770**

Thus Herman Melville, in *Moby Dick*, describes some of the mystical aura surrounding the horses of the West in the middle of the nineteenth century, although he himself had never seen the White Steed, nor had he even talked with men from the western plains who had reported such sightings. He was describing how the White Steed had captured the imagination of the American people of that period. Josiah Gregg, in his *Commerce of the Prairies*, his Journal for 1820–1840, supplies the following details that he secured firsthand from hunters on the plains.

The beauty of the mustang is proverbial, one in particular has been celebrated by hunters of which marvelous stories are told. He has been represented as a medium-sized stallion of perfect symmetry, milk white—save a pair of black ears—a natural "pacer." But I infer this story is somewhat mythical from the difficulty one finds in fixing the abiding place of this equine hero. He is familiarly known by common report, all over the great prairies. The trapper celebrates him in the vicinity of the Rocky Mountains; the hunter on the Arkansas, or in the midst of the plains, while others have him pacing at the rate of half a mile a minute on the borders of Texas. It is hardly surprising that a creature of such ubiquitary existence should never have been caught.

The Plains Indians had similar legends, tinged with deep superstition. The Kiowas felt that arrows or rifle balls could not touch the Phantom Mustang and that he could run unscathed through a prairie fire. The Blackfeet believed that he was "big medicine," and could, if he chose, breed war-horses that rendered their riders invulnerable in battle.

The White Steed of the Prairies is the great American contribution to the wonder horses of myth and legend that have enthralled the thoughts of men through the centuries. No other animal has ever attained the lofty heights held by these noble, spirited steeds.

The Golden Horses of the Sun, dashing across the sky each day with Apollo's chariot, are followed closely in the old legends by Pegasus, the snow-white winged horse whose flights through the clouds were the inspiration of poets. Of lesser rank, but still above the mundane flesh-and-blood animals, are the spotted war-horse Rakush, ridden by Persia's legendary hero Rustem, and Bucephalus, the great black war-horse of Alexander the Great.

[4]

Below these exalted ones come the herds of actual horses, but endowed by men with spiritual attributes, such as the sacred horses of Persia, cherished by King Xerxes, and the heavenly horses of Emperor Wu Ti of China.

Ever since the first bands of mounted nomads swept down from the Iranian Plateau some four thousand years ago to dominate the Fertile Crescent, the wild horsemen from beyond the farming frontiers have been held in high regard by the earthbound, plodding farmer folk. In America the dashing, colorful horsemen have been the Spanish conquerors of Mexico and the Southwest, and their northern neighbors, the spectacular mounted Indians of the Great Plains. After them came the cowboys who handled the range horses and the vast herds of cattle throughout the West. All these groups are now viewed through a romantic haze in songs and stories, movie and televison westerns.

But there is another important phase of horse culture, which for centuries has been epitomized by the sturdy plowman guiding a span of strong, heavy horses in the essential task of feeding mankind. While the draft horses have been largely neglected in myth and legend, they are powerful animals that furnished much of the muscle power for America's work until well into the twentieth century, entering into most phases of economic development. The draft breeds dominated the country east of the Mississippi almost as strongly as the riding horses did the American West. In both the East and the West, horses came in with the first settlers and aided materially in every stage of development of the new lands. Their contribution is worthy of attention and their importance is better understood if their dual roles—that of carrying man to adventure and that of doing much of the country's work by muscle power—are kept in mind.

Our modern horses of all kinds are descended from a small, four-toed, grass eater, *Eohippus*, whose earliest remains have been found in the strata of the Eocene period, laid down some sixty million years ago or more. In North America during the next fifty million years or so, *Eohippus* evolved into the present *Equus caballus*, which occupied the pasture lands just east of the Rocky Mountains in large numbers. This species was finally entirely destroyed by some unknown combination of factors, the last of the species in North America dying about 7000 B.C., and the continent was without horses of any kind until the Spanish brought in their domesticated animals by way of the West Indies, landing their first horses on the mainland in 1519.

[5]

A few million years ago some of the ancestors of *Equus caballus* had moved from North America across the land bridge into Siberia and then spread through the grasslands westward through Europe to the Atlantic. Somewhere along the way they evolved into two distinct types, still closely related. One was a small, rangy animal, which today is represented by the light riding horse. The other had heavier bones and was larger and stockier. Today it is represented by the draft horse, but both types have been crossbred so extensively that neither can be considered a pure type.

In the black-earth belt of southern Russia about 4000 B.C. men domesticated horses in small numbers, at first using them only for sacrificial ceremonies. Later they harnessed the horses to small carts, and then learned how to ride the animals. About the time the first mounted men were reported in southern Russia, mounted nomads were moving south from the Asian steppes, which indicates that perhaps the development of riding occurred in two widely separated places at about the same period.

About 2000 B.C. nomadic tribesmen from the Asian steppes crossed the Iranian Plateau on their horses and overran the entire Near East. In a thousand years they had occupied North Africa to the Straits of Gibraltar, while another prong of the movement went west through Europe and spread horse culture as far as Scandinavia, the British Isles, France, and Spain.

After the Roman Empire had been overrun by the barbarian horses, the warriors of Germany and France developed large, heavy horses to carry their armored knights into battle, while in Spain the preferred war-horse was the light, agile type. Hence when colonization began in the New World, the Spanish filled their new holdings with the light riding horses so well suited to their pattern of stock raising that had been developed on the Spanish Plateau and could be used with only minor changes on the open ranges of Mexico and the Southwest.

In a comparatively short time Indians from the buffalo-hunting tribes had learned from the Spanish how to train and ride horses. They also adopted the highly developed Spanish horse gear. Once mounted, several of the Plains tribes became true nomads, following the buffalo herds the year around, while other tribes became seminomadic, retaining their villages for winter quarters while living among the buffalo herds during the summer and fall. With the horse as a servant, the tribes prospered and increased in numbers. They used their new leisure time to develop the colorful culture that soon covered the plains and went even beyond. At the same time, the changes in material culture produced significant social changes within the tribes.

While the Spanish settlers were heavily dependent on the horse from the first, the English, French, and Dutch colonies along the Atlantic seaboard followed a somewhat different pattern that stressed the raising of cattle in small herds—the cows to supply milk and butter, the oxen for draft teams. Once the colonies became firmly established, horses were increasingly important and gradually replaced most of the oxen in transportation, and later, in farm work. Horses were not only more versatile than oxen but had a greater advantage—their superior speed at a walk. Since draft horses were needed to take over the work of the oxen, the heavy breeds of northern Europe were favored over the lighter Spanish type, although the seaboard colonies used many of the light riding horses for both riding and racing.

The draft horses continued as an important factor in the development of America until World War I. The horse was the prime small-power unit for all tasks. On land all transportation depended principally on the horse, not only for the movement of farm crops, but also for the many hauling chores in every town and city, and for interurban travel.

While the importance of the draft horse on the American farm is common knowledge, the large number of horses needed in even a small town comes as a surprise to people born in the age of the gasoline motor. Not only did the draft teams crowd the city streets with the large vans and drays they hauled, but they required barns, stables, and wagon lots for their off-duty hours, and these filled many blocks in the congested areas.

In the West, when the explorers, trappers, and traders reached the open plains, they needed a large supply of horses to carry themselves and their goods across the wide spaces. They were soon followed by settlers of all kinds seeking farmlands on the west coast or the mineral riches in the mountains. This whole westward movement was aided and accelerated by the presence on the plains of many thousands of extra horses owned by several tribes and readily available, usually at a reasonable price. Horses were particularly valuable for transportation throughout the West because the entire area was almost devoid of streams suitable for navigation.

With horses being raised in large numbers in northern Mexico, horse thieves became common. While Indian tribes were constantly trying to steal horses from their neighbors, the important thefts were from the settlements in southern Texas, Chihuahua, and California, where a single raid might net several thousand head in a few days. At first these raids were confined to Indian thieves, but after a time adventurers from the pioneer settlements in the Ohio Valley joined in for fun and profit. In the latter part of the nineteenth century horse rustlers on the western ranges received a great deal of publicity, but their best efforts were rather puny compared to those of the raiders of half a century earlier.

The English gentry who were early settlers in Virginia and the Carolinas brought with them a high regard for fine riding horses and enjoyed horse racing, usually for short distances. In the more puritanical northern colonies running-races were considered sinful, but in time harness racing was permissible. By the close of the Civil War the southern people, especially in Kentucky, had developed Thoroughbreds from imported stock for their racetracks, while in the north both trotters and pacers vied in harness races at all fairs and celebrations, which also featured matched teams of huge, beautiful draft horses in pulling contests. A large number of blooded horses of racing stock, but not quite good enough for the racetrack, were used to upgrade the horses being raised for the cavalry and as the pleasure horses of the upper classes, who liked polo ponies, stylish riding horses, and harness horses for pulling light rigs such as buggies, surreys, and carts. Wild West shows used many riding horses, while the circuses needed horses both for riding and for the important task of hauling the large wagons in the parades, and to and from the train sidings.

This post–Civil War period also marked the movement into the western range country of horses, cattle, and sheep. The ranchers moved in as fast as the extermination of the buffalo and the removal of the Indians permitted. The growing cities of the East and of Europe furnished a ready market for all the beef cattle the ranchers could produce. Handling of the herds on the open range required skilled riders and produced the colorful cowboys and their trained cow horses. Most of the other westerners, except in a few towns and cities, did their errands and made their friendly calls on horseback, a type of transportation more suited to the greater distances and fewer roads than the buggies and surreys of the East. The roundups, rodeos, and Pioneer Day shows of the West built up the cowboy as a romantic figure in the eyes of the eastern tourists.

[8]

The rapid improvement of steam locomotives and steam tractors had little effect on the use of draft horses. The locomotives were confined to distance hauling that increased rapidly as the population increased, but the draft teams still had a monopoly on farm work and on short hauls of all kinds. The internal-combustion engine, developed in the 1890's, soon became a serious competitor of the horse in many fields. The motor, applied first to autos, then to trucks and tractors, soon proved that for hauling jobs of all kinds the motorized vehicle was superior to the horse-drawn one in two important respects. The new vehicles required less room on the streets and in the parking lots, and needed a mineral fuel instead of grain that could be used to feed people.

The demands of World War I inspired a rapid improvement in gasoline motors as their many military uses soon became apparent. At the same time, European demands for food grains made it imperative that all possible grains be shipped to the starving millions in the war-torn countries. Consequently, there was a rapid displacement of horses by motors, especially in the urban areas. Then the use of motors spread to the farms, and in twenty years there were comparatively few draft horses left even in agriculture.

While the number of draft horses has steadily declined in America over the last sixty years, there has been a marked increase in the number of pleasure horses since World War II—most of them saddle horses with western equipment. Such horses have always been considered luxury items except on a stock ranch, but in recent years more people have been able to afford them, and they like the social prestige that goes with owning and riding a fine saddle horse. The strong influence of the western shows in the movies and on television has helped build up the romantic aura surrounding the western riding horse, making this animal especially appealing to teen-age girls. The desire for a horse that will look well in parades and shows has increased the demand for well-bred, registered horses of all the light riding horse breeds. In the light of this trend it would seem that at this time the number of horses in America will not increase very rapidly, but there will continue to be a marked increase in the average quality of the horses.

Above, a model of Eohippus, *which lived in North America some sixty million years ago. It is the oldest known ancestor of* Equus caballus, *the true horse, seen below in a Cro-Magnon portrayal, drawn some twenty thousand years ago in the Cavern of Font-de-Gaume, Dordogne, France.* (Courtesy, American Museum of Natural History)

2

Eohippus *and His Progeny* Encircle *the Globe*

LITTLE *Eohippus*, LITERALLY THE DAWN HORSE, lived in North America about sixty million years ago. This small creature, about the size of a fox terrier, is the oldest known ancestor of the modern horse, and the chain of descent from the Eocene mammal to the emergence of *Equus caballus* about six million years ago can be traced through fossil remains with only a few minor gaps in the sequence of its development.

The *Eohippus* that scampered through the shrubbery and underbrush of Nebraska in those early days, feeding on leaves and fronds, had a head like a sheep, large hindquarters like a jackrabbit, and multiple toes —four on each forefoot and three on each hind foot, and all fourteen toes equipped with pads of heavy cuticle shaped like miniature hooves. *Eohippus* was prolific and spread over the Northern Hemisphere through Asia and Europe to the British Isles, where it was known as *Hyracotherium* because in some respects it resembled a hare.

On the western plains of America over a period of about thirty million years, descendants of *Eohippus* evolved through several stages into the genus *Mesohippus*, a larger animal. The height increased to twenty-four inches, the head became more horselike, and the legs lengthened, increasing its speed. By this time each foot had three hooved, padded toes. The teeth were still short, low-crowned, and comparatively soft, adequate for a diet of leaves, new bark, and tubers, but still unsuitable for grazing.

Another twenty million years produced great geologic upheavals in the western mountains, which in turn made many changes in the climate and ecology of the plains to the east. Lush forests became open plains covered with grass, which presented new problems to *Mesohippus*. The silica in the stems and seeds of the grass and the small amounts of sand and dirt taken into the mouth while grazing caused rapid wear on the soft teeth, forcing a rapid adaptation to the new conditions if the progeny of *Mesohippus* were to survive. Under this environmental pressure *Mesohippus* evolved into *Merychippus*, which had high-crowned teeth covered with a much harder outer layer. This new animal was larger, too —about forty-two inches high, the size of a small pony of today.

After *Merychippus* spread over all the pastures of the Northern Hemisphere, there is a gap in the fossil records, from about six million years ago to about 600,000 B.C. No fossils of the evolving horse have been found in North America for this Pleistocene epoch, the Great Ice Age, that covered much of North America and northern Europe with huge glaciers. When these ice masses melted away, the resulting floods washed away the surface deposits that would have contained the fossil remains of any horses for the earlier period. Some paleontologists think the absence of the horse fossils indicates the absence of horses, while others still expect to find some of the fossil remains by further digging.

During this period of very scanty records—and those only in Eurasia —*Merychippus* evolved into *Equus caballus*, the true horse, with a single toe on each foot and that one equipped with a well-developed hoof. The two side toes still show faintly as vestigial remains in the fetlock.

During the entire Ice Age a wide land bridge connected Alaska and Siberia, furnishing an easy passage from one continent to the other for many animal species. Hence it is quite possible that *Equus caballus* evolved in Asia from some of the *Merychippus* stock that had crossed over from North America. Then some changes in conditions, which are not yet understood, brought a large number of the new horses back to the American West about 600,000 B.C., where they throve and multiplied until they had spread over a wide area. Their fossil remains are now found in many different places and have been dated from about 600,000 B.C. down to about 7000 B.C. About 25,000 B.C. the last ice sheet began melting, and by 15,000 B.C. it was gone, leaving large new pastures. At the same time the ice in northern Europe melted away, providing more pastures there. The wild horses occupied all these new grasslands.

Equus caballus was about fourteen hands high at the withers—the top of his shoulders—and weighed seven to eight hundred pounds when full-grown. Horsemen the world over liked to measure their horses' heights in hands, a measure that was used for centuries before inches were invented and one that has universal acceptance. Each hand is now set at four inches in the English-speaking world. *Equus caballus*, at fourteen hands, was right on the dividing line that now separates the horse from the pony, but ponies under twelve hands are frequently measured in inches.

While *Equus caballus* came with some color variations, according to the cave paintings in color of specimens in central France, the common pattern for wild horses was probably that which the western stockmen commonly call a line-back buckskin—dun colored with a heavy black dorsal stripe, black mane and tail, black muzzle, and legs black below the knees and hocks, with black hooves.

In the limestone formations of the Massif Central in France are many caverns carved out of the solid rock by the ground water. There Cro-Magnon hunters used the shallow caves for living quarters, while deep in the winding caverns their medicine men painted what were probably considered magic pictures of the game animals the hunters pursued. They hoped the magic would help bring the animals in plentiful numbers into the ambush of waiting hunters, or it would help the animals produce many offspring for future hunts. In order for the magic to be effective they believed the pictures had to be good likenesses of the living animals. These pictures in vivid colors that have not faded through the intervening centuries give the only eyewitness depictions of the wild horses of that period, about 18,000 B.C. as indicated by carbon 14 dating. The horses in the cave paintings are dark red with black points, or light colored and covered with dark spots. All of these horses resemble the modern light saddle horse type.

Over the last six thousand years since the horse has been domesticated, man has done so much selective breeding and crossbreeding that we can only speculate on the probable appearance of the first horses to be tamed, although from the skeletal remains we know a great deal about their general size and shape.

The melting of the ice sheet about fifteen thousand years ago changed the climate of North America and exposed a large expanse of land that was soon covered with grasses. The Southwest and northern Mexico became more arid, drastically reducing the pastures of those regions, but more new pasture was added in the plains than was lost to the desert. Conditions appeared to be better for grazing animals than before, but several species of large grass eaters vanished from North America in a comparatively short time in spite of the better food supply. Among the lost species was the horse, whose numbers diminished steadily until they were all gone, the latest fossil remains being carbon-dated at about 7000 B.C.

Several theories have been advanced to account for this selective destruction of the horses and mammoths, but none of them has won much acceptance. One theory is that a form of plague hit the animals. Another theory as to their disappearance is connected with the arrival of migrant hunters from Asia. Since the rapid decline of the vanished species occurred during the period these hunters reached the North American plains, and since the rate of decline seemed to keep pace with the increase in numbers of the hunting bands, some scholars feel that there must be some direct connection between the two, but the use of fire by a few dozen bands of hunters scattered over the great expanse of the plains does not seem adequate to explain the extinction of selected species while other large grass eaters prospered, multiplied, and extended their ranges.

While the melting of the ice sheet in Europe brought a corresponding increase in the grasslands there, it brought no destruction of species to match that on the western plains of North America. As Europe warmed, the forests encroached on the grasslands, forcing the grazing herds to move eastward onto the vast steppes of southern Russia and western Asia. Tribes of Paleolithic hunters followed the herds and established themselves in small villages along the woodland fringes, where they had shelter and fuel and were close to the hunting grounds. In time they became seminomadic, following the herds across the rolling steppes in summer and retiring to their wattle-and-daub huts in winter. They had hunting dogs, and by about 5000 B.C. had domesticated the reindeer and the onager, a small wild ass.

A large invasion of Indo-Europeans from the southeast then took over the whole region and the reindeer herds. Soon they had tamed a few horses, which at first they used only for religious purposes. These invaders are known as the Red Earth people, from their custom of coating the bodies of their dead with red ocher before placing them in crypts in huge mounds of earth now called kurgans.

The Red Earth people had some trade connections with the people of the Near East through the Black Sea and the Straits linking it to the Mediterranean. In the Fertile Crescent they found that the people had domesticated sheep, goats, cattle, and onagers. They used wheeled carts and wagons drawn by oxen and onagers. The Red Earth people borrowed all these innovations for their own use and trained a few of their horses to pull carts. This occurred about 4000 B.C.

The horse-drawn carts were a special feature of the great midsummer festival procession that moved from the village to the sacred grove for the ceremonies. Both horses and carts were decorated with garlands, and the carts were piled high with offerings. At the altar the offerings were unloaded and the horses unhitched and sacrificed, and everyone sat down to a feast that included a large part of the offerings and probably the horse meat. The carts and the rest of the offerings were burned before the altar.

After horses became more common they were used as draft animals throughout the year. Some of the carts for daily use were covered with light shelters, converting them into portable sleeping quarters at least as comfortable as the wattle-and-daub huts. For many of the bands the next step was to become truly nomadic, traveling in search of game and moving camp each day or two to secure clean campsites and fresh grass for the horses.

To handle a large horse herd in open country and to have the draft teams ready each morning as they were needed, a few mounted men were a necessity. This pattern of nomadism, dependent on using the horses each day, required mounted men to insure smooth functioning, as is evident from the combined experience of stockmen the world over. Only mounted men could keep the herds from straying and could bring the animals into camp when the teams were needed. The riders also had to control the many spare horses, mares with young foals and the half-grown colts as the band moved about the plains. These nomads on horseback were such a novel sight to the Greek traders to the Black Sea region that at first they were believed to be some strange new animal—half man, half horse—that the Greeks called centaurs.

The caravans of carts spread out toward the east across the steppes and in time some of them reached the foothills of the Asian mountain ranges.

There the native people rapidly adopted horses as servants, but in that hilly country found them more useful as mounts and pack animals than as draft animals. Whereas the larger, heavy-boned, long-legged Red Earth people had some difficulty in riding their small horses, the short, small-boned hill people—tough, wiry, and short-legged—soon became expert horsemen. Whole villages learned to ride and became mounted nomads, using only a few carts for baggage in open country. The whole life of the band centered around the horse herd that furnished mounts, pack animals, extra animals for trade, and a few to eat in times of need. Milk from the mares became a staple article of diet.

This type of horse culture spread north and east into Mongolia, turning hundreds of thousands of people into nomads. Then, over the centuries, came wave after wave of population increase among the nomads, and hordes of them moved out into the adjacent lands to conquer and hold vast areas, taking their horses along to stock any grasslands they could find.

Early accounts of the invasions by the nomadic horsemen into the settled valleys of the Near East are rather vague, having been written by men far from the scene, but it is evident that the first wave poured down from the Iranian Plateau into the fertile lowlands of Mesopotamia about 2000 B.C. In the next century other bands followed in sufficient numbers to establish a firm foothold. These fierce, tough fighters had little difficulty in overrunning the country, easily evading any large force sent against them, then turning and chopping up any small detachments of foot soldiers they could find as the army disbanded.

The invaders soon introduced a potent new weapon, the light war chariot with spoked wheels. Just where and when it was first used is not clear, but the invaders from the northeast used it extensively and might have borrowed it from India. The light chariot was much superior to the lowland carts with solid wheels. A span of horses could pull the chariot with a driver and a warrior across the flatlands at a gallop, thus giving the attackers great mobility and increasing the effectiveness of surprise attacks. By about 1600 B.C. the Mitanni in Syria, with the effective use of the chariots, had taken over a large area and had established a strong kingdom. With their chariots, horses, and improved tactics they dominated the entire region for about two centuries.

An earlier tribe of invaders who had entered Anatolia from the northeast had set up the Hittite kingdom there. Their respect for the Mitanni horses, chariots, and tactics was plainly shown when the Hittite king hired an expert Mitanni horseman, Kikkuli, to set up a training program for his war-horses that were to be used with chariots. The entire program was to be written down and copies were to be made for the Hittite men in charge of horse training. Kikkuli's program covered a period of 180 days for each group of horses and was designed to accustom the horses to go to work at any hour of the day or night, and to go for days on scanty rations of forage and water. The remarkable book outlining this program, the earliest known work devoted entirely to horses and horse training, has been recovered intact on clay tablets from the Hittite royal archives. It begins, "Thus speaks Kikkuli, the horse trainer from the land of the Mitanni. . . ."

While the Mitanni and Hittites were setting up their kingdoms, another large band of horsemen with war chariots overran Palestine and Egypt. They were the Hyksos, who brought the first horses into Africa just prior to 1700 B.C. A century or two later a seafaring people shipped some horses across the Mediterranean to Libya. The early presence of these horses west of Egypt has led some writers into the erroneous assumption that horses were indigenous to North Africa.

From the initial stock of horses in Egypt and Libya all the country west to the Atlantic coast secured horses by 1000 B.C. In Algeria and Morocco the natives preferred riding to war on horseback rather than in chariots. They trained their horses to work without bridles of any kind. Each rider guided his mount by tapping it on the neck or shoulder with a small stick. These horses attracted the attention of the Roman writers of the period, for they carried their heads much lower than those continually checked by bit and rein. They were docile and easily managed, but spirited and brave in battle. The North African horsemen, particularly the Numidians and Moors, used men on horseback in battle in preference to either foot soldiers or war chariots. In one battle the Numidians had eighty thousand cavalry in action against the Roman legions.

As the use of horses increased throughout the Near East and the Mediterranean world, horse raisers in various places tried to produce special types of animals for specific purposes. Frequently they imported stallions from other areas to aid in the breeding programs. The heavier, stockier horses from the steppes, such as are shown in early Persian carvings, were used to raise larger animals suitable for carrying an armored soldier into battle. The Persians also improved the saddle cloths, held in place by a cinch and a martingale, to protect the horse from being scarred by the armor and weapons carried by the rider. The cloths also provided more comfort for the rider.

By the fourth century B.C. the pad saddle was widely used, and the Scythians north of the Black Sea had invented a saddle with a rigid tree, but the stirrup, a most important item, did not appear for another thousand years. This is in sharp contrast to the early development of halters and bridles, which were both highly developed by 700 B.C., as is shown by pictures on vases, by bas-reliefs, and by specimens that have survived.

In the first two centuries of the Christian era, as the armies of Rome conquered one neighboring country after another, adding province after province to the empire, all the good breeding stock of the Mediterranean world became available to the wealthy Roman landowners. They recognized about a dozen distinct types of horses from as many areas, each with its own specific qualities. By securing stallions from this varied stock, the Romans were able to raise many beautiful horses for riding, racing, and chariot teams, as well as large numbers of lesser quality for their cavalry. After many generations of crossbreeding, pure strains of the original types were hard to find, and the horses of the empire had become a rather heterogeneous mixture.

Throughout the empire the horse-breeding industry suffered serious setbacks during the civil wars of the third and fourth centuries, as the warring generals moved their armies back and forth across the provinces striving for the imperial crown. An army moving through an agricultural district laid waste the fields and confiscated the livestock. In rounding up mounts for the cavalry they always took the best they could find, leaving mediocre stallions to restock the pastures. This process, continuing for more than two centuries, produced a marked deterioration in the quality of horses being raised throughout southern Europe.

After the civil wars had weakened the empire, the barbarian hordes—Germanic tribes from the northern woods—broke through the frontier guards and ravaged the Roman world. These blond invaders—Goths, Vandals, Franks, and the like—were huge men, much taller and heavier than the sturdy, stocky Mediterranean people. The invaders found the light riding horses of the south unsuitable for carrying heavy, long-legged men and their weapons. When they used horses they preferred the large, heavy horses of the northern woods, even though those animals were slower and clumsier.

The civil wars and barbarian invasions had much less effect on the horses of North Africa and the Near East. There the people pressing against the empire's boundaries were often desert tribes, pastoral people living on their flocks and herds beyond the settled farming lands. Their horses were not subject to confiscation by the armies, for they could be protected by being moved out into the desert until the danger had passed. This whole strategy had been well developed by some of the leaders, and was outlined years later by a Muslim general for his successor in these words quoted by Desmond Stewart in *Early Islam:* "Fight the enemy in the desert. There you will be victorious, or, even if defeated, you will have the friendly desert at your backs. The enemy cannot follow you there, and from there you can return to the attack."

All of these desert horsemen preferred mounts of the light riding type —tough, wiry animals accustomed to subsist on scanty forage and able to go a long time without water. The men themselves were also tough and wiry, living in a rough, harsh country with no accumulated stores of wealth to attract such invaders as the Visigoths who ravaged the North African coast from the Straits of Gibraltar to Carthage in the sixth century.

The desert horsemen had great military potential, but they needed an inspiring leader and a great common cause to unite the scattered bands into an effective fighting force. In time they got both. The leader was the prophet Mohammed, who started his career of conquest at Medina in A.D. 622. His religious message, recorded in the Koran, stressed the bonds of a common faith above the old blood ties of the tribe and brought an end to many of the tribal blood feuds. The Koran also had a message for the warriors: "Fight against those who follow not the religion of truth until they pay tribute." Coupled with this was the promise that anyone who died fighting in a holy war would be transported immediately to paradise. With the prospect of much loot in this world or paradise in the next, the warriors fought with fanatic zeal.

The enmity between the Byzantine and Persian empires had made the small states in Syria and Palestine a war zone between the two great powers. By the time the Muslims moved out from Medina to conquer the rest of the world, the people and armies of these little states were ripe for revolt, willing to join forces with the invaders. They were encouraged, too, by the lenient treatment accorded the city of Damascus, which surrendered after a siege when given these favorable terms by the Muslim commander, as quoted by Desmond Stewart.

In the name of Allah, the compassionate, the merciful, this is what Khalid ibn al-Walid would grant to the inhabitants of Damascus. . . . He promises to give them security for their lives, property and churches. Their city shall not be demolished, neither shall any Muslim be quartered in their houses. Thereunto we give to them the pact of Allah and the protection of His Prophet, the Caliphs and the believers. So long as they pay the tax, nothing but good shall befall them.

This pact became the standard set of terms to be offered any city or government in the future conquests, and its lenient terms, in dramatic contrast to the terms usually given a city taken by siege, allowed the Muslim armies to occupy many new places with very little fighting. Usually the people of a country under attack felt that they would be at least as well off under the Muslim rulers as they were under their old ones, and often they could see a real improvement in their living conditions.

Once the Muslim conquest was well under way, it moved on unchecked for a century until the crescent banners floated over a domain stretching from eastern India through the Near East and North Africa to the shores of the Atlantic. Ancient legend has it that the conquering general stood on the Atlantic beach looking out across the surging waters and said to Allah, "Were I not hindered by this sea, I would go forward to the unknown kingdoms of the West subduing those nations who worship other gods than Thee."

The pattern of conquest is exemplified by the conquest of North Africa. A force of cavalry, 3,500 strong, led by Amr ibn al-As, rode into Egypt in 639. The port city of Alexandria offered the only substantial resistance, and when it fell after a long siege the whole country was soon pacified. In 660 a nephew of Amr raised an army, largely from Egypt and including many sons of the original Muslim force by Egyptian wives. He moved west into Libya and on to the edge of Tunis. All along the way Berber tribesmen came in from the desert to join the Muslim forces, bringing with them large herds of fresh horses for themselves and as remounts for the army. By the time the Muslims moved on west about 680, a new generation of young men, sons of the soldiers by native mothers, was ready to join, and other Berber tribes along the way brought in their horses when they came to enlist.

By the time the Muslims had occupied Morocco, there were only a few men from Arabia, recent arrivals, in the armies. It is probable that some of the men fresh from Arabia rode across that wide country and managed to bring a few horses from their homeland along, but the number of such horses must have been small. Just as the blood of the conquerors had become greatly diluted by intermarriage with the women of North Africa, so did the blood of the war-horses from Arabia vanish in the large herds of Algeria and Morocco. This dilution would have been very rapid, for the Muslims usually preferred to ride mares to war.

The Berber tribesmen of Morocco, yearning for profitable new conquests, shunned any advance into the desert country of interior Africa. Instead they turned their attention to the wealthy lands of southern Spain just across the narrow straits, where some of the dis-affected nobles, angry at King Roderick, encouraged an attack from the outside and offered to help such a venture. This inspired a Muslim leader, Tarif, to cross the straits on such a raid in 710. He returned with much loot and reported that the whole country was ripe for invasion.

Another Muslim, Tariq, in 711 crossed to Spain with a force of seven thousand men, planning to conquer and occupy a portion of the coast. His initial success brought him five thousand more recruits from Morocco and inspired another leader to invade farther to the west the next year with eighteen thousand men. With these two armies and more reinforcements from North Africa, by 715 the Muslims had overrun all of Spain except the rough plateau and mountains in the northwest. The rapid, easy success of the Muslims was helped by many of the Visigoth nobles, the bulk of the Hispano-Romans, and the Jewish merchants, but a very important factor was the great superiority of the Muslims' cavalry over the Visigoth forces, especially their mounted men.

The weakness of the Visigoth armies came as a great shock to the Spanish ruling class and to their neighbors to the north. For three hundred years the Visigoths had been fighting and conquering. They had come into Spain from the northeast in 414, occupying Aragon in their first attack. Gradually they had increased their holdings until by 585 they had taken over the entire Iberian Peninsula and had organized it into a single powerful kingdom. There, safe behind the barriers of the Pyrenees and the ocean, they lived a life of ease, and their fighting forces degenerated.

The Visigoths came as conquerors and so became the landed nobility. In their northern forests and in their new home they had little use for war-horses. They liked to have easy-gaited mounts to ride about the country, horses sturdy enough to carry large, long-legged men. They brought in some of the heavy horses from the north and crossed them with the horses of Spain, producing a stout, easy-gaited, slow horse, very comfortable to ride at an amble, but one that was of little use in a battle. They ran herds of cattle on the plateau pastures but they followed their old practice of keeping them in small bands managed by men on foot. When the Moorish horsemen staged their invasions, the Visigoths had no horses able to cope with the swift, agile steeds of their enemies.

Although the Spanish in the rough northwest were able to hold their mountain passes against the Moorish horsemen, they were unable to fight them in open battle until they had adopted the horses, weapons, and battle tactics of their foes. In a hundred years or so the Spanish had made the change, and with the Moorish kingdoms to the south weakened from a variety of causes, the Spanish gradually drove the Moors back until the last Moorish fortress was captured in January 1492.

While the Spanish were developing their light riding horse for their new type of cavalry, the people in France, the Netherlands, and Germany followed a different pattern of horse breeding. In the northern woodlands and even in the clearings, divided as they were by dense hedgerows, cavalry was less effective than on the arid, open Spanish land. These northern people had been successful on several occasions when their massed infantry refused to break under the impact of a cavalry charge. At Chalons in 451 the army of Theodoric turned back the mounted hordes of Attila after a long, gruelling fight, and at Tours in 732 the spearmen fought off the Moorish cavalry in a seven-day battle.

As the feudal system developed in these lands, there was a change in the pattern of the armies. Each king and lord gathered his own forces, with the heavily armored mounted knights as the important nucleus. The knights and the lesser-ranking men-at-arms needed big, powerful horses to carry the large riders with their armor and weapons.

By the eleventh century a mounted Norman soldier wore a heavy iron helmet and a coat of chain mail, the standard equipment for the mounted men who followed William of Normandy across the Channel to England in 1066. William found the English horses too small for his army's needs and encouraged the importation of large, heavy stallions from across the Channel. One of his men, Roger de Bellesme, also imported several Spanish stallions.

A century and a half later King John brought in a hundred Flemish stallions at one time, but still England lagged in producing enough large horses for the army. When Edward III fought his wars in France in the fourteenth century, he had to buy many horses from Hainaut, an area now part of Belgium, to supply his cavalry.

As the war-horses in England, France, and Germany grew bigger and stronger through the selective breeding programs, their loads increased in proportion. Armor for the knights became more elaborate and heavier, and some protection was added for the horses. About 1200, in the reign of King John, the knight added long hose and gauntlets of chain mail to his body armor, and his helmet was made heavier and more elaborate. A century later armor of steel plate replaced the chain mail, and steel plates covered the horse's head, neck, and parts of his body. Then the knight rode ponderously forth to battle more like a slowly moving castle than a man. A cavalry charge was made at a slow gallop, the great horse with his burden of steel plates clanking and thundering along.

Before the armor could attain any further complexity and weight, the English longbow and the introduction of gunpowder made the whole system of armored knights obsolete, and the huge war-horses were no longer desired for riding. The heavy horses then became draft animals, pulling heavy coaches and diligences along the dirt roads. In time they gradually replaced the oxen for most farm work, but this change was very slow.

For all draft work the heavy type of horse has a definite advantage over the light riding type aside from its size and weight. The heavy horse has a straight, heavy shoulder that is easy to fit with a collar, and it affords a broad surface to take the thrust, while the riding horse, with its sloping shoulder, is difficult to fit with a collar that will not ride up and hamper its breathing by pressing against the base of the throat. When the light horse was used for light loads, such as pulling carts and buggies, a broad breast strap took the place of the collar.

Other characteristics useful in distinguishing between the heavy and light types of horses are interesting but of less practical importance. The draft horse has short, upright pasterns—the areas from the hooves to the first joints—giving it less spring to its step, while the riding type has long, sloping pasterns that put spring in its gait. The heavy horse also has larger, rounder hooves, a heavier and bushier mane and tail, and a large head, proportionately longer from poll—the top of the head between the ears—to nose. When the two types are crossed, the resulting animal usually shows all of the different draft characteristics, but in a modified form.

As the breeders worked to improve their draft animals, they usually tried to produce an animal that was chunky and close-coupled—short from shoulder to hip—weighing from twelve to fourteen hundred pounds. Such animals were in demand in the cities and towns for hauling loads and later for work on the more prosperous farms.

During the nearly eight hundred years of fighting a succession of invaders, the Spanish had developed riding horses, mostly from North African stock with some of the older Spanish blood used to increase the size. These horses were used in the cavalry and on the stock ranches, where the cattle were handled by mounted men, in contrast to the earlier practice of using men on foot. Thus, when Columbus returned from his first voyage of discovery, Spain had seasoned veterans from the recent wars eager to make their fortunes in the New World and fine horses to carry them, but the veterans were easier to find than the horses, for the latter were in short supply at the time. The wars had taken a heavy toll of the herds, and many of the stockmen had turned from raising war-horses to breeding riding mules, which many of the Spanish preferred for ordinary use, finding them more placid and easy-gaited than the cavalry stallions. The king finally had to decree that no one except women and the clergy were ever to ride mules except by special permission. Such permission was granted to Columbus after his fourth voyage because of his poor health.

This shortage of horses continued for several years and occurred just when many horses were needed for exploration, conquest, and settlement of the new territories. At the same time people from other European countries were in the market for Spanish horses and helped to run up the price of any animal offered for sale.

The glowing reports of Columbus on the wealth of the West Indies induced the king and queen to give him a large, well-equipped fleet for seizing and occupying the islands. An important addition to the expedition was a cavalry squadron that was expected to do more than just fight Indians. In the royal instructions was this passage: ". . . there will be sent twenty lancers with horses . . . and five of them shall take two horses each and these two horses which they take shall be mares."

In addition to the ten mares—and fifteen stallions—with the cavalry, Columbus had a few more horses of his own. From Hispaniola he complained by letter to the court that he had paid a high price for good horses at Seville, but the dealers had provided poor horses at the loading dock. In the same letter he stressed the importance of increasing the supply of brood mares on the islands as rapidly as possible and asked that some be sent on each ship. He knew there would be no shortage of stallions. This supply of mares was considered so important to the proper development of the new colonies that for several years the king provided free transportation for them.

When the Spanish had conquered and settled the Canary Islands about a century earlier, they had learned a great deal about transporting horses on lengthy ocean voyages on their small sailing ships. In fairly good weather with the northeast trade winds blowing steadily, the horses did fairly well, even though they had to be tied on the open deck for a month or more. Some of the more valuable animals were placed where an overhang gave them some shelter from the tropical sun and the occasional rainstorms, and often they were placed in broad slings to support and protect them when the ship rolled heavily in a storm, but the ordinary horses stood out in the weather day and night, drenched by the rains and buffeted by the winds.

The horses were in serious trouble whenever the ship was becalmed and lay motionless for days scorched by the tropical sun. Then the water supplies ran low, and as the horses died of thirst they were cast overboard. One expanse of the Atlantic north of the Canaries became known as the "Golfo de yegues," the gulf of the mares, from the number of animals lost there over the years. After voyages to the West Indies began, and many horses were lost in the belt of calms west of the Canaries, that belt was called the horse latitudes. In later years, when the English and Dutch lost horses farther to the north, between the thirtieth and thirty-fifth degrees of north latitude, between the northeast trades and the prevailing westerlies, they called that area the horse latitudes also.

Columbus was fortunate on his second voyage with his horses. The weather was favorable and he made a rapid crossing, taking only twenty-two days from the Canaries to landfall in the West Indies. When the ship was still many miles from land, the horses smelled it and became excited, pawing and neighing. The next day the fleet reached Guadaloupe and anchored for six days. The horses were put ashore for exercise and forage, then were reloaded to spend another four weeks aboard before being landed at La Navidad to be used against the local Indians, who were greatly impressed by the sight of the strange beasts, which they believed fed on human flesh. The horses were then taken by ship to the new colony of Isabela, where they finally finished their ocean travel on January 2, 1494—the first horses in the New World since their wild cousins had died off some 8,500 years earlier.

The island of Hispaniola had much good pasture land suitable for stock raising. Not only was the forage good and the climate mild, but there were no predatory animals to attack the colts and calves. The stockmen devoted most of their land to cattle raising, but they also raised many horses both for their own use in handling the cattle and for sale to new settlers planning to establish ranches of their own. With a good price being offered for any marketable horse, the stockmen took the best of care of their brood mares and imported as many more as they could. While there is no record of the specific number shipped from Spain to the islands during this period, several references indicate a rapid increase in the size and number of horse herds.

In the early stages of island settlement the king set up a number of crown–owned breeding farms to furnish stallion service for the settlers, and to supply brood mares that were to be repaid in kind. The first of these farms began operation in 1497. In 1499 Francisco Roldan received two mares from the king's herd, and a year later one of the royal farms reported sixty brood mares in service. After 1501 the tax collector was authorized to accept colts in lieu of money for tax payments. These scattered references in diverse documents indicate a thriving horse industry aided and supported by the government.

In 1507, as part of his preparations for war in Europe, the king placed a ban on further exports of any mares from Spain, but one man secured special exemption from the order when he proved that he had bought 106 mares and had prepared them for shipment before the ban was published. The situation finally eased and in 1510 the king recommended that mares be sent to the new colony of Puerto Rico. Horses were taken from Hispaniola to Jamaica with the first settlers in 1509, and royal farms were operating there by 1515. These farms in 1530 supplied Francisco Pizarro with twenty-five stallions and twenty-five mares for Peru. Horses were taken to Cuba in 1511, and several stock farms were established in time to provide horses for the invasion of Mexico in 1519.

[26]

Throughout the first half of the sixteenth century the cattle herds in the islands were highly profitable. Hides and tallow found a ready market with the skippers of vessels returning to Spain, who needed some cargo to help defray costs and who could sell these products profitably in Europe. The cattle also supplied dried beef for the emergency supplies of the explorers who went out to map new lands. With both horses and cattle doing well, many of the men who through luck or foresight devoted themselves to ranching became prosperous and built up large estates, while their more restless brethren, who bought up the excess cattle and horses for their treasure hunts, dashed about for years in great excitement, usually escaping death in the wilds but seldom ending up with a profit.

There is no way to determine how many horses the island ranches supplied for the conquest of Mexico, Central America, and Peru, and for the exploration of the southern United States, but the total would be in the thousands. Since most of the horses were purchased with gold, the ranchers experienced great prosperity and had the coins necessary to buy what they wanted from Spain. In many cases they secured good stallions to upgrade their herds. This economic pattern explains why the ranches of the West Indies built up a reputation for raising fine horses during the sixteenth century.

Horses had been extinct in the New World for about 8,500 years when Cortez landed in Mexico in 1519. His small troupe of cavalry terrified the Indians, playing a decisive role in his first crucial battles. (Detail from seventeenth-century Spanish painting, New York Public Library Picture Collection)

3

Horses for the New World

HORSES WERE STILL IN SHORT SUPPLY and high in price in Cuba in the spring of 1519, when Hernando Cortez sailed from Havana with ten ships and 508 soldiers, hoping to find much golden treasure in Mexico. His men were well equipped for fighting. They carried thirteen arquebuses, thirty-two crossbows, ten small brass cannon, and four falconets, in addition to swords, lances, and pikes, but altogether they had only sixteen horses, six of which were mares and one heavy with foal. The colt arrived during the voyage, leaving the mare unfit for active fighting for several weeks and underlining one of the reasons the Spanish preferred stallions for military use, especially for a protracted campaign. The ratio here of one horse to about thirty men is unusual, for the Spanish on later expeditions, when horses were plentiful, took one horse for each two men. Even so, these ten stallions and six mares made the difference between victory and defeat in the first critical fights.

One of the men with Cortez, Bernal Díaz del Castillo, in his *The Discovery and Conquest of Mexico, 1517–1521*, has left a vivid eyewitness account of the many battles. He had a high regard for the horses and their achievements and recorded their stories in some deail. The following two quotes are from his work. Soon after Cortez reached the mainland he learned that a force of several thousand Indians was forming to attack him. Díaz describes the situation.

As soon as Cortés knew this for certain he ordered all the horses to be landed from the ships without delay, and the crossbowmen and musketeers and all of us soldiers, even those who were wounded, to have arms ready for use.

When the horses were brought on shore they were very stiff and afraid to move, for they had been many days on board ship, but the next day they moved quite freely. . . .

The best horses and riders were chosen to form the cavalry, and the horses had little bells attached to their breastplates. The men were ordered not to stop to spear those who were down, but to aim their lances at the faces of the enemy.

Thirteen gentlemen were chosen to go on horseback with Cortés in command of them. . . .

Cortés ordered Mesa the artilleryman to have his guns ready, and he placed Diego de Ordas in command of us foot soldiers and he also had command of the musketeers and bowmen, for he was no horseman. . . .

Cortés [and the horsemen] were separated a short distance from us on account of some swamps which could not be crossed by the horses, and as we were marching along we came on the whole force of Indian warriors who were on the way to attack us in our camp. It was near the town of Cintla that we met them on the open plain.

As they approached us their squadrons were so numerous that they covered the whole plain, and they rushed on us like mad dogs completely surrounding us, and they let fly such a cloud of arrows, javelins and stones that on the first assault they wounded over seventy of us, and fighting hand to hand they did great damage with their lances, and one soldier fell dead at once from an arrow wound in the ear, and they kept on shooting and wounding us. With our muskets and with our crossbows and with good sword play we did not fail as stout fighters, and when they came to feel the edge of our swords, little by little they fell back, but it was only so as to shoot at us in greater safety. Mesa, our artillery man, killed many of them with his cannon, for they were formed in great squadrons and they did not open out so he could fire at them as he pleased, but with all the hurts and wounds which we gave them, we could not drive them off. . . .

Just at this time we caught sight of our horsemen, and as the Indian host was crazed with its attack on us, it did not at once perceive them coming up behind their backs, and as the plain was level ground and the horsemen were good riders, and many of the horses were very handy and fine gallopers, they came quickly on the enemy and speared them as they chose. As soon as we saw the horsemen we fell on the Indians with such energy that with us attacking on one side and the horsemen on the other, they soon turned tail. . . .

After we had defeated the enemy, Cortés told us that he had not been able to come to us sooner as there was a swamp in the way, and he had to fight his way through another force of warriors before he could reach us, and three horsemen and five horses had been wounded. . . .

The battle lasted over an hour and the Indians fought all the time like brave warriors, until the horsemen came up.

In this first fight in which the horses were used, the thirteen mounted men had more effect on the Indians than did four hundred foot soldiers with cannon.

In his remarkable conquest of the Aztec empire Cortez continued to put great reliance on his horses, but he had two other important factors helping him. Montezuma, the Aztec ruler, firmly believed that Cortez was the god Quetzalcoatl, whom the prophets had foretold. This belief was reinforced for a time by the guns and horses of the Spanish, both of which seemed supernatural to the Aztecs. In addition, many powerful tribes held in subjection by the Aztecs were ready to rebel, and they rose up in arms to support the invaders who promised them freedom from the harsh Aztec rule.

After establishing a settlement at Veracruz and enlisting several of the neighboring tribes as allies, Cortez set out on his march across the mountains to the Aztec capital of Tenochtitlán (now the site of Mexico City) in August 1519. One of his horses had died at Veracruz, but a ship had brought in ten more, so he had an effective force of twenty-five mounted men with which to attack the massed armies of unfriendly Indians along the road. In these battles his greatest difficulty was in maneuvering his foes onto ground suitable for a cavalry charge. He lost one of his horses in this fighting along the line of march.

On the way to Mexico City Cortez had his fiercest fight with the brave Tlascalans, powerful Indians who resented their subjugation to Montezuma but at the same time were fearful of the Spanish. They barred his advance with the forces of five great chiefs, each leading an army of ten thousand men. As the Spanish approached this great assemblage of enemies, Cortez arranged his men for the battle and gave them their instructions. Díaz has the story:

The next morning, the 5th September, 1519, we mustered the horses. There was not one of the wounded men who did not come forward to join the ranks and give as much help as he could. The crossbowmen were warned to use the store of darts very cautiously, some of them loading while the others were shooting, and the musketeers were to act in the same way, and the men with sword and shield were instructed to aim their cuts and thrusts at the bowels [of their enemies] so they would not dare to come as close to us as they did before. . . .

All the plain was swarming with warriors and we stood four hundred men in number, and of these many sick and wounded. And we knew for certain that this time our foe came with the determination to leave none of us alive excepting those who would be sacrificed to their idols.

How they began to charge on us! What a hail of stones sped from their slings! As for their bowmen, the javelins lay like corn on the threshing floor; all of them barbed and fire hardened, which would pierce any armour and would reach the vitals where there is no protection; the men with swords and shields and other arms larger than swords, such as broadswords and lances, how they pressed on us and with what valor and what mighty shouts and yells they charged upon us. The steady bearing of our artillery, musketeers, and crossbowmen, was indeed a help to us, and we did the enemy much damage, and those of them who came close to us with their swords and broadswords met with such sword play from us they were forced back and they did not close in on us so often as in the last battle. The horsemen were so skilful and bore themselves so valiantly that, after God who protected us, they were our bulwark.

And all of that was accomplished by twenty-four good horses with their skilled, determined riders. Every horse was wounded in this fight, but they all recovered. In a later minor skirmish one of the horses was less fortunate. Cortez, in his third letter to the king, cited in his *Five Letters, 1518–1526*, wrote:

Our people were in no danger that day, except during the time when we left the ambush. Some horses collided and a man fell from his mare. She galloped off toward the enemy, who severely wounded her with arrows. When she saw the bad treatment she was receiving, though badly hurt she came back to us. That night she died. Although we felt her death deeply, for the horses and mares were our salvation, our grief was less because she did not die in the hands of the enemy, as we had feared would be the case.

After Cortez finally reached Mexico City and made peace there, he had to return hurriedly to Veracruz, where Pánfilo de Narváez had arrived with a fleet of nineteen ships, eighty horses, and fourteen hundred men to capture him and and bring him back to Cuba. Narváez was acting on the orders of the governor of Cuba, who was furious with Cortez for ignoring his authority. Cortez managed to defeat Narváez by clever strategy and by suborning many of his men with Aztec gold. Then he returned to Mexico City with the combined forces, arriving there on St. John's Day, 1520. Díaz reported, "We entered that city with upward of 1300 soldiers, cavalry included, which latter body was 97 in number, and of our infantry, eighty were crossbowmen, and as many musketeers."

Two weeks later they were in full retreat, having lost 870 men, all their cannon, and all but twenty-three of the horses, most of the losses occurring on the rain-drenched causeway as they attempted to escape in the night. This battered fragment of the army managed to reach the country of the Tlascalans, who had come over to the Spanish side. Here they recuperated and received reinforcements from the West Indies and from their Indian allies. All the while the smallpox scourge was weakening the Aztec army, killing them in untold thousands.

When Cortez had fought his way back into Mexico City, the weeks of bitter fighting from street to street and house to house left that proud capital a mass of ruins. The Spanish thoroughly looted the place, then turned their attention to other matters.

The great store of Aztec gold and gems flowing from Mexico further excited the cupidity of the Spanish and led many of them to hope that further search might turn up another Mexico along the Gulf coast of the United States. The search turned north to Florida just across the narrow channel from Havana. There a man might hope to find piles of treasure and perhaps even a Northwest Passage to the Pacific. While leaders schemed and planned, striving for royal permission for a quest, many Spanish slave ships moved along the coast capturing Indian slaves for the island plantations. In a few years the Spaniards had so embittered all the Florida tribes that they hated all white men and mounted fierce attacks against any colony set up on their shores. Their lasting enmity was the chief cause of the many failures of colonies attempted in this region.

First with a royal grant to colonize in Florida was Juan Ponce de León, who led the way north in 1521 with 250 men, fifty horses, other domestic animals, and farming implements. His men were attacked as they left their ships and Ponce de León was fatally wounded when he went to their relief. The survivors sailed back to Hispaniola, the expedition a total failure.

Five years later Lucas Vásquez de Ayllón tried again at a different location farther up the coast. He had five hundred men and women, eighty-nine horses, and adequate equipment for the new colony. He found a fairly good location on the coast of South Carolina and began building, but the colony was buffeted by a series of very cold northern storms that brought disease and death to Ayllón and many of his settlers. After one mutiny and several Indian attacks the survivors sailed away in a winter storm that froze many of them to death. About one hundred and fifty of the original five hundred reached Hispaniola. In both of these attempts the horses proved of little value in fighting the Indians, for the attacks came from foes concealed in swamps and thickets where the horses could not follow.

Ayllón's grant was then given to Pánfilo de Narváez, who had vainly tried to arrest Cortez at Veracruz. Narváez enlisted his settlers in Spain, then sailed to the West Indies, buying his horses and additional supplies from Puerto Rico and Hispaniola. In the spring of 1528 he sailed up the west coast of Florida and landed at Tampa Bay on Good Friday. The local Indians told him he could find heaps of gold off to the north, so away he went with three hundred of his men, forty of them mounted soldiers in armor. The women all decided to stay with the ships that were to sail on up the coast and find a good harbor, where they could wait for the arrival of the land forces.

Food gave out for both men and horses as they marched through the Florida swamps and thickets, but they finally reached the reputed treasure-filled land of Appalachen, only to find it a small, poor village surrounded by fields of ripening corn that saved them from starvation. They moved on to the northwest, drowning a horse at the Suwanee River crossing. The animal was pulled out and eaten, as meat was very scarce. After weeks of wandering and fighting the Indians, the Spanish finally reached the coast and looked for their ships, but the sailors had given them up and had returned to Cuba.

Narváez then decided to build boats and sail west to Mexico, which he thought was near at hand. He and his men took all the iron from the crossbows, stirrups, spurs, and bits to make axes, saws, and nails. From makeshift materials they finally built boat frames of timber and covered them with the hides of the horses that they butchered one by one to feed themselves. In September, after they had eaten their last horse, they embarked from the Bay of Horses leaving the bones of their slaughtered mounts gleaming in the sand.

They sailed west and into disaster. The way was much longer than they expected and the weather was stormy. All the boats sank in the Gulf, or were cast ashore on the sandbanks of the Texas coast. The few survivors became slaves of the local Indians. Four of them, led by Álvar Núñez Cabeza de Vaca, walked across Texas, New Mexico, and half of Arizona. Then they turned south and in a few hundred miles found some Spanish soldiers who took them back to the settlements.

When Cabeza de Vaca finally arrived in Spain he had wondrous tales to tell at court and hinted to the king that there were vast treasures off to the north of his path across the continent. His tales inspired two other important Spanish expeditions, those of Hernando de Soto and Francisco Vásquez de Coronado. The stories of these two men will be given here in some detail, for their adventures gave rise in later times to a popular legend of the West that recounted how stray horses from the explorers' two herds managed to unite on the plains of Texas and in time filled the whole western grasslands with wild horses and so made horsemen of the Plains Indians—a legend with no basis in fact. De Soto, the new governor of Cuba, left Havana in May 1539 and sailed north to Tampa Bay with 600 armed soldiers and 213 horses. There, in the dirt of an Indian hut, he found a few pearls, and from the villagers he heard stories of wealthy cities off to the north full of pearls. Leaving fifty men and thirty horses in a fortified camp, De Soto set out on his treasure hunt.

He marched at the head of an imposing cavalcade of 550 men and nearly 200 horses across northern Florida, searching for a land so rich the warriors wore helmets of gold. The route led across a low, flat country full of thickets, bogs, and marshes—very difficult traveling for horses burdened with armored riders. The men crossed the deep rivers by paddling on logs, while the horses had to swim. The land offered scanty provisions for either man or beast until they finally reached a large Indian village surrounded by fields of growing corn, but the Indians had all fled and the soldiers had to harvest and grind their own corn, tasks which they resented. A search for slaves embroiled them in a pitched battle with Indians who were strong fighters and difficult to subdue. They rose in revolt even after they had been captured and chained.

In October De Soto decided to spend the winter near Tallahassee. He wrote letters home to be forwarded from Tampa Bay and with them sent orders to his soldiers at the post to come to him at once with all their supplies. The trail to Tampa Bay led through more than three hundred miles of difficult terrain crossed by deep rivers and inhabited by hostile Indians. For messengers on the dangerous ride De Soto chose thirty of his best horsemen, among them Gonzalo Silvestre, who rode a dark chestnut stallion reputed to be the best in all the Indies.

Lightly armed, with no bedding or spare clothes and very little food, they set out early on an October morning at the steady running walk that eats up the miles while conserving the strength of the horses. On the afternoon of the second day they hid near an Indian town and skirted it in the dusk. They rested a few hours and galloped fifteen miles to the first river crossing before the Indians could gather to dispute their passage. When the other horses balked at entering the chilling current, Silvestre led the way on his willing steed.

On the fourth day they reached a larger river with a bitter north wind blowing and an Indian attack expected at any moment. All the horses except two for the rear guard were unsaddled, and a small raft was quickly made of branches to carry the saddles and other gear across the stream. Twelve good swimmers stripped to their shirts and crossed with their horses, lances, and swords to hold the landing place, shivering on their wet horses as they beat back the Indians. Then the raft made four trips, with four strong swimmers pushing it across and back. Silvestre and a companion, both in full armor, guarded the rear until the raft shoved off for the last time. Then, as Silvestre charged the approaching Indians, his companion put his armor and saddle on the raft and swam with his horse. Silvestre turned his horse and dashed for the river, plunging in with all his armor, submerging his horse until only its head rose above the icy waters. Indian arrows showered harmlessly against Silvestre's fine plate armor, while the water protected his horse, and they crossed safely.

A freezing wind drove the men to scanty shelter in the ruins of an Indian town. There they alternately huddled around blazing fires or gleaned corn from the fields to feed the hungry horses and to fill the saddlebags. Then on they rode through the storm, with one man dying in his saddle from exposure and lack of food. The next day another man died, and finally one of the horses collapsed and had to be abandoned beside the trail.

On the evening of the eleventh day the weary riders approached the post in time to see a line of horsemen riding two by two out of the gate. They also formed in pairs and each pair, starting separately, dashed to the gate at full gallop, twirling their lances to show the spirit of their horses after such a ride. Three days later, to their great pleasure, a friendly Indian led in the horse which had been abandoned by the trail. With a little rest it had recovered and seemed not much the worse for wear. Even for the best of De Soto's herd, the journey through the wilderness to Tampa Bay had been a remarkable feat of endurance.

De Soto wintered near Tallahassee and explored some of the country. His men found Narváez' Bay of Horses, recognizable from the heaps of bleached bones on the sand. In the spring, rejecting all pleas from his men to turn back, he marched on northeastward into Georgia, where he found the warmest welcome of his entire journey. A large, prosperous tribe led by an attractive chieftainess furnished the Spanish with food and gave them many presents, including 350 pounds of freshwater pearls. When De Soto moved on toward the west he repaid this hospitality by marching the chieftainess and her female slaves along on foot and under guard, but after a few days she escaped in the night, taking a large chest of the fine pearls.

Months later in Alabama De Soto had a fierce fight with Indians who attacked at night while the soldiers slept in their town. Before the Spanish could recover from their surprise they had been driven from the town and had lost all their baggage and provisions, and a large number of pearls. Then they counterattacked and regained the town, killing almost all the defenders, but in the process the houses burned and the soldiers lost all the captured supplies in the fire. In addition to having many soldiers killed and wounded in the fight, De Soto lost twelve horses, and seventy more were injured.

A few months later, on the Yazoo River, the Indians again burned De Soto's encampment at night, destroying his small store of food, the men's clothing, and more horses. When they finally reached the Mississippi, De Soto and his men were a tired band of tattered, footsore adventurers, but they still had to discover what lay beyond the great river. They built a fleet of barges and crossed over, sending four mounted men in each of the leading three barges. They plunged their mounts into the shallows on the far side and took up a position on a firm sand spit to protect the landing.

De Soto spent several months west of the Mississippi hunting for Indian towns. He found several, but none of them had any gold for him. He reached the fringe of the buffalo plains without seeing any of the herds. After spending a winter in Arkansas he returned to the west bank of the Mississippi, worn out and discouraged. He had lost 250 men and 150 horses since leaving Tampa Bay three years earlier. There on the river bank he died of fever in May 1542.

His men then set out to march overland to Mexico, which they knew was off to the southwest. After traveling far into Texas they became discouraged and turned back to the Mississippi, where they spent the winter building seven brigantines to carry them back. As they worked they killed all their hogs and all but twenty-two of their horses, eating what they needed and preserving the rest for rations on the voyage. Then the 322 survivors embarked with their horses and sailed down the river, beating off attacks by Indians who killed and wounded both men and horses with their arrows. Finally the last five horses, the best of the mounts that had started from Cuba, were turned loose along the river in an open glade, only to be shot down by the Indians before the boats were out of sight downstream. The brigantines finally reached Pánuco, Mexico, on September 10, 1543, with 310 survivors.

While De Soto was camped near the Bay of Horses, Francisco Vásquez de Coronado was mustering his forces at Compostela west of Mexico City as he prepared to follow the back trail—that is, the same trail in reverse direction—of Cabeza de Vaca. Coronado had 336 men, several women, and a few hundred Indian allies and servants. His livestock included 550 stallions, 3 mares, about 500 pack animals (mostly mules), a large herd of cattle, and a larger flock of sheep. Both the cattle and sheep were taken to stock the farms of any settlement that might be established, but more importantly they were the traveling meat supply for the expedition, to be slaughtered along the way as the need arose. If the march went well, usually no more animals were butchered than were replaced by calves and lambs born along the trail.

In traveling through strange country such an expedition had to move slowly enough to allow all the animals to forage each day, moving from twelve to fifteen miles a day in about eight hours where the trail was good. The rest of the day was spent in camp, with the flocks and herds pasturing nearby. The whole caravan moved at a slow walk, and the footmen had little difficulty in keeping the pace.

After advancing up the west coast between the mountains and the sea, Coronado reached Culiacan. He then chose eighty of his best horsemen, thirty foot soldiers, and a large contingent of Indian allies to advance rapidly ahead of the main force and investigate the land of Cibola, which turned out to be the Zuñi villages of Arizona. Along the way he lost most of his small flock of sheep and several horses on the rough trail. Three months of steady traveling brought him to the fabulous Seven Cities only to find them villages devoid of treasure and inhabited by unfriendly Indians. A small advance scouting party was attacked at night by the Zuñis, who stampeded the loose horses, but luckily the two men on guard had remained on their mounts and they easily rounded up the scattered horses the next day.

By the judicious use of his eighty horsemen Coronado was able to send out three parties at different times to explore the country. One party rode west to the Colorado River and explored from Yuma for some distance downstream. A second group advanced to the northwest until stopped by the abyss of the Grand Canyon of the Colorado River, while a third party, under Hernando Alvarado, went east to the buffalo country. They all returned safely with marvelous tales of the country they had seen, but with no hint of treasure. However, Alvarado, who had found the buffalo herds, reported that a Plains Indian held captive at one of the pueblos told him of a wealthy land of Quivira far out on the plains to the northeast, where the people had much gold.

The Pueblo Indians resented the continual presence of the strangers in their lands and in the fall began a series of attacks, first turning their attention to the horses. One pueblo village on the Rio Grande sent out a war party to destroy a small horse herd pasturing near by. The herder escaped with minor wounds and bruises, but the Indians drove off all the horses, killing some of them on the way back to the pueblo. There they penned the rest of the herd inside their palisade and had a great time shooting the frightened animals full of arrows. The tails were taken as trophies. In retaliation the Spanish attacked the pueblo and after hard fighting set fire to the place and killed most of the people. They also attacked other hostile pueblos and took many captives for slaves.

Before winter set in, the main body of the expedition arrived and the whole force went into winter quarters at Tiguex on the Rio Grande. In April 1541 Coronado started east toward the buffalo country with most of his forces, hoping to find the gold of Quivira. He had a thousand horses, five hundred cattle, five thousand sheep, and fifteen hundred people, most of them Indians from Mexico or slaves taken in the recent fighting. To round out the party, three of the Spanish soldiers had their wives and children along.

They were surprised both by the immensity of the plains and the great number of buffalo. They reported that in traveling for more than a thousand miles on the open plains there was not a single day that they did not sight buffalo. They dashed through the herds killing for meat and sport, but they soon learned that buffalo could be dangerous. Several of the hunters had their horses badly gored when they rode too close to wounded animals, and once, in chasing a herd, three hunters following in the cloud of dust fell into a barranca filled to the rim with squirming bodies of buffalo that had dashed blindly to their destruction. The horsemen who fell into the churning mass lost their mounts and gear, but they managed to escape.

After traveling to the east in Texas across the flat expanse of the Panhandle, Coronado's party began to realize that they were on the wrong route to Quivira. They reasoned that their guide must be a liar who was deliberately leading them astray. Then they met with a severe hailstorm, with stones so big that all the pottery and gourds in the camp were broken, steel helmets were dented, and many horses were badly bruised. Coronado decided he should send most of his forces back to Tiguex, where they could rest safely while he went off to the northeast with a small party in search of the elusive Quivira. He chose thirty of his best horsemen and six foot soldiers for his party. In addition he had about forty wranglers and servants.

He went northward through the Texas Panhandle, across Oklahoma, and into Kansas, where he crossed the Arkansas River at the big bend. Finally he found Quivira, a prosperous farming village with large grass huts but no palace and no gold. At the same time De Soto, also seeking gold, was about three hundred miles farther down the river to the southeast, but neither of them had any report of the other.

Coronado turned back from Quivira, his last chance for a golden fortune gone. He reached the pueblos on the Rio Grande safely and rejoined his main force. The following spring the whole army retraced its steps to Culiacan, where it was disbanded. Although it had found no treasure it survived in much better shape than did De Soto's party.

In northern Mexico the Spanish repeated on a much vaster scale the pattern of their occupation of Hispaniola. Here again the soldiers and adventurers made a quick dash for treasure and sudden wealth that often ended in disappointment and death for many of them. They were followed by the stockmen with their slower, steadier exploitation of the millions of acres of rangeland and the establishment of a solid economy based on raising livestock, horses, mules, cattle, and sheep.

The immense plateau of northern Mexico required two centuries or more of sustained effort for its occupation and development and stimulated the institution of new methods of handling livestock on the open range. The Spanish stockmen, the rancheros, tried many new practices, and the successful ones were incorporated into their system. Many of these practices were so well conceived and well applied that they were used widely throughout western North America to the end of the nineteenth century and are still common in some areas today. While the older records are explicit on the many details of the system, some of the more interesting accounts of Mexican ranching practices were written by travelers in the middle of the nineteenth century. These depict a pattern of life that had existed with little change for two hundred years or more, and they are valid descriptions of the old way of life on the Mexican plateau.

After the Aztec capital had been subdued in 1521, the Spanish fanned out in all directions in search of more treasure, but in northern Mexico and the Southwest there were no piled-up hoards of gold and gems waiting to be grabbed. Instead the restless adventurers found rich lodes of ore embedded in the solid rock of the rugged mountains, some of the ore rich with gold but more with large amounts of silver. These mines offered much wealth at the cost of wresting it from its rocky fastnesses and refining the metals. Mining in these mountains required some bravery, a great deal of skill, and much backbreaking labor.

To the northwest of Mexico City the great range of the Sierra Madre mountains stretched away a thousand miles or more, with access across the central plateau to the mouths of the mountain canyons. The whole was through country held by tough, wild Indians who fought the Spanish intruders. The rich mineral strikes all along the way, first in Nueva Galicia, then on to the great district around Zacatecas, opened up in 1548, and the even richer finds at Durango, in 1563, brought in enough soldiers to beat back the Indians and enough miners to take over the country. A hundred smaller strikes dotted the foothills and canyons between the large centers, each to be worked until the ore was exhausted. Then the miners moved on to new strikes, leaving the old pits, tunnels, and waste dumps around the ghost towns while a small farming village at the edge of the plateau still eked out a bare existence by using the water trickling from the old diggings.

All the new mining camps demanded large quantities of food and could pay for it in hard cash. High on the list of necessities were cattle in large numbers to furnish meat, and equally important, to supply the rawhide and leather for a hundred uses and tallow for candles, soap, and lubrication.

Horses were needed for all sorts of work. They carried riders, pulled carts, packed goods, furnished the power to hoist the ore from the depths of the mines, and dragged the heavy stones that crushed the ore to a fine powder and thus allowed the precious metals to be separated from the waste. In many of these mines much of the concentration of the metal was achieved by amalgamating it with quicksilver, then distilling the quicksilver to be used again, while the metal remained in the bottom of the crucible. To secure a good mix of the ground ore and the quicksilver, the whole mass was made into a thick mud.

The heavy mud was spread to the depth of a foot or two on a well-paved courtyard surrounded by high walls. Then a bunch of unbroken horses right off the range—the wilder the better—were driven into the courtyard and kept in a state of panic by men waving blankets and lashing them with whips. As the horses slowed from fatigue, some of the bolder men would jump on them and ride them about. The horses' hooves churned the mud thoroughly while the heavy mixture rapidly wore away the hair, hide, and flesh just above the hooves, completely crippling the animals, which were then taken out and slaughtered, their hides being used for leather and their meat going to feed the miners. When the next batch of mud was ready, a new band of unbroken horses culled from the range herds was brought in and the process was repeated. The well-mixed mud was gathered up carefully and washed in a sluice to separate the heavy amalgam from the lighter waste.

The quicksilver process was very good for refining free milling ores, but often the precious metals were locked in with other elements and required a different treatment of the mud. George Ruxton, an English traveler, mentions such a process in his *Adventures in Mexico and the Rocky Mountains.*

> Two thousand mules are daily at work in the hacienda de beneficios, and 2,500 men are employed in the mines. . . . The patio, or yard . . . where the porphyritic crushing mills are at work, contain[s] 32,000 square yards. In undergoing one process, the crushed ore, mixed with copper and salt, is made into mud puddings, and trodden out by mules, which are back deep in the paste. . . .

This was in 1846, when mules had replaced horses for many of the jobs in the mining districts.

In the Spanish colonies horses were often used to thresh grain in a manner similar to that used on the ores. One of the last of such threshings was reported in the newspaper *Daily Alta California* in 1853.

> Did you ever see the Californians thresh? . . . The whole harvest was carried to the corral, a yard about a hundred feet square and a substantial fence, and sometimes the straw would overtop the fence. A drove of from thirty to sixty wild mares was then driven into the straw, the colts being caught with a lasso and taken out, for fear they might be injured. Half a dozen Indians would get into the center of the corral, and perhaps one or two on horseback, and the fun would commence. In a few hours the horses are completely exhausted and not unfrequently some of them ruined or maimed. It was a very speedy method of threshing but the work was only half done, large quantities of grain being lost.

Whenever there is a ready market that promises a profit for a commodity, suppliers soon appear, and such was the situation in the mining country. In a short time large haciendas dotted the foothills and spread across the plateau to the east, each owner locating wherever there was an adequate supply of water for his stock. At the same time many millions of acres of good grass went untouched, for they were too far from the water. A hacienda might be quite large and pasture 100,000 head of cattle. The records of 1586 list one owned by Diego de Ibarra that branded 33,000 head of stock one season, while a neighbor, Governor Rodrigo del Rio, tallied 42,000 head, and there were hundreds of smaller herds throughout the provinces.

These stockmen followed the system of handling cattle that had been developed on the Spanish Plateau after the Moorish invasion—that of ranging stock in large herds instead of the more common practice in most countries of herding the animals in small bands with one or two herdsmen on foot in constant charge. This Spanish system of ranging is of special interest, for it was brought to the American Southwest and was used, with minor variations, from the Mississippi to the Pacific Coast and north into Canada.

This system, which in its essential features still exists today, worked as follows: Ranging stock were turned out on unfenced pasture and allowed to graze at will over the countryside. They soon found a favorite watering place and fed around it in all directions for a few miles. This feeding area became known as the range for that herd. Every few days a vaquero, or cowboy, rode out to look at the herd, turn it back if it tended to stray off the range, and search for predators and thieves. Under the range system the cattle became rather wild, but they required very little supervision through most of the year and were still accustomed to being handled by mounted men, although they could be dangerous to men on foot.

Twice each year the cattle were rounded up and driven to a central point on the range. In the late spring roundup the calves were tallied and branded, and most of the bull calves were castrated. In the fall, when the cattle were fat, the herd was again rounded up and the stock to be sold or slaughtered was cut out. This cut included all the mature steers, usually four-year-olds, and the old cows. In Mexico the meat from these animals was sun-dried in thin strips and packed in rawhide bags. The tallow was melted and packed in standard-size rawhide bags. The skins were spread out flat to dry and were later made into rawhide or tanned into leather.

In addition to this autumn harvest, the haciendas near the mining camps usually drove a small herd of beef stock into the camp each week or two to furnish the miners with fresh meat. Steers were in marketable shape for about six months of each year, from late April until November. The rest of the year the miners ate dried meat or horse meat.

The owner of the hacienda needed a large number of well-broken horses to carry him, his family, and his vaqueros wherever they needed to go. In addition, much of the ranch work had to be done on horseback, especially the handling of horses and cattle on the range. The riding horses had to subsist by grazing, except in unusual instances, when they might be fed a little grain. A horse needed about three days' grazing to recuperate after a hard day's work, although a horse ridden for only a few hours a day could be used each day. If the riding was over hard, rocky ground the horse might need several days extra for its hooves to heal, since very few of these ranch horses were shod.

The hardest work for a horse came at roundup time, when he had to carry a rider for several hours at a stretch, and much of the time was spent in a series of short dashes to turn the cattle. Half a day of such work and the vaquero needed a fresh mount for the afternoon ride. If he was too far from camp to make a change of mounts at noon, his horse might need two or three extra days of rest before working again. Hence a top hand might need seven or eight horses for range work and two trained roping and cutting horses to handle the chores around the branding fire.

Horses raised on the open range matured more slowly than those that were raised in small enclosures and fed some grain, but they developed fine bones, good muscles, and great endurance. They were not ready to be broken for riding until they were four or five years old, and then they were good for about five or six years of steady work on the range. After that they were suitable for light work for a few more years around the ranch, or they could be sold for duty in a town. A stockman who raised some horses for market and some for the mines, in addition to all his own riding stock, and a supply of mules, required a large herd of brood mares to supply all these needs.

Out on the range the brood mares were grouped in small bands of about twenty to twenty-five head, each band led by a stallion. The foals, yearlings, and two-year-olds stayed with the mares, making a total of about fifty head in each band that had its own range. Unlike cattle, range horses seldom assembled in large herds.

Brood mares might be used at any time for riding or packing, but for the most part none of the range band ever felt a saddle. Such untrained animals and the young unbroken stallions were called broncos, and were quite different from the true wild horses, often known as mustangs. An unbroken horse of this kind was a bronco no matter what his age or breeding. He might even be of pedigreed stock, such as Arabian or Thoroughbred.

All of these range horses were corraled a few times each year. In early summer the foals were all roped and branded. Horses to be broken to ride were cut out early in the spring. Riding stock that had joined a range band for company could be recovered only by roping it in a wild chase or by putting the entire band in a corral. When the four-year-olds were cut out for breaking they were snorty and wild-eyed for a time, but they did not have the hysterical fear shown by most wild horses when they are corraled and roped.

The quality of the horses raised on the Mexican Plateau was good. It was maintained by culling out the poorer horses for the mines, and by importing good stallions from Spain. Ruxton recorded these details about his own horses.

I selected and purchased two horses from his stud, and better animals never felt the saddle: one [Panchito] I rode upwards of 3,000 miles and brought it to the end of the journey without flinching; . . . We entered a large plain well covered with grass, on which were immense flocks of sheep. A coyote lazily crossed the road, and, stopping within a few yards, sat down on its haunches, and cooly regarded us as we passed. Panchito had had a four day's rest and was in fine condition and spirits, and I determined to try the mettle of the wolf; the level plain, with its springy turf, offering a fine field for the course. Cantering gently at first, the coyote allowed me to approach within a hundred yards before he loped lazily away; but finding I was on his traces, he looked around and, gathering himself up, bowled away at full speed. Then I gave Panchito the spur, and answering it with a bound, we were soon at the stern of the wolf. Then for the first time, the animal saw we were in earnest, and, with a sweep of his bushy tail, pushed for his life across the plain. . . . Panchito bounded along like the wind itself, and soon proved to the wolf that his race was run. After trying in vain to double, he made one desperate rush, upon which, lifting Panchito with rein and leg, we came up and passed the panting beast. . . .

Ruxton also attended a fiesta at a hacienda:

We arrived at the rancho of La Putna in the afternoon, in time to witness the truly national sport of colea de toros—in English, bull-tailing. . . . When all was ready the bars were withdrawn from the entrance of the corral, and a bull was driven out. . . . With a shout the horsemen pursued the flying animal. . . . At least a dozen horse-men were now striving for the honour, but the roan distanced them all, and its rider . . . dashed up to the bull, threw his right leg over the tail, which he seized in his right hand, and, wheeling his horse suddenly outward, upset the bull in the midst of his career, and the huge animal rolled over and over in the dust bellowing with pain and fright.

This type of fiesta in the range country of Mexico was the progenitor of the rodeo of the West.

Above, Coronado's army attacks a pueblo. The legend that the Plains Indians first obtained horses from wild herds that were descended from strays from the Coronado and DeSoto expeditions has been discredited. No wild herds, such as the one below, were reported on the Plains until 1705, more than half a century after dispersal of horses among the Indians had begun. (Above, pen and ink by Charles M. Russell, Courtesy, Amon Carter Museum, Fort Worth, Texas; below, painting by A. J. Miller, The Walters Art Gallery)

4

Horses for the Indians

AT THE END OF THE SIXTEENTH CENTURY the ranching frontier stopped abruptly just beyond the northernmost of the mining camps, for where there was no mining there was no market for the rancher's livestock. The last post on the central plateau was Santa Barbara at the head of the Conchos River. Slave catchers and prospectors had made several excursions from this town down the Conchos and across the Rio Grande into Texas. In 1581 a missionary enterprise followed this route and reached the pueblo villages on the upper Rio Grande, but the friars were soon killed by the Indians. A military party sent to rescue the friars arrived too late to help them, but its leader, Antonio de Espejo, in searching westward into Arizona for an imaginary lake of gold, found rich veins of ore at Prescott. The potential mines were too far from any settlements to be worked until many years later.

Thirteen years after Espejo, Juan de Oñate led a party of 130 soldier-settlers and their families, together with many Negro and Indian slaves and several thousand head of livestock, to establish a permanent settlement in Otro Mexico, later New Mexico, so called because the pueblo village structures, visited and described by Coronado, resembled the buildings of the Aztecs in general appearance. Instead of following down the Conchos, Oñate decided to open up a new, shorter route directly to the north across the plateau. His trail led over several small ridges between the flat stretches and through great sand dunes directly to El Paso del Norte, where the Rio Grande del Norte broke through a high mountain barrier in a great gap. Three hundred miles to the north of El Paso

[49]

near the pueblos of Tiguex, Oñate put his first settlement. Ten years later the village of Santa Fe was located a distance away to the northeast toward the mountains on a side stream.

Oñate's colony was not very successful but it did survive, and in thirty years was surrounded by twenty-five flourishing Indian missions serving sixty pueblos with about sixty thousand people. The Spanish stockmen had ample pastures for large herds of cattle, sheep, and horses, but they had no ready market for the wool, hides, tallow, and meat. An attempt to domesticate buffalo failed miserably. The mature buffalo could not be herded or handled, and while the young calves were docile and easily captured, they became unruly and dangerous at the age of two years, even though they had been raised in the farmyard with goats for foster mothers.

For eighty years the colony continued its slow growth, producing no more than a fair living for its people, but it holds an important place in western history as the gateway to the Great Plains for two centuries. Its most important contribution to the development of the West was its mission of supplying horses to the Plains Indians long before white settlers from the East swarmed across the Mississippi, thus giving the nomadic tribes the opportunity to develop in isolation their elaborate culture complex centered around the horse and the buffalo.

A rather widespread, colorful legend explains in some detail how horses from De Soto's and Coronado's expeditions escaped on the Texas Plains and by natural increase stocked the entire Great Plains with wild herds by 1600 for the Indians to capture and use, but this legend has been thoroughly discredited. There is not a single fact to support it, while there are many pertinent objections.

A very important objection is that there was not one mare among De Soto's horses, nor any mention of any of his horses surviving. Even the five released on the bank of the lower Mississippi were shot down from ambush that same day by the Indians. Coronado's muster rolls list a total of three mares at Compostela, but there is no mention that any of them were taken beyond Tiguex when Coronado went east into the buffalo country, and in the careful records of the expedition, although horses are mentioned as being injured or killed, there is no mention of two or more animals straying away at one time.

Even if two or three horses had been lost on the plains of Texas they would have survived only with fantastic luck in that harsh environment before they became adjusted to its dangers. Exposed to winter storms and attacked by cougars and wolves, they were extremely vulnerable. But if the horses had managed to survive and multiply on the high plains of Texas, they would have had to make use of every water hole from time to time, and their sign near the water would have been plainly visible for fifteen or twenty years after their last visit—yet Spanish explorers crossing those plains several times in the next century never found a single trace of any horse, and no wild horses were reported in the whole region before 1705, more than a century and a half after Coronado and many years after the Indians in the Texas Panhandle had secured tame horses from the Spanish.

Intelligent and adaptable as the Plains Indians were, it is expecting too much of them that they should have been able, without instructions, to catch, tame, train, and use horses and to invent the necessary specialized horse gear in half a century—an accomplishment that took the combined experience of several million people more than five thousand years to accomplish in the Near East and the Mediterranean area. It is evident both from the rapid spread of the horse culture to the many tribes and its very close relationship in all major items to the horse culture of the Spanish colony in New Mexico that the Plains Indians must have borrowed both their horses and their horse culture from that colony.

During the first thirty years of the seventeenth century, the Indian missions along the Rio Grande Valley prospered more than did the settlers. In the twenty-five prosperous missions, schools were established where Indian children could learn to read and write in addition to having instruction in the manual arts and in agriculture. The mission farms and herds were all managed by the Indians with some supervision from the friars, and the young men had the breaking, training, and using of horses as part of their regular duties.

As the settlers gradually increased in numbers they drafted Pueblo Indians for farm labor and to help with the livestock. Boys were used around the corrals, especially to handle the riding stock, to groom and saddle the animals, and to bring them in from the range as they were needed. Some of these Indians learned to ride and in time became vaqueros. For a time in New Spain both the law and custom had frowned on any Indian ever being allowed to ride a horse, but in far-off New Mexico such restrictions gave way before the pressing need for more men to handle the increasing herds. If any of the skilled horsemen from either the missions or the ranches became irked with their Spanish masters, the horses offered them a ready means of escape from their bondage.

With all the pueblos and the surrounding country dominated by the Spanish, the fugitive had to seek refuge at quite a distance, and the buffalo plains offered the most attractive prospect. Buffalo hunters came to the pueblos each year, especially to Taos, to trade robes, dried meat, and captives for steel knives, needles, cloth, and the like. During these yearly visits they stayed several days and became friendly with some of the local Indians. It is probable that many an Indian planning an escape first asked the visitors for asylum before he ever left his home.

At times the Pueblos slipped away in a group. Such an instance is recorded in 1642, when some families went northeast to Kansas and settled with the Apaches in their farming villages. There they instructed their hosts in improved methods of gardening and pottery making. They might have taken along some horses too.

Some fugitives were less fortunate and became captives of some Plains band, sometimes becoming slaves but often being accepted as useful members of the band. In either case even one fugitive with a gentle, well-broken horse could instruct the whole band in the training, handling, and care of the animal, and then give riding instructions. In a short time the more ambitious young men would be ready to secure horses for themselves. They might trade for an animal at Taos if they could offer a Christian Indian captive in exchange, or they might steal a horse or two from the open range. While they were thus borrowing Spanish horses they also borrowed all the basic items of the horse complex, including the sophisticated horse gear developed in the Old World.

Each small village or band was on friendly terms with a few other bands, meeting them each year to visit and trade. After a band had secured a small horse herd of perhaps twenty animals, it could offer one of the gentle old ones in trade for various articles and give the necessary instructions for its care and use. The recipient band in turn would build up a small herd and trade off a few, always to Indians farther from the Spanish settlements. In this way the use of horses spread across the plains, hampered somewhat by the limited basic supply but proceeding rather rapidly because the entire plains was occupied by only a comparatively few small bands in the period of the horse dispersal, 1650–1780.

In 1680 the Pueblo Indians, with some help from visiting Apaches, rose up in revolt. They killed off or drove out all the Spanish and captured most of the range stock, including a few thousand horses. After the Spanish had gone, the Pueblos fell to bickering among themselves over the division of the spoils, and in the resulting turmoil the Apaches drove off many of the horses. Since the Pueblos did not value the horses very highly, they guarded them carelessly and lost many animals to raiders. They also traded off many more for Plains products and as ransom for captive relatives. As a result the Plains Indians secured more horses in a few months in 1680 than they had accumulated in thirty years. This increase in the horse supply was reflected at once in the more rapid movement outward of the horse frontier, which reached the Gulf coast in Texas by 1685 and northeastern Texas by 1690.

Although the horse was introduced into several new tribes at this time, the southward movement of some of those Plains tribes, particularly the Kiowas and Comanches, nearly canceled the movement, and the horse frontier remained almost stationary for a time. Also, as the horses moved radially from their distribution center, each hundred-mile advance brought an increasingly greater area to be occupied. Even with all the Spanish horses acquired in 1680 and new animals secured each year through trading and raids, plus the natural increase in the Indian herds, it required a century for the horses to reach the northern limits of the Great Plains in Canada.

In the nineteenth century any one of the larger tribes, such as the Comanches, Sioux, or Blackfeet, had more horses than all the herds from New Mexico in 1680, but at that early period the Plains tribes were fewer in number and smaller in size, with a total population south of Nebraska of about twenty thousand people. Since those tribes at first considered a horse or two for each hunter real wealth, five thousand horses would have sufficed to equip them all, yet a century later any one of the tribes would have felt poor indeed with fewer than five to ten horses for each hunter. As each tribe desired more and more horses with the passing years, its wants were supplied in part by the natural increase of its herds and in part by new stock from the settlements.

West of the Rocky Mountains the spread of the horse is a story separate from that of the plains. From Taos north to the Upper Snake Valley only the Navahos and the Utes were across the distribution route, and both tribes were small and had little use for horses at first. Since the Navahos had enough horses in 1659 to stage a mounted raid almost to Santa Fe, it is probable that they had already traded a few animals to the Utes by that time, who in turn could have passed them along to the

Shoshonis along the Bear River by 1670. From that point north into the upper Missouri drainage, the whole area is highly suitable for range horses, and the Shoshonis controlled it all. Their herds prospered in the favorable environment. Soon horses from their ranges were moving out to the east, north, and west—to the Wind River Shoshonis through South Pass, down the Yellowstone to the Crows, north along the eastern face of the Rockies to the Blackfeet in Alberta, directly north to the Flatheads in the Bitterroot country, and west and then northwest to the Nez Percés and Cayuses in the Columbia Basin. All the tribes mentioned had at least a few horses by 1730, when the horse frontier on the plains had barely reached the Platte River in Nebraska.

While the horses were spreading throughout the West from the Spanish colony in New Mexico, a similar movement of horses on a much smaller scale occurred east of the Mississippi. Several Spanish expeditions, notably those led by Narváez and De Soto, rode their horses through the country, but there is not a shred of evidence to indicate that any of their horses were left behind to start a local band. About the time Oñate moved to the Rio Grande, Franciscan missionaries established a chain of missions in Georgia. By 1615 these Guale missions numbered more than twenty, with farms and livestock at each one. Detailed reports of their activities are lacking, but it is known that they prospered for many years before they were overrun and destroyed by slavers and stock rustlers from the Carolina settlements.

On these mission farms, the Indians learned to handle and use horses as part of their regular duties. In time these farms were the source of horses and other livestock for the Indians to the northwest—principally the Creeks, Cherokees, and Chickasaws, who were trained in their care and use by the missions' Indians. All of these tribes had horses early in the seventeenth century.

These tribes were farming people, living in permanent villages surrounded by cornfields. Since they had few buffalo to hunt in the small glades and no wide plains to roam, they had no incentive to become even seminomadic and needed fewer horses for their occasional rides than did the Plains tribes, but they did use a large number for pack animals. They had established friendly relations with traders along the Georgia coast as early as 1603, when a merchant ship secured a cargo of deer hides from them. After that the Indians offered bundles of hides in exchange for trade goods, bringing to market about 200,000 hides a year over a long period. The deer hides were in great demand in England at the time, where they were tanned into soft buckskin for use in making clothing.

After the English colony was established at Charleston in 1670 the hide trade moved through that port, an important item of trade. The settlers bought horses from the Indians as well, to use on their farms. In many of the old records these are called Chickasaw horses, although sometimes a distinction is made between the horses from the south toward Florida and those from the west. Here is a firsthand account of the horses as recorded in 1774 by John Bartram, a naturalist who visited the horse-using tribes.

The Seminole horses [from Florida] are the most beautiful and sprightly species of that noble creature, perhaps anywhere to be seen; but are of a small breed and as delicately formed as the American roe-buck. . . . The Seminole horses are said to descend originally from the Andalusian breed, brought here by the Spaniards when they first established the colony of East Florida. From the forehead to their nose is a little arched or aquiline, and so are the Choctaw horses among the Upper Creeks, which are said to have been brought across the Mississippi, by those nations of Indians who emigrated from the West, beyond the river. Those horses are everywhere like the Seminole breed, only larger, and perhaps not so lively and capricious. It is a matter of conjecture and inquiry, whether or not the different soil and situation of the country have contributed in some measure, in forming and establishing the difference in size and other qualities between them. I have observed the horses and other animals in the high hilly country of Carolina, Georgia and Virginia and all along our shores are of much larger and stronger make than those which are bred in the flat country next the sea coast.

The Shawnee Indians who were driven from Tennessee north into Kentucky and Ohio also had horses of the Chickasaw stock.

5

Horses of the Atlantic Seaboard

DURING THE SIXTEENTH CENTURY English, Dutch, and French ships, manned by pirates according to the Spanish, and by freebooters according to themselves, sailed to the Atlantic coast and to the West Indies to lie in wait for the treasure galleons carrying gold and silver from Peru and Mexico to Spain. For pastime and profit while they waited, they slaughtered Spanish cattle on the islands for their hides and tallow, and dried the meat into boucan—thus earning for themselves the new name, buccaneers. Their continued depredations over many years brought ruin to the stockmen of Puerto Rico and Hispaniola.

The defeat of the Spanish Armada by the English navy in 1588 opened the way for England and other nations to begin establishing colonies in the New World. Virginia was settled by the English in 1607, the first permanent settlement in Canada was made by the French at Quebec in 1608, and New York was first settled by the Dutch in 1624. However, lands in the West Indies, where cane for sugar and rum provided a quick and high profit, were preferable. England colonized Barbados in 1627 and seized Jamaica from the Spanish in 1655; Curaçao was taken by the Dutch from the Spanish in 1634. In time the Spanish horses and cattle on these islands were taken to the mainland colonies, for it was much cheaper and easier to ship stock from the West Indies than from Europe.

The Spanish cattle were smaller and trimmer than the Dutch and English stock, and produced a poorer grade of oxen, so bulls were brought from Europe to increase the size of the draft stock. During the first half-century cattle and oxen were considered of more value to the new settlers than horses, for the cattle could produce milk, meat, and hides in addition to serving as work teams.

The story of the horse in colonial Virginia divides naturally into three periods. In the first, from 1607 to about 1675, horses were considered of little value and were raised only in small numbers. Several small shipments of horses were brought to Jamestown between 1608 and 1625, including one group of twenty mares from England. All the first horses were either lost to Indian attack or eaten by the starving settlers. After 1625 more horses were brought over, this time from Ireland, where the native horses of the period were rather stocky and heavy-boned, and grew heavy, shaggy coats in winter.

The small amount of work for horses on the tidewater plantations, along with their higher cost of maintenance as compared to oxen, kept horse production at a low level. In the winter they could not subsist on forage but required some grain or hay supplement. Most of the horses in the colony were found on the newer farms back from the navigable streams, where they were used in pack trains to transport goods to and from the riverboats. These outlying farms suffered severely from Indian attacks. In a short but bloody war in 1622 they lost five hundred settlers and almost all their livestock. Another such war in 1644 also ravaged the border farms, and it is probable that many of the horses escaped in the turmoil and moved westward to the hills, where they had better forage for the winter. In a few years they became wild and remained so until their range was occupied by settlers.

After the Indians had been subdued in fierce fighting and had been forced off the farms by the repeated destruction of their crops, the settlers moved back to their own farms, but some of the effects of the war are evident in the census of 1649, when the colony reported a total of two hundred horses for fifteen thousand people. No mention is made of the number of horses lost in the war, but two hundred horses would have been a scant number for even a small hacienda in New Mexico.

During Cromwell's rule in England (1649–1660) many of the king's followers and some others who wished to escape the civil disturbances flocked to Virginia, increasing the population from fifteen thousand to forty thousand in seventeen years. This great number of new settlers had to find lands to the west of the settled areas and soon extended the settlements to the base of the Blue Ridge Mountains. On the hills there they found bands of wild horses, which soon became a nuisance to the crops. Some of them were captured and tamed, some were hunted down with packs of dogs, and some were shot. The law held that any farmer could shoot without penalty any free-ranging horse that came into his orchard for the third time.

This push to the west brought new conflict with the Indians on the border, who were being squeezed on the other side by Senecas from the Mohawk Valley. Disagreements on how to handle the Indians, along with other points of friction, led to Bacon's Rebellion in 1676. After the border settled down again, the new growth continued, always pushing to the west and southwest and increasing the need for more horses. The breeding farms stepped up their production and some animals were brought in from the Spanish West Indies, contrary to Spanish law. These imports were accurately described as of Spanish blood and were often brought by ships from England that had stopped off at the islands to trade on their way to Virginia. Soon, and often by deliberate intent, these imported horses were listed as horses from Spain by way of England, or even as pure Arabian blood from Spain. A few stallions were also imported directly from England.

This clandestine trade with the West Indies left only a few vague records, but the circumstantial evidence for it is strong. It has also left its mark on two small offshore islands, where many ships have been wrecked. According to legend, a Spanish ship with a load of horses from Spain was wrecked on Sable Island near the coast of Nova Scotia. The horses swam ashore and adapted themselves to the new environment, where their offspring survive to this day. At about the same time, again according to legend, a Spanish ship with horses from Spain was wrecked on Assateague Island off the Virginia coast. Again the horses swam ashore, and their offspring have survived. The only legendary item in each story is the Spanish ship, for no Spanish ship carrying horses from Spain would ever have been in those waters, even if driven off course by a great storm. Instead the ships were English or Dutch, bringing horses from the West Indies, and were only two of many such ships in the trade.

In New York and Pennsylvania the introduction of horses followed a pattern somewhat different from that of Virginia. From the first the Dutch preferred horses over oxen as draft animals for many tasks and brought in some of the heavy draft stock from the Netherlands to cross with the Spanish stock from Curaçao. Their herds, especially those on Long Island, were safe from attacks by Indians.

Pennsylvania had a few settlers before William Penn took it over in 1682. He brought over thousands of farmers from the lower Rhine, who found the rich, rolling lands southwest of Philadelphia desirable, but the farms there were far from water transport. These Germans, or Pennsylvania Dutch, favored draft horses over oxen for hauling their produce to market and bred up heavier horses for their needs as did the Dutch in New York.

In New England horses were used very little in the early period. They were expensive to keep and riding horses were considered somewhat sinful by the Puritans, who objected to many of the things favored by the landed gentry of England. In Connecticut horse racing was banned by law, and it was discouraged by social pressure in Massachusetts and Rhode Island. During the same period racing was a popular sport from New York to Georgia and was favored by colonial officials.

In the seventeenth century racing was confined to short distances on straightaway tracks, which were usually just rough dirt strips with the trees and brush removed. The tracks were about a quarter of a mile long and favored sprint horses that, from the length of the race, became known as quarter horses. For these races the gentlemen of South Carolina and Virginia found the Chickasaw horses very good, especially if they were bred up a little in size by the use of imported stallions.

No one has seen fit to leave a detailed record or even a description of the early race meets, but such events must have been common, as is shown by the casual references that have survived. In the earliest known mention of racing in Virginia, a justice of the peace in 1674 fined a tailor for racing with a physician, ruling that racing was a sport reserved for gentlemen. At the small fairs and celebrations horse racing was always an important part of the program even when it was not the primary purpose of the gathering. To break the monotony of many races, a number of innovations were introduced to entertain the crowd. In one kind of race the last horse to cross the finish line was declared the winner. In order to make such a race a real contest, each man who entered a horse had to ride an opponent's horse, and his own horse could win the prize only if he drove his mount ahead.

Back from the tidewater the farmers raised grain as a chief crop. For a century or more the common method of threshing was to place the grain on a well-packed circular path about fourteen feet wide and a hundred feet in diameter. The horses were then led around the circle at a sober trot until the grain had been separated from the straw. Oxen were considered unsatisfactory for this work, presumably because they could not trot for a long time at a stretch.

As early as 1657 the West Indies, especially the sugar islands of Nevis, Barbados, and Jamaica, became large importers of horses to use in the many sugar cane crushing mills. The island horse herds dwindled rapidly as the land was put into sugar plantations, cutting down on the available pasture, and the horses used in the mills died off rapidly from overwork and poor care. To supply this new market, prosperous merchants in New England turned to raising horses as a sideline. They sold their poorer horses to the sugar mills, but the pick of their herds went to the wealthy plantation owners to be used as riding horses.

A point of land jutting into the tidewater made a good safe pasture, needing only a strong fence or stone wall across a narrow neck to provide several hundred acres of good range land where horses could be raised with little supervision. This practice is illustrated in a letter from John Hull to Governor Arnold of Rhode Island.

> Procure a very good breed of large and fine mares and stallions for Point Judith and fence off the neck with a stone wall at the north end thereof—that noe mungrell breed might come among them—We might have a very choice breed of coach horses, for saddle some and for draught others, and in a very few years might draw off considerable numbers and ship them to Barbados, Nevis and such parts of the Indies where they would vend.

In 1685 Hull also stocked Boston Neck with horses in the same fashion. Nearly a century later a famous running horse, Old Snipe, was foaled on Point Judith in the old pasture.

The Narragansett pacer was a type of horse credited to the New England horse breeders for its development. The foundation stock came either from Spain, imported by Governor Robinson of Rhode Island, or from the West Indies, possibly by the way of New York and the Dutch traders. These pacers were in great demand as riding horses for use on smooth ground, their gait being especially pleasing to women riders, but a pacer is useless for rough country or for handling stock. A few of the Narragansett breed found their way to Virginia and

South Carolina, but most of them sold at good prices in the West Indies. Only one or two specimens of this strain were known in New England after the American Revolution.

About 1730, horsemen in England stepped up their program for raising superior racing horses by importing several good stallions from the continent, northern Africa, and the Near East, and they started keeping more exact breeding records by listing the dams as well as the sires of their foals. In a few years wealthy Virginia planters began buying some of the fine stallions produced under the new program. In 1746 Janus, a spotted stallion, was brought to Virginia, where he sired a large number of exceptional colts, most of them spotted as he was. These colts were from Virginia-raised mares, most of them carrying a heavy concentration of the Chickasaw strain, or from mares from the West Indies and Rhode Island. There is no indication that mares were imported directly from England at this time.

A few more potent sires were imported about 1750, and these good stallions altogether produced a few hundred good colts by the time of the Revolution, furnishing a heritage of English blood to several thousand American horses that also carried one half or more of the old Virginia and Chickasaw blood.

Breeders in South Carolina also imported some sires directly from England and several more from Rhode Island to cross with their local Chickasaw mares. Only a small percentage of these horses actually came from the Chickasaw country. The great majority were stolen from the Spanish missions in Guale. Although both English and colonial officials banned any attacks on the Spanish in time of peace, the large-scale raids continued. The droves of horses and cattle brought back as plunder were classed as wild, unclaimed animals from the backwoods. By the time England finally acquired Florida in 1763, the entire group of prosperous missions with their several thousand peaceful Christian Indians had been destroyed.

From the tidewater clear back to the mountains, South Carolina had fine ranges for its stock, and the growers prospered. They found a ready market for all their surplus horses in the West Indies, where they could undersell the New Englanders because they were much closer to the market. They shipped the hides and tallow from their cattle to England, and sold some dried beef to the sugar plantations on the islands.

The French and Indian War, 1754–1763, brought a steady demand for heavy draft horses from New York, Pennsylvania, and Virginia to haul artillery and supply trains for several military expeditions. When General Edward Braddock, in May 1755, moved west from Virginia and across the mountain ridges in southern Pennsylvania in his attempt to capture Fort Duquesne, he had a large party of axmen proceed in advance to cut a swath through the timber and brush from Fort Cumberland westward. At first called Braddock's Trace, it later became the Cumberland Road. Braddock found the Alleghenies too rough for his wagons, and after advancing thirty miles across the first ridge he abandoned them and used pack trains for the rest of the way. Three years later General John Forbes led a successful advance against Fort Duquesne. He went across the mountains north of Braddock's route, from Harrisburg west, cutting a new trace across the ridges that became Forbes' Road.

The outbreak of the American Revolution in 1775 brought an increased demand for horses. To put down the rebel movement, the British moved large armies across the Atlantic to Boston, New York, and South Carolina. In each case the British needed horses as mounts for their officers, cavalry, and scouts; as teams for their artillery and supply trains; and as pack animals in rough country. Their procedure was to occupy a good harbor in settled country, then send out men to procure a supply of animals. If the port was in Loyalist country all the necessary horses could be purchased with little trouble, the farmers swarming into the market with their stock. In neutral areas the buyers who went out to the farms with ready cash were welcome, while in areas filled with patriot sympathizers the horses were captured by mounted raiders. In New England and Pennsylvania the British used a great many draft animals, while in the Carolinas during the closing years of the war the cavalry and mounted raiders became increasingly important.

Throughout the war, horses were more important to the colonial forces than to the British, just from the nature of the armies. The British had a supply of trained infantry, a substantial force of cavalry, and additional Loyalist scouts, guides, packers, teamsters, and the like. They always had an effective force ready for battle on short notice. Although the colonial army in time built up several regiments of well-trained infantry, they could not match the British in numbers of regiments of well-disciplined men. The American army as a whole worked mostly on a different pattern, often quite exasperating to the officers, but it was the only pattern the bulk of the men would follow.

Each spring after the crops were in, or any time of year when some special excitement was forecast, the American militia gathered in large numbers. Each man mounted his horse and rode away to war for a time, but he was poorly trained for fighting pitched battles. He and his friends fought well from cover, and made good forces to attack outposts and supply trains. They could gather quickly where the enemy least expected them and could vanish just as quickly if they were pursued or if they felt like going home.

To illustrate how deadly such a force might be under good leadership and the right conditions, consider two of the largest engagements fought in the Carolina back country—King's Mountain and Cowpens.

The King's Mountain fight, on October 7, 1780, was a bitter struggle between a British foraging party of about 1,100 men under Major Patrick Ferguson and 930 militia hurriedly assembled from the piedmont country of North and South Carolina and from the Watagua settlement in eastern Tennessee. When Ferguson had marched out to pacify the western Carolinas by hanging all the rebels and destroying their farms, he had sent an arrogant message across to the Wataguans threatening to attack their settlement and hang them all if they did not stay home and behave.

Smarting under this threat and anxious to help their compatriots east of the mountains, a large contingent of local militia assembled and rode east across the mountains on a long, difficult route to conceal their movements from Ferguson's scouts. At Cowpens in northwestern South Carolina they met a few hundred of the Carolinians who had come from all directions to join them. They chose 930 of their best men and moved directly against King's Mountain, thirty miles away, where Ferguson had taken up a strong position on the extreme eastern spur of the mountain ridge. This spur rose sharply about sixty feet above the open country. It was flat on top, with the sides covered with boulders, brush, and some trees. The Americans rode up, dismounted and tied their horses, and surrounded the spur. Then they fought their way up the brushy slopes, being more than a match for Ferguson's men when they could fight from cover. They wiped out the entire force, their riflemen pouring out a deadly fire from behind trees and other shelter on the British, who were massed in the open.

A similar hasty gathering of a few hundred militia helped General Daniel Morgan defeat the redoubtable Colonel Banastre "Bloody"

Tarleton in January 1781 at Cowpens, a complex of corrals for rounding up and branding cattle that ranged the hill country among the scattered trees. Here in the open glade of several hundred acres General Morgan set a trap for the British, who were pursuing him closely. He had his militia tie their horses in the rear and then put them well down the slope in the first line. There they had a little cover in the deep grass and a few scanty shrubs. They had orders to wait until the British approached within range; then each was to shoot twice and retreat up the hill to new cover, where Morgan had about three hundred regular troops and eighty dragoons under Colonel William Washington. Tarleton's force was of about equal size, but he had three hundred dragoons, three cannon, and a fine regiment of Royal Highlanders. When he advanced to the attack the accurate rifle fire from the militia mowed down his officers and threw the troops into confusion, allowing Washington's cavalry to make a devastating charge. The British were completely disorganized and were driven from the field with heavy losses.

During the war in the South the British, with help from the local Loyalists, dashed about the countryside on foraging expeditions, killing any rebels they could catch and laying waste the farms. When outnumbered, the local militia scattered and hid in the swamps, only to regroup and attack any foragers they could surprise, and often they succeeded in inflicting heavy losses. For two years much of the military action was carried out by parties of mounted men from both armies, who, by their combined efforts, captured almost every horse in the country. This guerrilla warfare provided many incidents such as the following: A prosperous Loyalist owned a very fine horse that he offered to Tarleton as a present. One afternoon an orderly rode in to the plantation and said he had come for the colonel's horse. Only after he had vanished down the road did the duped Loyalist learn that the orderly was from the American camp.

In the small-scale but often spectacular operations west of the Alleghenies horses were of little use in the war except occasionally as pack animals. The Shawnee Indians of southern Ohio owned some horses they had brought from Tennessee when they were driven from their old homes by the Cherokees. The French settlements in southern Illinois had a few horses secured from west of the Mississippi, but no horses had as yet reached Detroit.

Even at this early date stories had crossed the Alleghenies about the fine Spanish horses among the Plains Indians just west of the Mississippi.

After hearing such reports, Governor Patrick Henry of Virginia, on December 12, 1778, wrote to George Rogers Clark, commander of the Virginia forces west of the mountains, to purchase two stallions and eight mares of the best Spanish blood even if he had to send men into Iowa to get them. The governor wanted them in Virginia in time for the spring breeding season. Clark answered from Vincennes early in the spring:

> ... there being no such horses as you request me to get. The Pawnee and Chicsa [Chickasaw] Horses are very good and some of them are delicate. ... The finest stallion by far that is in the country I purchased some time ago and rode him on this expedition [from Kaskaskia to Vincennes]. He came first from New Mexico. ... I could soon get five or six mares at the Illinois [settlements] very fine but I think they are hurt by usage.

For most of the settlements in the Atlantic colonies in the early period, transportation was by sea, tidewater estuaries, and navigable streams. The various colonies were often annoyed at each other, the hostile Dutch occupied New York, and the roads, just dirt tracks through the woods, usually led from the wharfs to farms a few miles away. Finally the English took New York from the Dutch in 1664, and by 1704 they had laid out a post road from Boston to New York. This was a primitive track through the woods most of the way, with streams to be forded or ferried. Gradually the post road was extended south to Philadelphia, Baltimore, and eventually to Georgia. Along the entire route, except at New York and Philadelphia, the road kept well back from tidewater areas to avoid estuaries, swamps, and marshes.

The Revolution brought a rapid development of new routes of travel although it did nothing for road improvement. When one of the armies took a long march across country, as Lord Cornwallis did with his troops from Charleston, South Carolina, to Yorktown, Virginia, the passage of his thousands of troops, hundreds of mounted men, and artillery trains and supply wagons left a broad track through the trees and brush from one good river crossing to the next that could easily be followed by later travelers. In the same way the march of the French troops from Rhode Island and Washington's forces from northern New Jersey to Yorktown also left a well-marked track to the head of Chesapeake Bay. Additional shorter routes were cut across New Jersey,

Pennsylvania, and the southern states—some of them from the ports to the back country—and where the army had gone civilians could follow.

During the war the armies had secured draft horses whenever they could be found. As the continual demand for heavier horses increased, so did the price, and the stockmen were soon breeding more of the larger animals. When the war ended the demand for draft horses continued, for peace brought an increase in population and a need for better lines of communication across the land. The old Post Road between New York and Boston was improved and extended. Stagecoaches and freight wagons had much new work to do, and replaced most of the pack trains on the older trails. Although a good deal of travel was still done on horseback, the stage lines rapidly built up their passenger business.

Better roads brought an increase in private vehicles too. Coaches, carts, and wagons moved more people and more produce. All of these needed larger horses than the light riding type. The larger Chickasaw mares were crossed with draft stallions from the Dutch stock or from new imports. Enough larger stallions were soon available to cover all the larger mares, and this selective breeding soon produced a good supply of draft stock that weighed eleven hundred to twelve hundred pounds each. Such horses were also in demand in the towns, moving heavy loads to and from the docks, hauling building materials, and bringing in large loads of farm produce. This steady demand continued, and the breeders continued to meet it, until the whole pattern was drastically changed in the twentieth century by the gasoline motor.

6

Mounted Warriors
of the Plains

AFTER THE REVOLUTION the great valleys across the Appalachians beckoned the land-hungry migrants moving westward from the Atlantic seaboard and from Europe. On foot, trudging alongside their pack strings or carts and herding a few cattle, or on horseback and supervising a caravan, they swarmed up the Mohawk Valley into northern Ohio, or along the Forbes Road and the Cumberland Road to the forks of the Ohio and on down the great river, or along the Valley of Virginia into Kentucky and Tennessee, or westward from Georgia south of the mountain chain. For this sort of cross-country travel horses were superior to oxen, and they were ridden, or hitched to carts, or loaded with packs, while the loose cattle were herded along the rough tracks.

The new settlers cried loudly to the army to clear the new frontiers of Indians, then found themselves blocked in their expansion by the Spanish, who owned the entire west bank of the Mississippi and the port of New Orleans and thus had a stranglehold on all the produce shipped down the river to market. Finally Napoleon tricked Spain out of Louisiana and offered the entire Louisiana Territory to the United States. When Thomas Jefferson authorized the purchase, the United States not only doubled its land size but got forty million buffalo and other more important natural resources too numerous to mention. In 1804 the whole American West to the crest of the Rockies lay open to the settlers who moved out from St. Louis to explore and exploit the new land. There they encountered tribes of mounted Indians, nomads of the plains, with their elaborate culture complex based on horses and buffalo. The newcomers accepted the Indians without question, assuming that the red men had lived that way for centuries, not realizing that this culture of the plains was something new, and just coming into full flower. Not always had the Indians followed the buffalo the year around.

In earlier times, when the bitter cold winds blew in from the north and drifting snows swept across the plains, even the hardiest of the buffalo hunters had needed more shelter than their little tipis provided and more food than they could find each day on a hunt for the elusive buffalo shrouded by the storm. Some of the bands from the Texas Panhandle moved west and visited the friendly pueblos in New Mexico for the winter months. Others, like the Comanches, found refuge in the foothills of the Rockies, where they had cached their food reserves of seeds and nuts from their autumn gleanings and their dried meat and buffalo robes from their big fall hunt.

The Apaches, scattered in little villages of earth lodges along the streams in western Kansas, followed the buffalo herds for several months of each year, but they raised some garden vegetables and corn for the lean winter months. Many other villages of several different tribes, such as the Mandans, were also scattered throughout the plains with their permanent villages and garden patches, and they followed much the same pattern as the Apaches, hunting buffalo for their meat supplies.

Along the eastern fringe of the grasslands, sheltered among the scattered groves, several large tribes lived in permanent villages, their dwellings made with heavy timber frames covered with mats. They raised large fields of corn for their staple food supply and usually went out on the plains on a short hunt in midsummer and a longer hunt in the fall. This group included the Pawnees and Osages.

Until the coming of the horse, none of the people mentioned were truly nomadic, for each group had a permanent wintering place that it occupied for at least three months each year. After the horse came, the whole plains country was occupied by tribes of true nomads following the buffalo herds the year around. They traded with their farming neighbors for any grain and vegetables they used.

Picketing horses. Plains Indians kept some riding horses near camp at all times, especially for rounding up and bringing in their herds. At least one horse would be picketed on a long rope tied to a halter or a front foot, while several others might be fitted with hobbles of leather or buffalo hide. (Painting by A. J. Miller, The Walters Art Gallery)

Hunters like the Comanches, who raised no gardens or grain, quickly adjusted to the new nomadic pattern. The only incentive they needed for the change from the old ways was the surety of more food to be harvested from the buffalo herds by using horses. Tribes with permanent houses and staple grain crops were reluctant to make such a drastic change. They used their horses to travel farther after buffalo and to stay longer than before on the open plains, but they moved from their permanent homes only under heavy pressure from their enemies. The Sioux, for instance, had horses for a century before the last of the tribe gave up their old homes in the Minnesota lake country. Other tribes on the forest fringe, such as the Osages, were out of the main stream of the westward-moving whites and kept their homes until the buffalo were gone and the tribe had to move to a reservation. It is evident from a consideration of the many tribes using horses to hunt buffalo that this did not automatically induce them to become nomads.

All of the tribes, nomadic or seminomadic, rather quickly adopted the body of economic and social practices typical of the new buffalo and horse culture. Then they added most of the stylized warfare patterns and adopted similar colorful costumes until it was difficult to believe that they did not all come from closely related parent stocks, when in reality they came from various ethnic groups that differed greatly from one another in language and physical characteristics.

A tribe just getting its first horses found them useful at once as pack animals for moving camp or for carrying in game. One horse was at least as easy to manage as the tamest dog and could carry five or six times the load. More importantly, the horse lived on forage while the dog ate meat. In times of good hunting, dogs could live well on the odds and ends from the kills, but in hard times the people ate all the scraps and left the dogs to starve, or ate the dogs too.

In a year or so, an Indian with a new horse had learned to ride well enough to chase buffalo. While good buffalo horses were always scarce, even in a herd of several thousand animals, a fairly good riding horse could catch one buffalo in a short sprint if the animal did not have too much of a head start. Then an arrow or two in the paunch or a well-placed thrust of the lance brought down the prey. An ordinary riding horse could not dash through the herd and put the hunter near the choicest animals, but even the lagging tough old bull buffalo could provide acceptable, nutritious meat for a hundred people for a day.

A small Indian band with just a few horses never had to starve in the buffalo country, although the people might be on short rations at times during a severe winter storm when the buffalo were scrawny and hard to find. And a band with an assured food supply could raise more babies to healthy adulthood and could afford to keep feeble old people until they died a natural death. In hunting tribes, in times of actual starvation, the first to die were the old people, then the youngest children, for they could best be spared, while the young adults, especially the hunters, had to live to insure the survival of the band.

Once the Indians became skilled at hunting on horseback they found that one good man on a good horse could kill enough buffalo in a morning's run to feed a family group of twenty or so for several days, with plenty of meat for the drying racks and piles of scraps for the dogs. This left the successful hunter with a great deal of leisure time to be spent visiting with his cronies, making weapons and ornaments, handling his horses, or going off with a few kindred souls to raid an enemy camp.

A hunter felt that he had finished his day's work as soon as he had killed the buffalo. When he found smaller game he dressed it out and took it into camp, but the buffalo lay where they had fallen until the women arrived with knives and pack horses to do the butchering and take the meat and hides back to camp, although the men sometimes helped in skinning and packing the meat onto the horses. More often they just stayed near, alert for any sign of enemy raiders.

The women dried the surplus meat, dressed the hides into rawhide, robes, or leather, and made the tipi coverings and all the clothes. They collected fuel for the fires, usually buffalo "chips" (dried dung), and carried the water. They cut the tipi poles, put up and took down the tipis, saddled and unsaddled the pack string, loaded and unloaded the animals—a regular set of chores when camp was moved every day or two. In addition to these tasks, they did the cooking and raised the children.

As the regular kill of buffalo increased, the work of caring for all the products from the animals also increased until there was much more work in a family than any one woman could possibly manage. The full-time efforts of three women barely sufficed, while five or six were not too many, if the head of the family was a successful hunter. In a nomad band there were always extra women, for the dangers of plains life killed off many men. War, hunting, and horsebreaking took their toll, leaving many widows, and more girls than young men. The older widow found a welcome in the home of a sister, daughter, or niece. Younger widows and the extra girls became the second or third wives of successful hunters, often at the suggestion of the first wife. In this way the family unit was about twice as large as it had been in the old days, an increase born of necessity and retained because it was an obvious benefit to all concerned, as well as being a source of strength for the whole band.

Visitors from other cultures were often annoyed at what they considered the extreme laziness of the Indian men and the hard lot of their women, who worked long hours with never a helping hand being offered except in some extreme emergency. There sat the idle men in a tipi or on a sunlit knoll, yet the women never complained, for those idle loungers were the guardians of the group's safety, ready at a moment's notice to ward off any danger, and the women definitely preferred to stay alive rather than be helped with their tasks.

As the food supply increased, the size of the individual hunting bands also increased until the old custom of maintaining discipline and order by social pressure from the group was inadequate, especially if two or three of the bands gathered for a common hunt or for visiting and trading. Then more formal controls were needed to keep order among several hundred people. All of the Plains tribes adopted some sort of police who were specifically given the responsibility of keeping peace in the camp and order on the hunt. These police groups were patterned after that used by the Sioux for many years before they moved west from Illinois into Minnesota.

Since Indians did not levy fines as penalties, and could not imprison anyone, culprits were commonly punished by whippings, which were physically painful and carried a heavy burden of social disapproval. Flagrant violations of the hunting code resulted in the man's being deprived of all his meat, which was then distributed around the camp. He also might have his bow and arrows broken, and in extreme cases, have a horse killed and his tipi slashed. While friends of the culprit might ask that he be given a light punishment, there is no record that they ever intervened after the decision had been made.

Among the Plains tribes war was a highly stylized game with an elaborate system of scoring points while escaping injury. Seldom did a tribe embark on a war of conquest, and pitched battles on a large scale were rare. Even a warlike tribe might have a major fight only once in fifteen or twenty years, but each year hundreds of small raiding parties roamed the plains in search of honor and horses, more anxious to return safely with a little loot than to lose one or two warriors in securing a fortune. The individual preferred to win his honors by stealth and trickery, especially in stealing horses.

A horse raid usually began with a warrior having a dream about a successful venture. He then invited any of his friends who wanted adventure to accompany him, and according to his reputation as a good dreamer and a lucky leader, he would get some followers. If fewer than five volunteered he usually called off the raid. If more than thirty liked him for a leader he expanded its scope into a hit-and-run attack on an enemy camp.

The men then took their ritual sweat baths, bundled up several pairs of moccasins each, a small robe, a little dried meat, and their weapons, and slipped away into the darkness to avoid the notice of any enemy scout who might be in the area. If the raiding party happened to be Blackfeet from Alberta on their way to the Spanish ranches in New Mexico, eleven hundred miles to the south, they might need a few dogs to carry the extra moccasins and dried meat needed for such a long trip. They went on foot, for they could travel faster and with less risk of discovery than could mounted men. Their feet left only a dim trail, and they could do much of their traveling at night, slipping by enemy camps undetected.

The raiders always wanted all the horses they could find, but they were constantly on the lookout for some special war-horse or buffalo runner. In a strange camp these could be recognized from a distance, for they were always kept on a picket line and in the evening were tied near the owners' tipis with little girls assigned to pick grass to feed them. If the owner of a special horse sensed danger, he might even put his prized mount inside the tipi for the night, moving some little girls out to make the necessary room, because such a horse was one in a thousand, or even one in ten thousand, while more little girls could be much more easily had. A horse thief who could evade the people and the dogs, and cut loose such a horse, had both honor and profit for his skill and daring.

When a scouting party went out from a camp searching for game and signs of the enemy they were mounted and often carried their war regalia. If they met a similar party of some enemy tribe, they would attack if they had the advantage. In such an encounter the chief objective was for a warrior to "count coup" on an enemy. The highest-ranking coup was achieved by an unarmed man dashing up to an armed enemy, striking him with a small coup stick, and escaping unscathed. This feat required a good horse, great skill and courage, and a modicum of luck. To wrest a weapon from an unwounded enemy and kill him with it rated almost as highly.

Always in such encounters, if time permitted, all the Indians of both parties put on their war paint and feathers before the attack. If the scouting party expected trouble, they rode ordinary horses and led their war-horses to keep them fresh for the fight. Although the resulting action might be a long-range skirmish with little damage to either side, it was a highly colorful affair and eminently satisfying to the warriors.

The many small raiding parties scurrying around the plains and busily transferring horses from the herds of one tribe to those of another often made a blurred and confusing pattern, like the eddies in a stream that flows steadily onward. Here the stream of horses flowed from the southwest—from the ranches of Texas, New Mexico, and Chihuahua to Canada in the north and across the Mississippi to the northeast, the flow dwindling steadily as the trail lengthened.

By 1770 all the Plains Indians had breeding stock well suited to the environment. Seemingly the natural increase of the herds should have filled all the grasslands to overflowing in half a century, yet the horse population leveled off and it required the addition of thousands of new animals each year from the southwest just to maintain its numbers, for the losses were high.

Each year several hundred animals were traded across the Mississippi, and in times of famine a number of horses were killed for food. The herds were subjected to attacks by wolves and were harmed by winter storms and neglect. Some horses died on the buffalo hunts and some were killed in battle, but the severe losses came from the abuse of the mares. Pregnant mares were run to exhaustion in the buffalo hunts, or worked too much in the pack strings while the foals were very young. In some tribes both of these practices caused heavy losses of both mares and foals. Other tribes with the same basic breeding stock, notably the Cayuses and the Nez Percés, took care of their brood mares and were rewarded with more and better foals.

While the Indian raiders and traders were securing horses from the Spanish settlements they also acquired all sorts of horse gear. A few specimens of Spanish halters, bits, and saddles found their way as far north as Alberta by 1790. With the Spanish items as patterns, the Indians soon learned to make adequate duplicates from their own materials.

Of prime importance in working horses on the open range was a good lasso, about forty feet of braided rawhide rope three eighths of an inch in diameter with a slip noose on one end. After the Indians caught a horse in the noose and choked it down it was fitted with a halter of rawhide or leather and a lead rope of buffalo hair. A hackamore (a head-stall without a bit) could be fashioned of rawhide, although in later times it was usually of woven horsehair, and reins could be either raw-hide or leather. Most Indians preferred to use stock bridles if they could be secured. Such a bridle required a steel bit secured from a trader, but the headstall could be of Indian leather or rawhide. For some work with a well-reined horse a war bridle, a thin rawhide thong with a loop over the lower jaw, was ample.

It was necessary to keep a few riding horses near the camp at all times, especially for rounding up and bringing in the herds. At least one of these was picketed on a long rope tied to the halter or to a front foot, while several other horses might be fitted with leather or buffalo-hair hobbles so they could graze nearby.

Although Indians often rode bareback in racing and fighting, they preferred some sort of riding pad or saddle for ordinary work. A rid-ing pad was a tanned robe held in place by a wide, soft strap or cinch. Pad saddles were made with two kidney-shaped pads stuffed with buf-falo hair, and they could be fitted with stirrups.

Heavier saddles for both riding and packing were made from two shaped boards held in place front and rear by forks of elkhorn or shaped wood, and the whole covered with close-fitting, damp rawhide. When this dried and shrank it held the parts of the saddle firmly in place. When such a saddle was used for riding it was covered with a folded robe. Stirrups were made of strips of green wood that could be bent to shape and dried. They were then covered with rawhide.

Apishamores were the Indian equivalent of the saddlebags of the white men but were used chiefly as ornaments or trappings in parades. Each was made of a wide strip of soft leather with long fringes on each end. It was decorated with dyed quill work, and in later times with beadwork. It was draped across the horse just behind the saddle.

Horse collars of soft leather were also decorated with quill work. After the traders came, a few small brass bells were added. Some In-dians liked to use a tuft of feathers held upright between the horse's ears by the headstall, and a few long feathers tied to the base of the tail. Parfleches, carrying cases of folded rawhide, and bags made of soft leather held spare clothes and food.

Quirts, or riding whips, were made from some good hardwood or from elkhorn, the handle usually about twenty inches long, with two heavy lashes of leather on the end. When not in use, a quirt dangled from the wrist by a thong.

When the tipis were moved, the tips of the poles were tied to the saddle while the heavy butts dragged on the ground. Sometimes two of the poles were linked together by two lashed crossbars near the lower ends, thus forming a travois on which large bundles could be carried. Old people and invalids often rode on a travois from one camping site to the next.

As the use of horses increased throughout the plains, the Indians could assemble in large numbers for ceremonies, visiting, and trading. These encampments were held in late June and might attract five thousand people, with possibly twice that many horses. With no system of camp sanitation, the area soon became too soiled for further use, even though each band moved its tipis two or three times. Also, the horses ate all the grass for miles around. Food was no great problem, since each family brought a large reserve of dried meat in case no buffalo were killed.

The great religious observance of the gathering was a complex of councils, ritual dancing, and purification ceremonies. White visitors called the whole affair the Sun Dance because several young men always danced around the great center pole of the ceremonial lodge, tied to it by thongs in their flesh, while they gazed intently at the sun. To the Indian this was only one of the important features. The Sun Dance ceremony and the elaborate war game of counting coup were less popular with tribes living around the edges of the buffalo country than were the other features of the Plains culture, such as war bonnets and tipis, that they adopted readily.

West of the Rockies in the Columbia Basin the Indians had much less trouble raising a large number of horses. They often owned several head for each man, woman, and child in the band, even though they had little use for so many animals. Before they had adjusted to new ways through the use of horses, they had felt that one or two animals to a village was enough. This early attitude is shown by Dr. G. Suckley in the *Pacific Railway Reports:*

There are old men now living at the Dalles [1855] and among kindred tribes in the vicinity who say they remember seeing other old men who were living when the horse was first introduced among them. They say that the first horses obtained were looked upon as great curiosities, and as their use was not known, the animals were kept merely for show and for pets. They were led about in festive processions, and were present at all dances and fetes. This must have been about 125 years ago.

After the Columbia Basin tribes became accustomed to horses, the men rode out hunting, and whole families used them when going to other villages to trade and visit. They also rode horses and used others as pack animals when going to and from the summer camp grounds on the plateau, where they gathered camas bulbs and berries for the winter. With more horses than they could use regularly, they had no need to work the brood mares and so were able to produce large crops of good foals, enough to increase their herds each year until they had their ranges full and had a surplus to trade. The Nez Percés, the best stockmen of all the tribes, usually traded off 5 percent or more of their herds each year and still had plenty of young horses growing up to replace the animals lost by old age or accidents.

While the Nez Percés did not plan it that way, the disposal each year of about five hundred of their poorer horses kept their breeding stock at a high level. In addition, they gelded some of their poorer stallions. This rather casual breeding program, combined with their excellent range land well protected from predators and enemy raiders, produced good horses larger than those raised by most other tribes and much larger than those raised on the plains. The Nez Percés also raised a higher proportion of good running horses than did any of the other tribes. Their close neighbors—the Flatheads, Cayuses, and Yakimas— did nearly as well with their stock.

After they had become good horsemen the Nez Percés rode north each year to the Indian trading center below Spokane Falls, where they met new tribes, including the Flatheads from Montana, who brought in the first buffalo robes the Nez Percés had ever seen. Although the Flatheads and Nez Percés were of totally different linguistic stock and differed a great deal in culture, they were friends from the first. The Nez Percés were invited to hunt buffalo with the Flatheads on the Montana plains, and in the friendly intimacy of the hunting camps the two groups intermingled until they were soon intermarrying like two bands of a single tribe.

The Nez Percés then opened up the Lolo Trail directly east across the Bitterroot Mountains to shorten the distance to the Flathead country and to the buffalo plains. Each summer, when the people assembled at the big camas grounds on Weippe Prairie at the western end of the Lolo Trail, some of the leaders would organize a large hunting party to go across the mountains. Sometimes an entire family joined the group, but usually the hardier adults and adventurous adolescents from several villages united, leaving their less active relatives to watch the home village while they set out on an August morning toward the buffalo land, planning to stay at least a year, and often two or three, in Montana. About a tenth of the tribe was east of the Bitterroots at any given time, learning new ways and trading for new goods.

In a few years these hunting trips made many obvious changes in the social structure of the Nez Percés. Each family began to live in its own tipi rather than in the large community building. More of the property was owned by individuals, less by the community. The hunting parties, being made up of people from several different villages, had to choose a leader for the group to be responsible for the defense of the camp and to supervise the hunters. Also, on the plains the Nez Percés learned a whole new set of social practices, especially several new dances that soon replaced their simpler ones.

While they were in Montana the Nez Percés were true nomads for the duration of their stay, living off the buffalo. Once they returned across the mountains they became settled fishing folk, with salmon and camas as their staple foods, for they could not carry home enough dried buffalo meat to last them for more than a few days. They adopted so many items of Plains dress and trappings that they seemed quite like Plains Indians to the casual observer, but underneath, their basic culture was still that of the old fishing tribe. They did not adopt the Plains type of stylized war game or the Sun Dance complex.

Several other tribes from the Columbia Basin—including the Cayuses, Wallawallas, Yakimas, Spokanes, and Coeur d'Alenes—followed the Nez Percés to the buffalo country and also adopted the tipis and culture trappings of the plains.

7

Building a Nation on Horse Power

In 1783 the last british troops were withdrawn from New York, once more allowing people to move freely from New England to New York and on through to Philadelphia and Baltimore. Small sailing vessels often made voyages from port to port along the Atlantic seaboard, but they frequently were delayed for days or even weeks by adverse winds and storms. The general public wanted a faster and more dependable means of travel and welcomed the new stage service started in 1783 by Levi Pease. With two wagons, each drawn by four horses, he began regular runs between Boston and Hartford, a distance of about 120 miles. Each wagon required about four days for the trip, stopping for the night at towns along the way. The next year the route was extended to New York.

Josiah Quincy, as quoted by Stewart Holbrook in *The Old Post Road*, wrote of his trip in 1785:

> The journey took up a week which in that day was considered a record of wonderful expedition. The carriages were old and worn. The harness was made of ropes. One pair of horses carried the stage 18 miles. We generally reached our resting place for the night, if no accident intervened, at 10 o'clock; and, after a frugal supper went

to bed with a notice that we should be called at 3 next morning, which generally proved to be half-past two.

Then, whether it snowed or rained, the traveler must rise and make ready by the help of a horn-lantern and a farthing candle, and proceed on his way over bad roads, sometimes with a driver showing symptoms of drunkenness, which good hearted passengers never failed to improve at every stopping place by urging upon him another glass of toddy.

Thus we traveled 10 miles a stage, sometimes obliged to get out and help the coachman lift the coach out of a quagmire or rut, wondering at the ease as well as the expedition of our journey.

Customarily the stage stopped about 6:30 A.M. for breakfast, and again at noon for dinner. In the fall and winter about half the travel was done in darkness. As travel increased, both the equipment and the roads improved, greatly speeding up the journey, but about half the travelers still preferred to ride horseback rather than in the stages.

In 1785 Congress established a postal service for the country, and Levi Pease won the first contract to carry mail between Boston and New York, using light wagons instead of post riders. He promised a schedule of five and a half days in winter and four days in summer. As the roads improved the time was cut to a day and a half. Such speed was possible only by changing teams each ten miles. A total of four passengers, at extra fare, were allowed to ride on each mail wagon. The mail contract proved so profitable that Pease extended both his mail and passenger service to many other New England towns. Other stage lines developed rapidly in competition with him.

After forty years of using the wagons with their light tops and leather side curtains, the stage companies were able finally to buy real stage-coaches. The first of the famous Concord coaches was made in Concord, New Hampshire, in 1826, and was modeled after the English coaches of the period. The Concord coach was light, durable, and completely enclosed, with the driver and some passengers riding on the roof. The mailbags and luggage were carried in an enclosed boot at the rear. The design was fundamentally sound, the workmanship and materials were superior, and the resulting vehicle became the standard for American coaches for the next seventy years. The same style of Concord coach can be seen today—horses, driver, and all—much as it was in 1826, in various western motion pictures and television shows.

*A peaceful Sunday in New York. Most nineteenth-century men con-
sidered it a sign of masculinity to ride and drive well. During the week,
many traveled by saddle horse between home and office; on the day of
rest, they indulged in more exciting rides.* (Courtesy, Kenneth M.
Newman, Old Print Shop, New York City)

*The Concord Coach. First built in Concord, New Hampshire, in 1826,
coaches of this design usually held six people inside and more on the
roof. The record coach load was a party of girls from Worcester,
Massachusetts, who hired a coach for a blackberry excursion—sixty-
two of them.* (Courtesy, The New-York Historical Society, New York
City)

The body of the coach was a sturdy, rounded container capable of holding six people, who sat three to a seat facing one another. Several more could be accommodated on the roof. The record load for a coach on a good road was a party of sixty-two girls, who chartered a coach in Worcester for a blackberry excursion. A team of eight horses handled the load.

The coach body was made independent of the running gear. It was suspended as in a cradle on two wide, thick leather straps, called thoroughbraces, attached to the running gear front and rear. While the coach body swayed and bounced, the worst of the road shocks never reached the passengers. The leather-strap springing was greatly superior to any steel spring of that time and was used even on the royal coach of Great Britain. The straps furnished a smoother ride, and if one broke it could be repaired by any fairly skilled person with a leather punch, a sharp knife, and a tanned cowhide, while a broken spring required the services of a highly skilled blacksmith with his forge and special steel stock. A coach with a broken steel spring might be only a great annoyance in settled country, while it could be the cause of near-disaster on the frontier.

On very good roads, such as a few of the turnpikes, a coach could be drawn by two horses, but the ordinary road required a team of four, and rough, hilly roads demanded six. The coach customarily proceeded at a brisk trot or a steady gallop, the metal parts of the harness jingling merrily. Quoting again from Holbrook: "it was voted [by the directors of the stage company] that our drivers shall be furnished with Horns or trumpets that shall be blown on approach of the Stage at any Post Office, and the places where they Dine, breakfast, etc., etc., and if any Driver refuses to comply, he must be dismissed by his employer." This order was easy to enforce, for most drivers greatly enjoyed making a dashing approach—trumpet sounding, chains jingling—to the admiration of the waiting crowd.

Along the Atlantic seaboard the stagecoach lines reached their peak in the 1830's, to be replaced in time on the longer runs by the new steam railroads. Boston, the transportation and trade center of New England, had about 350 coaches moving in and out of the city each working day. Each afternoon and evening 175 coaches, each drawn by four or six horses, drove into the city across the narrow Boston Neck, dropping their passengers along the way until they finally reached the end of the run at Scollay Square. There they unloaded and were cleaned and washed, their axles greased, their wheels checked, and were prepared for the next day's run, which might start within four to six hours after their arrival.

The horses were unhitched, unharnessed, rubbed down, fed, and watered. Careful attention was given to any cuts, sores, sprains, or loose shoes. The harnesses were cleaned, oiled, and hung up where the pads could dry. Any badly worn straps were replaced. All of this work had to be done in a short time and required a large staff of hostlers and stableboys at each important stage terminal, as well as a blacksmith on call to shoe horses, tighten loose wheel rims, mend trace chains, and take care of any other metal part in need of attention. Stables for the horses, with grain-storage bins and haymows, and sheds for the coaches filled many city lots in the business district.

Much of the forage for Boston stables was brought in by provision ships from the coastal farming communities and was moved from the docks by horse-drawn wagons. Loads of forage also came in from the up-country farms. In a large place like Boston it was seldom possible to take a loaded wagon to town, unload, secure some return load, and get out of the city again in one day, so all the teams bringing in forage, farm produce, firewood, and the like needed stabling for the night.

The busy Boston docks needed a large number of drays and carts to haul the incoming and outgoing cargoes of the great sailing ships that plied the seven seas with merchandise from the far corners of the world. Even when the goods were carried into and out of the harbor on the smaller coastal ships, much of them had to be moved from one dock to another in the exchange process.

In the 1830's a new vehicle appeared on the streets of the large cities. This was the recently developed omnibus that was so popular in England and France. It was drawn by two or three horses and carried about eighteen passengers on long benches running the length of the vehicle on each side. The whole body was enclosed to protect the passengers from the weather. The omnibus was more common in New York than in the other cities, and brought some added problems to the congested streets. John Anderson Miller, in *Fares Please,* quotes a New York newspaper:

> The character of the omnibus drivers has become brutal and dangerous to the highest degree. They race up and down Broadway and through Chatham Street with the utmost fury. Broadway spe-

cially, between Park and Wall street, is almost daily the scene of some outrage in which the lives of citizens riding in light vehicles are put in imminent hazard. Not content with running down everything that comes in their way, they turn out of their course to break down other carriages. Yesterday a gentleman driving down Broadway and keeping near the west side was run down by an omnibus going up, the street being perfectly clear at the time, the omnibus leaving full twice its width of empty space on the right of its track. At the same spot a hackney-coach was crushed between two of them the day before. It is but a few days since we published the account of a physician being run down near the same spot, his gig ruined, and his horse nearly so, and his own life placed in the most imminent hazard. A ferocious spirit appears to have taken possession of the drivers, which defies law and delights in destruction. It is indispensable that a decisive police should be held on these men, or the consequences of their conduct will result in acts which will shock the whole city.

Passengers also had their trials in riding on the omnibus. *The New York Herald*, on October 2, 1864, had this account:

Modern martyrdom may be succinctly defined as riding in a New York omnibus. The discomforts, inconveniences, and annoyances of a trip on one of these vehicles are almost intolerable. From the beginning to the end of the journey a constant quarrel is progressing. The driver quarrels with the passengers, and the passengers quarrel with the driver. There are quarrels about getting out and quarrels about getting in. There are quarrels about change and about the ticket swindle. The driver swears at the passengers and the passengers harangue the driver through the strap hole—a position in which even Demosthenes could not be eloquent. Respectable clergymen in white chokers are obliged to listen to loud oaths. Ladies are disgusted, frightened and insulted. Children are alarmed and lift up their voices and weep. Indignant gentlemen rise to remonstrate with the irate Jehu and are suddenly bumped back into their seats, twice as indignant as before, besides being in supplementary quarrels with those other passengers upon whose corns they have accidently trodden. Thus the omnibus rolls along a perfect bedlam on wheels.

Soon after the introduction of the omnibus, horsecars were added to the congested streets. While one horse could pull the car along its steel track, compared to the two or three needed for the omnibus, the driver had no leeway in dodging obstacles.

Livery stables, with riding and driving horses for hire, offered essential services in every city, town, and village. In addition, many business and professional men rode horses to the store or office each morning, leaving them at the livery stable during the day. Their wives had light carriages and carts for shopping and afternoon calls. As a result each middle-class townhouse needed a combined carriage house and stable at the rear of the lot on the alley, with a loft for hay and sleeping quarters for the handyman on the second floor. When one considers the large number of horses needed daily in even a small town for customary tasks, the old phrase "one-horse town" takes on added meaning.

Although the items described above were found specifically in Boston and New York, most of them, with minor variations, were typical of all the cities and towns in the United States. In the busy streets the congestion from the many horse-drawn vehicles was acute. An added factor, considered less serious then than now, was the presence of countless swarms of flies. Also, during dry spells any little puff of wind filled the air with powdered horse manure that settled on the passersby and had to be wiped from eyes and lips.

Philadelphia differed from Boston and New York in that little farm produce came to its markets in provision boats. Up-country to the southwest lay the rich farming lands of eastern Pennsylvania that could produce more crops than all the small hill farms of New England combined. Six days a week the heavily loaded wagons and carts rolled down from the German settlements, drawn by teams of large, sleek horses, their progress made easier by the Lancaster Turnpike.

That famous road had been built from Philadelphia to Lancaster, sixty-two miles away, to tap the rich farming area. A private stock company secured a charter from the state and had no difficulty in securing funds through the sale of stock. In four years, by 1795, the road had been completed, and it fully justified the optimism of the promoters by paying good dividends from the first.

The twenty-four-foot-wide road was built and surfaced by the macadam process: the pavement was made of a thick layer of crushed rock with a clay binder. This offered a hard, smooth surface for vehicles and stock in any weather. On either side of the pavement a six-foot-wide shoulder of packed earth provided ample parking space for any vehicle in temporary trouble. On this road a light rig or a horseman could average ten miles an hour with little difficulty, stopping only to pay a toll at each tollhouse.

A long pike pole, often ornamented with a steel point, was used as the toll bar, extending across the roadway about three and a half feet from the ground. When the toll was paid, the gatekeeper swung the pole out of the way—hence the name "turnpike." People who did not choose to pay tolls still used the old roads nearby, soon called shunpikes. In later years any well-surfaced road, even without toll charges, might be called simply a pike.

The steady, heavy flow of traffic on the Lancaster Turnpike brought prosperity to the farmers, to Philadelphia, and to the company. This quick success led to a proliferation of turnpikes throughout New York and New England. None of them was ever as profitable as the Lancaster pike and many of them went broke after a time. Some were constructed in the wrong places, some cost too much to build and maintain, and some were soon superseded by steam railroads, but their construction provided better transportation facilities and thus benefited the whole country.

The smooth turnpikes attracted a great deal of carriage trade as well as more passengers on the stage lines. These people soon preempted the inns along the way, leaving the rougher common people—the drovers, drivers, teamsters, hostlers, and hucksters—to the more primitive accommodations of the roadhouses.

A turnpike across the Alleghenies was considered unfeasible, but some improvement in the travel routes to the west was urgently needed. After General Anthony Wayne had defeated the Indian tribes of Ohio and, by treaties in 1795, taken much of their land, settlers swarmed across the mountains to occupy the rich farming country. Some families moved on horseback with pack trains and a few cows. Others used teams of horses or oxen to draw their wagons along the old Braddock's Trace, renamed the Cumberland Road but still just a track across the mountains, streams, and bog holes.

Along the road's length on either side, in the little coves and mountain valleys, earlier pioneers had occupied small plots of farmland. They raised scanty crops and eked out a living by hunting and trapping. Although they could raise more grain than they could use, it was not worth carrying it to market when a full load for a packhorse was only worth a dollar. If the same grain was made into high-proof whiskey, really an almost pure grain alcohol, the same horse could carry a load worth fifteen dollars or more. Hence many a bushel of grain from the Pennsylvania mountain country went to the eastern cities in kegs, to be traded for salt and iron. Joseph Doddridge, in his *Notes*, as quoted by Thomas B. Seabright in *The Old Pike*, gives this picture of the operation:

In the fall of the year, after seeding time, every family formed an association with some of their neighbors, for starting the little caravan. A master driver was to be selected from among them, who was to be assisted by one or more young men and sometimes a boy or two. The horses were fitted out with packsaddles, to the latter part of which was fastened a pair of hobbles made of hickory withes, a bell and collar ornamented their necks. The bags provided for the conveyance of the salt [on the return trip] were filled with bread, jerk, boiled ham and cheese furnished a provision for the drivers. At night, after feeding, the horses, whether put in pasture or turned out in the woods, were hobbled and the bells were opened [the cloth or hay stuffed in the bells during the day to prevent the clappers from ringing was removed]. The barter for salt and iron was made first at Baltimore; Fredrick, Hagerstown, Oldtown and Fort Cumberland, in succession, became places of exchange. Each horse carried two bushels of alum salt, weighing eighty-four pounds to the bushel. This, to be sure, was not a heavy load for the horses, but it was enough, considering the scant subsistence allowed them on the journey. The common price of a bushel of alum salt, at an early period, was a good cow and a calf.

Pack trains such as these could not handle the increased needs of the mountain people, and were totally inadequate to supply the new settlements in the Ohio Valley with the many thousands of tons of market goods they wanted each year. The old road, with its ruts, bog holes, steep grades, and stumps, made freighting by wagon trains a slow and costly process. The unrest of the western people over the transportation problem, coupled with the Aaron Burr conspiracy (seemingly a plot to take some of the country's western lands out of the Union) and with other secessionist talk in the western country, induced the federal government to take over the Cumberland Road, rename it the National

Road, and improve its entire length by grading it and laying a surface of crushed rock. The road building was begun in 1811 and continued even through the War of 1812. By 1817 it was ready for the traffic between Cumberland, Maryland, and Wheeling, Virginia (now West Virginia) on the Ohio River, and it proved its worth from the first.

Soon large new freight wagons laden with merchandise were rolling in trains west to Pittsburgh and Wheeling. With such a fine road surface a team of four horses could haul a freight wagon carrying two tons of cargo, and one firm alone in Pittsburgh received a thousand such loads in 1822. It was possible by driving long hours and changing teams along the way to haul a loaded freight wagon from Philadelphia to Pittsburgh in twenty days. Stage service along the road increased rapidly too, and the stages made excellent time. The record run was made by a coach carrying news of the War with Mexico in 1846. It traveled 131 miles in twelve hours.

This brief sketch by Seabright gives a good picture of the large, broad-wheeled Conestoga wagons covered with white canvas as they rolled along:

> [The wagons were] visible all the day long, at every point, making the highway look more like a leading avenue of a great city than a road through rural districts. . . . I have staid over night with William Cheets on Nigger Mountain when there were about thirty six-horse teams in the wagon yard, a hundred Kentucky mules in an adjoining lot, a thousand hogs in their enclosure, and as many fat cattle in adjoining fields. The music made by this large number of hogs eating corn on a frosty night I shall never forget. After supper and attention to the teams, the wagoners would gather in the barroom and listen to the music on the violin furnished by one of their fellows, have a Virginia hoe-down, sing songs, tell anecdotes, and hear the experiences of drivers and drovers from all points of the road, and, when it was over, unroll their beds, lay them down on the floor before the bar-room fire side by side, and sleep with their feet near the blaze as soundly as under the paternal roof.

Another highway, largely unimproved, led southwestward from the National Road at Harper's Ferry into Tennessee. It followed the Valley of Virginia instead of crossing the mountain ridges. This road had a western branch that led into central Kentucky along the old Wilderness

Trail through Cumberland Gap, which is about three hundred miles southwest of Cumberland and the same distance from the Cumberland Road. While there are few details of travel along most of these roads, it is certain that the people and their belongings, and the freight wagons, stagecoaches, and carts were usually moved by horses of several kinds —saddle horses, carriage horses, draft horses, and packhorses.

In the midst of the turnpike-building era, New York State undertook the huge task of digging the Erie Canal to connect Lake Erie with the Hudson River. The canal followed up the Mohawk Valley and crossed the low gap to the lake drainage. It was completed in 1825 and was prosperous from the first. Its example led other states to dig canals, many of which operated successfully for a long period, but none of them even approached the importance of the Erie Canal, which linked the West, through the Great Lakes, with the East and the ocean port of New York City. For motive power the boats depended on horses plodding along the towpaths. A single horse sufficed for a freight boat, while some of the passenger boats, moving at a higher speed, used a team. The speed of all boats was severely restricted, for the bow wave from a boat traveling more than about three miles an hour rapidly eroded the canal banks.

On the canal a break in the dike was a serious affair, for the escaping water cut a deep gouge, draining the entire length between two locks and leaving the canalboats helpless in the mud. To repair such breaks quickly, the canal operators had farmers all along the way with teams on call. They also stocked logs up to sixty or seventy feet long that could be hauled into place across a gap to help hold the new fill.

It is evident that in the first half of the nineteenth century the entire country depended on the muscle power of horses for a large number of important tasks and hundreds of minor ones. Even though oxen and mules furnished an important part of the labor, hundreds of thousands of new horses were needed each year to replace those lost through old age, accidents, and disease; yet there was no area east of the Mississippi where range horses could be raised in large herds by the ranching system used in the Spanish colonies. Instead the new animals had to come from a multitude of small farms throughout the land, each furnishing a supplementary colt or two each year, or they were supplied from the range herds in the West.

The steady demand over the years for draft horses at a good price brought a significant and lasting change in farming methods and gradually eliminated oxen for most work. A man who raised a colt or two for market had enough horses for all his farm work. He found, too, that one man with horses could do more work in a day than one with oxen, for the horse's working gait was about twice as speedy, and horses were more maneuverable. Also, the steady gait of the horse was of special value in pulling some of the new machines that were designed to operate at a constant speed. The reaper, invented in 1831, needed a steady rhythm of the sickle-bar for best results. It left the grain in a neat row, ready for the men to tie it into sheaves.

In winter workhorses had a great advantage on packed snow or ice, though the oxen were very good in deep, soft snow or in brush. Horses could be fitted with steel shoes studded with sharp caulks—sharp-shod in common parlance—that enabled them to work well on slippery footings where oxen would flounder helplessly. The teams of horses could haul enormous loads over icy roads on bobsleds, the bells on their harnesses jingling merrily as they trotted along.

When the contractors were building the Erie Canal they found it much easier to move all their heavy materials, equipment, and supplies to the building sites in winter, when the snow lay thick on the ground. The broad steel runners of the bobsleds soon made a wide, smooth roadbed of packed snow, free from ruts, bog holes, stumps, and rocks. A light sprinkling of water on the track each crisp winter evening kept the surface in good order, while a rough-lock on the sled runner prevented the heavy load from crowding the horses on a down grade. This system was developed to a high degree in the Maine woods and later was borrowed for use in other areas where the snow lay deep on the ground throughout the winter.

On the average small farm a stallion was a nuisance and potentially dangerous. In a farming community, only a few of the horse raisers kept stallions, and they supplied the breeding service for the area, or a skilled horseman might own a good stallion and spend his spring and summer months driving around the country offering service. Everyone in the area soon knew if a stallion sired superior foals, and such an animal was in constant demand at a good fee. A sire left his stamp on the horses raised in his area. If the offspring proved speedy on the racetracks the fame of the sire spread over the whole country, while a good draft stallion was seldom known beyond his immediate neighborhood.

Conestoga in southern Pennsylvania produced fine draft stock from the time of the first settlements. Stallions of Dutch stock were secured from New York, and with some crossing the Conestoga horses evolved. They were tall and rangy, with long, trim legs and springy pasterns. They looked much like the old war-horses of the Netherlands or over-sized riding horses. They sometimes measured seventeen and a half hands and weighed up to eighteen hundred pounds. In general appearance they were quite unlike the heavy-boned, stock draft animals developed in England and France. During the first half of the nineteenth century the Conestoga horses were the kings of the freight ways, as they pulled their fine Conestoga wagons heavily laden with goods consigned to distant markets.

The Lancaster farmers around Conestoga never attempted to establish a common type for their horses. Instead each good stallion was allowed to dominate his own area. A little work and planning could have made the Conestoga horse into a true registered breed, but instead the American farmers turned their attention to the draft breeds imported from England and France—the Shires, Clydesdales, and Percherons.

In Vermont a very different pattern was followed. There the off-spring of one extraordinary horse were used to establish a distinct breed —something most unusual in horse raising. This remarkable horse is known by the name of one of his owners, Justin Morgan, who called him Figure. Justin Morgan, the horse, was foaled in 1789 or 1793, sire unknown but guessed at by a number of people, each making a different guess. His whole career is so surrounded by legend that it is difficult to establish the facts of his great performances, but he did impress the men who saw him in action and he did leave descendants of major importance in the horse world. It is generally agreed that he was rather small—about fourteen hands, one inch—and weighed about 950 pounds. He was a neat, beautifully muscled, close-coupled animal, blood bay in color with black points, and noted for his speed in sprint races and his ability to pull large loads. He passed these qualities along to his offspring and thus influenced the horses of today. His important descendants finally became the foundation stock of the Morgan breed.

A trapper and his Indian wife. The mountain men rendezvoused each summer with Indians to trade for the three or four horses that each trapper needed for his winter operations. (Painting by A. J. Miller, The Walters Art Gallery)

Attack on a wagon train. The real objective of most such Indian attacks was not the wagon train itself, but the horse herd traveling with it. (Painting by A. J. Miller, The Walters Art Gallery)

8

Horses in the Pioneer West

BEGINNING IN THE MIDDLE of the eighteenth century a fairly steady stream of horses flowed from the Texas plains across the Mississippi near Natchez, while a smaller number passed near St. Louis. The southern horses first went to the Chickasaw Indians, then they and their progeny spread eastward through Tennessee and into Virginia and the Carolinas, or they moved northward into Kentucky and the Ohio Valley.

The Osage Indians living on the edge of the buffalo country were the middlemen in this trade for many years; then white traders from New Orleans took over much of the Natchez trade. Some of the eastern Indians sought new homes in Arkansas and Oklahoma and cut the Osages off from the south, turning them to more northern trade routes. European treaties affecting the Mississippi drainage initiated many of these changes in the trading patterns. In 1763 the Treaty of Paris transferred the French colony of Louisiana to Spain, ending most of the friction between Louisiana and Texas. The trade barrier between these two Spanish colonies was lowered slightly, and the bureaucrats allowed some trade in horses across the border.

An adventurous young American of Irish stock, Philip Nolan, saw an opportunity for profit and excitement in this border trade. In New Orleans he secured some trade goods, a passport, and a commission from Governor Esteban Miró to provide the Spanish troops with horses from Texas, but the Spanish officials in Texas refused to honor the passport.

Instead they seized Nolan's entire stock of trade goods and confiscated his passport.

Nolan then slipped away and went west to join the Indian bands. He lived on the plains with them for two years, learning a great deal about Indians, the country, and especially about Texas horses, both wild and tame. In 1793, on his return to New Orleans, he evaded the Texas border guards and brought back fifty horses for the Spanish troops. He decided that with such a large supply of low-cost horses in Texas and a demand for them at fair prices on the Natchez market, he could soon make his fortune as the middleman matching supply with demand. In 1794, with six companions and a new passport, he again went to Texas, where the border guards at Nacogdoches passed him through. Soon he returned with 250 horses that he sold at a nice profit.

On his next large venture, in 1797, he brought back 1,300 horses to Louisiana, with a few hundred more left in pastures at the border for future sale. But then the luck of the Irish ran out. He went to Texas again in 1800, arousing the suspicions of the Spanish officials, who decided, from sound evidence, that Nolan was involved in much deeper schemes than simply rounding up wild horses. A force of Spanish soldiers intercepted him, and when Nolan chose to fight rather than surrender he was killed in the resulting skirmish.

Details of Nolan's career survived in the official records because he was involved in the dubious enterprises of Aaron Burr and General James Wilkinson to invade Spanish territory and found a new nation. But many another American horse trader traveled the same trails, bringing back droves of horses, without leaving any exact records concerning the transactions. After the United States purchased Louisiana in 1803, horses could move more freely from the Texas plains to Natchez. The border was loosely guarded and there was little concern over the movement of wild horses captured in the Indian country.

By 1800 these wild horses, commonly called mustangs, roamed the Texas plains in great numbers and could be claimed by any man, red or white, able to catch them. During the same period there were many herds of range horses to the south around the Spanish ranches. While the Americans claimed that they captured nothing but wild horses, ranchers were certain that many of their tame horses were being driven off, because their losses were heavy. All of the captured horses, wild or tame, moved across Louisiana to the ready market at Natchez or were sold around New Orleans for the sugar plantations.

Natchez had grown apace once Pinckney's Treaty in 1795 recognized American possession and opened up the market at New Orleans to American products from the Ohio Valley. Each year heavily laden barges, flatboats, and rafts came from the many coves and tributary streams into the Ohio River and downstream to the New Orleans market, to be sold, cargo and all, while their crews returned by boat up the river to Natchez, where they usually bought horses and proceeded homeward along the old Natchez Trace. Hence the earlier flow of Chickasaw horses from the western plains to the eastern farms was greatly increased by the droves of Texas horses going to the Natchez market. This influx enabled the new settlers west of the Alleghenies to acquire the necessary workhorses at modest prices instead of having to compete in the eastern markets with buyers for stage lines, freight lines, and other nonfarm operations.

The farmers of the Midwest continued buying horses from the plains until World War I. They upgraded their western stock by crossing them with superior stallions from the East or from Europe, and thus were able to supply most of their own needs and still send a large number east across the mountains to meet the demands of the rapidly growing urban areas of the Atlantic seaboard.

After Thomas Jefferson made his bargain purchase of the Louisiana Territory, he sent out expeditions to explore the new lands. The most important one, led by Meriwether Lewis and William Clark, went up the Missouri, planning to continue on to its source and to determine the limits of the United States at the Continental Divide. Then they were to enter foreign territory and continue their explorations westward through the mountains to the Pacific Ocean. The success of this expedition earned it a high place among the great explorations of history—a success dependent largely on the presence of available horses among the Indian tribes in the Rocky Mountains.

As many another explorer had done in strange, trackless lands, Lewis and Clark used a river, the Missouri, for a highway—ascending it in boats, then in canoes, until they reached the foot of the Divide. The boats enabled them to carry adequate supplies, medicines, trade goods, and scientific instruments. But when they reached the headwaters of the Jefferson fork of the Missouri in southwestern Montana, they had to leave their canoes. Here they faced a series of formidable mountain ranges whoses passes would soon be blocked by snow. Unless they could secure a number of pack animals to carry their instruments and trade goods, they would be forced to retrace their journey with their mission only half completed, for their men could not possibly carry more than their weapons, ammunition, blankets, spare clothing, and enough food to take them across the mountains. Without their scientific instruments they could not make adequate observations, and with no trade goods they could not expect to secure necessary items from the Indian tribes along the way. They would have no means of carrying specimens of plants and animals, and would be hampered by the lack of writing materials for keeping adequate records.

At this juncture Sacagawea, a young Shoshoni woman and the wife of the party's interpreter, Toussaint Charbonneau, performed her most valuable services—not as a guide, but as the sister of a Lemhi Shoshoni leader, for at this point the party was on land held by Sacagawea's people. Through her efforts the whites were able to trade for twenty-nine packhorses of poor quality. This Shoshoni band owned about seven hundred horses for its three hundred people, barely enough to transport the people and their belongings, for about a third of the animals were too young to be used. The band was feeling very poor at this time because the Blackfeet had stolen about half its herd earlier that summer.

With these packhorses and a few more secured from the Flatheads in the Bitterroot Valley, Lewis and Clark were able to cross the mountains, where they were hospitably received by the Nez Percés, who took care of their horses and saddles for the winter, returning them in good condition the next May. Lewis, in his journal, gives several interesting details about Nez Percé horses.

They [the horses] appear to be of excellent race, lofty, elegantly formed, active, and durable; many of them appear like fine English coursers; some of them are pied with large spots of white irregularly mixed with a dark brown bay; the greater part, however, are of a uniform color, marked with stars and white feet, and resemble in fleetness and bottom, as well as in form and color, the best blooded horses of Virginia. . . . The abundance and cheapness of horses will be extremely advantageous to those who may hereafter attempt the fur trade to the East Indies, by way of the Columbia river and the Pacific ocean. . . .

The stone horses [stallions] we found so troublesome that we endeavored to exchange them for either mares or geldings; but although we offered two for one, they were unwilling to barter. It was therefore determined to castrate them . . . two were gelded in the usual manner, while one of the natives tried the experiment in the Indian way. . . . All of the horses recovered but we afterwards found that those on which the Indian mode had been tried . . . recovered sooner, so we are fully persuaded that the Indian method is preferable to our own.

On the return trip, Clark and most of the party used the horses until they reached the Yellowstone River. There they made dugout canoes and embarked most of the party. A few men drove the horses along the north bank for a distance; then the herd was stolen by the Indians.

The method of travel used by Lewis and Clark was adopted independently in 1806 by Lieutenant Zebulon M. Pike, who was sent west from the Missouri River to explore the central plains. Pike started up the Kansas River in boats with his seventy-four men, but soon reached the head of navigable water. He then traded with Pawnees for horses, left his boats behind, and proceeded westward to discover Pikes Peak, and later to get himself captured by the Spanish in New Mexico.

In 1811 Wilson Price Hunt planned to take his party of fur men up the Missouri and along the trail opened by Lewis and Clark to the mouth of the Columbia River. On his way up the Missouri he heard disturbing news of Blackfoot attacks against trappers in the Three Forks area and decided to avoid possible conflict with that tribe by crossing the Rockies well south of their range. At the Arikara villages in South Dakota he bought riding horses and packhorses for his men and set out due west through uncharted country. This led him across the high mountain ranges of northern Wyoming and finally to the headwaters of the Snake River, where his men, tired of riding horses by day and herding them by night, insisted on making dugout canoes for the rest of the journey. In emulation of Lewis and Clark, Hunt left his large herd of horses in the care of a band of friendly Shoshonis, who were quite willing to take charge of them.

Down the broad, smooth Snake River the fur men rode for days, paddling only enough to keep their canoes on course, finding this a most delightful change from traversing the rough Wyoming mountains on horseback and herding a pack string. Then out in the Snake River plain the placid stream suddenly plunged into a deep box canyon in a series of wild rapids interspersed by three high, vertical falls. Hunt soon realized that he had abandoned his horses too soon, but by that time they were beyond recovery, for the Shoshoni herders had moved on to new camping grounds. They never did return the horses, claiming later that they had all been stolen by the Blackfeet. Without horses, and with the river too wild for boating, Hunt had a great deal of difficulty and hardship in traversing the wild, rugged terrain of the Columbia Basin before he finally reached the new fur post of Astoria.

While explorers and traders were busily opening the whole Missouri drainage and the northern Rockies to travel, other Americans, from St. Louis, were charting a way across the southern plains to the Spanish settlements in New Mexico, looking for a new source of profitable trade. A few attempts between 1803 and 1821 failed or were blocked by Spanish officials enforcing the strict Spanish laws, but when Mexico threw off Spanish rule in 1821, the Americans were encouraged to try again. First on the trail to Santa Fe with a large pack train loaded with trade goods was William Becknell, who set out in 1821. He found the way such easy traveling that on his next trip in 1822 he used wagons. He found that wagons with broad steel tires rolled more easily across the open southern plains than they did along the dirt roads of the eastern farming country. Encouraged by Becknell's success, other traders followed, and the Santa Fe trade boomed. While New Mexico was sparsely settled and could use only a limited quantity of goods, other Mexican towns farther south gladly took the surplus stock from the Americans.

In return for cloth, hardware, and other manufactured items the Americans received silver coins. These were plentiful in Mexico, where great quantities of the metal were mined each year, whereas money of any kind was scarce in the Midwest. The traders also brought back many mules, which were in demand on the sugar plantations of Louisiana and the cotton plantations throughout the South. They also brought back jacks and jennets for breeding stock so that they could raise mules in Missouri, the eastern end of the Santa Fe Trail. These imports soon made Missouri the mule-breeding center of the United States, a distinction that endured for a century.

The new trail led through the heart of the Comanche country, but that tribe seldom was a problem to the strong, alert wagon trains. The Comanches were continually raiding the Texas settlements for horses, an activity they continued for another fifty years, but they liked to keep their northern land peaceful so that they could trade there for guns, ammunition, and other supplies. Most of the attacks on wagon trains along the trail were against the horse herds and were staged by war parties from other tribes farther to the north, notably the Cheyennes and Arapahos, but an occasional raid was made by visitors from as far away as Alberta. The Blackfeet from that area began their deep southern raids even before the Santa Fe Trail was opened, as this account from the journal of David Thompson shows. He was a Northwest Fur Company man camping with the tribe near the Bow River at the time.

In the year 1787 in the early part of September a party of about 250 warriors . . . went off to war on the Snake Indians. They proceeded southward . . . and found no natives. They continued further than usual very unwilling to return without having done something. At length the scouts came in with word they had seen a long file of horses and mules led by Black men (Spaniards) and not far off. . . . [they] approached to near the front of the file before being discovered, when giving the war whoop and making a rush on the front of the file, the Spaniards all rode off leaving the loaded horses and mules to the war party. . . . they were loaded with bags containing a great weight of white stone (silver) which they quickly threw off the animals. . . . I never could learn the number of animals. Those that came to camp at which I resided were about 30 horses and a dozen mules, with a few saddles and bridles. . . . The place this party started from . . . and the place they met the Spaniards . . . is about a distance of 1500 miles in a straight line.

Josiah Gregg mentioned two raids by Blackfeet during his travels. This tribe continued to raid the southern plains and deep into the Great Basin until it was seriously weakened by the smallpox scourge in 1837.

Seventeen-year-old Lewis Garrard, who traveled to Taos in 1846, in his account, *Wah-to-yah and the Taos Trail*, made special mention of the horses.

The maneuvers of the Mexicans of our company are really astonishing in lassoing unruly mules and horses; dodge as they may, or run about, the lariat noose is sure to fall on their unwilling necks; a loop thrown over the nose, the gagging Spanish bit forced into the mouth, the saddle clapped on, and the rider firmly in that, with galling spurs tickles the side ribs, and flies and curvettes on the open plain in less time than it can be written. But it does confound an

[99]

animal to have a Mexican horse furniture and rider strapped on him.

Garrard had some trouble with his own horse:

So soon as a faint streak of light appears in the east, the cry "turn out" is given by De Lisle; all rise, and, in half an hour, the oxen are yoked, hitched and started. For the purpose of bringing everything within a small compass, the wagons are corralled, that is, arranged in the form of a pen, when camp is made; and as no animals in that country are caught without a lasso, they are much easier noosed if driven in the corral. There, no dependence must be placed on any-one but one's self; and the sooner he rises when the cry is given, the easier he can get his horse.

Like all persons on the first trip, I was green in the use of the lasso, and Paint [his horse] was given to all sorts of malicious dodg-ing; perhaps I have worked myself into a profound perspiration with vexation a hundred and one times in a vain attempt to catch him.

Not being able to catch my horse this morning, I hung my saddle on a wagon and walked. . . . .

Later Garrard had trouble with Paint on a buffalo hunt:

To the south were several hundred buffalo, confused by the sight of the wagons and us; as we drew near, their bewilderment in-creased and they scattered, a few within a hundred yards. We hur-riedly dismounted, not holding our animals, and fired, while off with the clattering herd galloped Chadwick's horse and Paint, the meat flapping at their sides, accelerating their speed with every jump. I did not shout "my kingdom for a horse" to pursue the runaway Paint, but felt like sending a rifle ball as a check, though, fortunately, my gun was unloaded. Blas, our Mexican, seeing the mishap, came from the wagons with lasso in hand, and soon recap-tured the fugitives, after a chase of two miles. . . .

For a few days Garrard's party rode with a band of Cheyenne In-dians. This is how they handled their horses on the trail:

Each lodge had its own band of horses, which presented a strange appearance; eighteen or more bands close to each other, walking along but not mixing; each band following a favorite mare, or, perchance, a woebegone, scrawny mule, not worth the powder and ball to kill it. It is a strange and general fact that caballadas are mostly led by a no-account mare or mule—the greatest devil in the drove. They follow their erratic leader everywhere, like sheep, whether jumping, running, or grazing.

The successful use of wagons on the Sante Fe Trail soon attracted the attention of the fur men working in the Rocky Mountains of Wyoming. At first all the trapping in those mountains was handled by parties of fur men ascending the Missouri and Yellowstone Rivers to the mouth of the Bighorn in the heart of the Crow country. There they left the river and moved south up into the high country, returning in the spring with their winter catch, buying horses from the Crows for the mountain work. When William Ashley entered the fur trade in 1824 he found himself in bitter competition with the American Fur Company, which had a trading post on Crow land. The trader in charge induced the Crows to harass Ashley's men until Ashley decided it would be easier to use the shorter overland route to market down the Platte River. This would bypass both the troublesome Crows and the more obnoxious Arikaras farther down the Missouri.

On his way west in 1824 Ashley had traveled up the Platte in the fall, trailing a wagon behind his pack train, the first wheeled vehicle of record on what later became the Oregon Trail. He brought his first season's catch of furs down the Yellowstone and the Missouri to take advantage of the water transport, for the Platte was too shallow and full of sand for boats to operate on it. After some trouble in the Crow country, Ashley determined to bring his furs down the Platte on pack animals, although he would need a strong guard with the train to ward off marauding war parties. Soon he found that he could use a wagon for much of the way.

In addition to taking a wagon up the Platte, Ashley had other new ideas, such as his pattern for mountain trapping. In the fall he sent out several small parties of trappers, each assigned to a certain area. Before they left, he had set up a meeting place for the following summer, where all the trappers would turn in their furs and receive supplies and assignments for the following year. He expected to attract many free trappers and some Indian trade as well. While the Indians did not have many furs, they did have plenty of horses that the trappers needed.

Prime consideration for the meeting place was a good pasture for the large horse herds, with an abundance of grass and running water. The first year the trappers met on the Green River branch of the Colorado and so instituted the famous Green River *rendezvous,* the term being supplied by the French creoles in Ashley's party, who, with their Canadian cousins, left many French names and terms scattered throughout the western country. Although the rendezvous was later moved to Great Salt Lake, Pierre's Hole in Idaho, and the Wind River fork of the Bighorn in Wyoming, it has remained the "Green River rendezvous" in the minds of most western readers.

When Ashley took his caravan with the yearly supply of goods up the Platte in 1827, he also had a four-pound cannon on a sturdy carriage, the first wheeled vehicle to cross South Pass. Three years later William Sublette brought the trade goods all the way to the rendezvous on Wind River by wagon, and Captain Benjamin Louis Eulalie de Bonneville followed the same track with twenty wagons, then branched off to the left across South Pass and on to Pierre's Hole. Bonneville found the trail easy for the wagons to travel until he reached the North Platte. There he met with canyons, steep rocky ridges, and dangerous river crossings. A source of much trouble was the dry mountain air that shrank the wagon spokes, wheel rims, and wagon sideboards, forcing frequent tightening of the bolts and many repairs. The steel tires had to be cut down also. At some camps the wagon wheels were removed and soaked in the river overnight to keep them tight. Bonneville's troubles induced the rival traders, Robert Campbell and Lucien Fontanelle, to use pack trains again in 1833, but after that wagons rolled west each year with the trade goods and east with the bales of fur for market.

The large-scale operations of the mountain men in the Rockies depended on horses in large numbers at reasonable prices. These were readily available from the Indian bands that visited the camp each summer. In addition to packhorses and teams needed for the supply trains, each trapper leaving the encampment for another winter on the streams needed a horse to ride, another to carry his traps and supplies, and a third to help bring in his anticipated winter catch of furs. If the trapper had an Indian wife, as many of them did, she too needed a horse to ride and another to carry the family tipi. Since ordinary horses easily met the requirements for all this work, a trapper could purchase them for only a few dollars' worth of trade goods.

Trapping parties in the field were always attracting horse thieves from the various Indian tribes. One instance of such activity on the part of a Crow war party took place in March 1831, when about sixty young men stole fifty-seven horses from Tom Fitzpatrick's camp. Jim Bridger led the volunteers to recover them, about fifty men on foot, who traveled day and night along the well-marked trail and caught up with the thieves about dusk the second day. The Indians were camped on a bend of a flood-swollen tributary of the Bighorn, protected on three sides by the stream; the horses were in a pen of piled-up driftwood. Bob Newell and Antoine Godin sneaked into the horse pen, made a breach in the wall, led out the bell mare with the bell carefully silenced, and had the horses on the run before the startled Crows could interfere. The rest of the mountain men were lying along the edge of the cutbank just across the stream, rifles ready for any Crow who might show against the campfires. In the first burst of firing seven Crows were killed. The leg-weary trappers rode hurriedly back to their main camp to escape possible pursuit by the main Crow force. This is but one of the many such incidents that dot the tales of the mountain men.

Sometimes the stealing pattern was more complicated. In the winter of 1839 some Cheyennes raided the horse herd at Fort Davy Crockett in northern Colorado. Philip Thompson then led some of the men from the fort across the mountains to Fort Hall, some three hundred miles away on the upper Snake River, to steal replacements from a camp of friendly Nez Percés, but failed to get even one horse from their well-guarded herd. On their return Thompson and his men lifted fourteen horses from the herd at Fort Hall and thirty more from a camp of friendly Shoshonis on Bear River.

The Shoshonis went at once to Fort Crockett to protest, demanding the return of their horses. By stealing from friends, Thompson had violated the code of the mountain men, and his theft was also bad for business. A party of fur-trade notables sallied forth from the fort and tracked down Thompson's band, who were huddled with the horses on an island in the Uinta River a hundred miles off to the southwest. After a little skirmishing and a trick or two, the rescue party secured all the horses without a fight, when the Utes in a nearby village refused to help the thieves. The disgruntled Thompson and his party then left for California.

The caravan of freight wagons to the rendezvous in 1836 was trailed by a light wagon carrying two missionary couples, Marcus and Narcissa Whitman and Henry and Eliza Spalding. As the first two white women ever to cross the plains, Mrs. Whitman and Mrs. Spalding created quite a sensation at the rendezvous, where Narcissa held court and received the homage of the mountain men while Eliza spent her time becoming acquainted with the Nez Percé women who were soon to be her charges. She also started learning the Nez Percé language, to help in the mission work.

Against the advice of the mountain men Whitman insisted on taking his wagon on west, only to have it break down on the Bear River. He then made a cart of the hind wheels and axle, piled the front wheels on top, and continued on to Fort Hall. After hauling the cart through three hundred more miles of rough country covered with sagebrush, he finally admitted defeat and abandoned the rig at Fort Boise.

Four years later a party of three missionary families traveling in two wagons reached the rendezvous. There they engaged Robert Newell to guide them on to Fort Hall, where they left the wagons and put their baggage on packhorses for the rest of the way. Newell took the wagons and harnesses as his pay for guiding them. He decided he would quit the fur trade and go west with his wagons to the Willamette Valley. He took along his old friend Joe Meek as a driver. Newell's Nez Percé wife, Kitty M., and their three sons, together with Meek's Nez Percé wife, Virginia, and their daughter were with the party. Caleb Williams drove a third wagon.

The way through the tough desert scrub and over lava rocks was so rugged that they had to put all their goods on packhorses and discard the wagon beds. Even the light running gear was difficult for the teams to pull through the brush.

After the party crossed the Snake River at Fort Boise the artemesia scrub was scantier, with frequent patches of grass interspersed, and the wagons rolled easier. The party struggled up the rough, narrow canyon of the Burnt River and crossed the wide valleys of the Powder and the Grand Ronde. They climbed the last ridge of the Blue Mountains and drove on to the Whitman mission, where apparently no one was at all impressed with their arrival. Then they followed down the Walla Walla River to old Fort Nez Percé, often called old Fort Walla Walla, on the Columbia. Two of the wagons were left there for the time, while the third was dismantled and loaded on a boat that arrived at Fort Vancouver December 15, 1840. Newell left this note in his diary concerning his feat: "This is to be remembered that I, Robert Newell, was the first who brought wagons across the Rocky mountains and up to this place 19th April, 1841, and have it [the third wagon] at this time on my farm about 25 miles from Vancouver west."

Once the word spread in the East that white women had successfully braved the Oregon Trail and that wagons had crossed the mountains to the banks of the Columbia, the migration to Oregon, then outside the boundaries of the United States, was under way. A few wagons started west in 1841 and a few more in 1842, but bickering and poor planning stopped them along the way. Then in 1843 came a group so large it has been called the Great Migration.

At the crossing of the Kansas River this group reached its full size as the last of the stragglers caught up with the main body. No exact count was made, but one of the leaders stated that there were more than 100 wagons and about 250 men, 130 women, and 610 children. Five thousand cattle belonging to various members of the train were herded along the trail by a body of horsemen.

From the first the people suffered a variety of troubles, some of their own making. They bickered and squabbled until the train divided into two, then into four different groups, with some lone wagons straggling along behind each of the four trains, but on they went through storms of rain and hail and heavy winds, with Indian scares nearly every day, yet determined to reach the Promised Land beyond the western mountains. The passage of their hundred broad-tired wagons and 5,000 cattle left a well-marked trail across the western vastness, a guide to any who chose to follow. Several of the travelers were imbued with the conviction that they were taking part in an important historical event and kept diaries and journals to record their achievements, an example followed by thousands who followed the trail during the next thirty years.

While horses were essential for the hunters, guides, and cowherds, most of the wagons were drawn by three or four yoke of oxen plodding along day after day in the heat and dust. All the good sections of the trail, with ample grass and water, came in the first several hundred miles.

Then came rough terrain, sparse pastures, barren, rocky ridges, and the desert plains of southern Idaho shimmering under the rays of the August sun.

Finally the tired, footsore teams crossed the Snake River and toiled up Burnt River Canyon and across a steep ridge to the sun-baked valley of the Powder River. With their animals gaunt and exhausted, worn and lame, the travelers faced the steep ramparts of the Blue Mountains athwart their path. They did not dare tarry to rest their suffering animals, for early snows would soon cover the mountain ridges, and they might become snowbound. At this extremity, as a crowning touch to their mountain of troubles, hundreds of mounted Indians came dashing down on them.

Here the guides quickly allayed their fears, telling the travelers that these were friendly Nez Percés with flour from their mission gristmill, apples from their orchards, salmon fresh-caught from the river, and, to cap it all, plenty of good fresh horses—all to be traded off to the white people for cloth and clothing, tools, knives, and pots and pans, but the horses were usually offered in exchange for the weak, limping cows that would be as good as new after a month's rest on good grass. Such trades were of real benefit to both the Indian and the traveler, and many a covered wagon crossed the last high ridge of the Blue Mountains with horses fresh from the Indian herds furnishing the necessary extra power for the steep pitches.

When the settlers finally reached the Willamette Valley, nearly every family had an Indian horse or two from the lands claimed by the Cayuse tribe, although most of the animals had been purchased from the visiting Nez Percés. At first these were called Cayuse Indian horses, then Cayuse horses. After most of the Cayuse tribe had been wiped out by disease and war and the survivors had been absorbed by other tribes, the horses became simply cayuses, and have so been known on the western ranges for a century or more.

In the 1890's, half a century after the Great Migration, the survivors met each year and recalled many incidents of their grand adventure. Understandably a body of folklore grew up around their actual experiences, adding touches of color to the reminiscences. One group of such tales might well be called Goldilocks on the Oregon Trail. The framework of these stories is always the same: a beautiful blond child in the camp enchants a visiting Indian chief, who then offers a number of horses in trade for her. In each story the girl has a different name and her age varies from three to seventeen, although she is usually quite young. In two of the stories she has red instead of yellow hair, and in a very few cases she turns into a boy. The number of horses offered also varies from two to two hundred. The most fascinating aspect of this thrilling episode is that it was never considered important enough at the time to be recorded in any diary or journal, and was never mentioned publicly until the 1890's. Outside of folklore, no one in the Columbia Basin has ever found an Indian chief of any tribe who would have taken such a child even as a gift.

Immediately after the Seven Years' War (1756–63) Spain made a determined effort to colonize California to forestall any possible encroachment by other nations. Small ports and settlements were developed at San Diego, Monterey, and San Francisco. A string of missions, twenty-one in all, were established near the coast along the Camino Real, the King's Highway, a winding dirt road. The initial breeding stock for the mission farms—horses, cattle, and sheep—was donated by the older missions in Lower California and was driven up the coast to the new mission sites.

In 1775 Juan Bautista de Anza brought in 250 settlers for a new pueblo on San Francisco Bay. He opened an overland route from Sonora across the desert by way of the Yuma crossing of the Colorado River, and brought in his own livestock.

The coast range from San Francisco to Los Angeles was an excellent area for stock, with mild winters and few predators. All the livestock prospered with very little care and filled the grazing lands around each mission, but these were located far enough from each other that the growing herds did not crowd one another for fifty years. In 1800 the missions reported a total of 24,000 horses, 74,000 cattle, and 88,000 sheep. This averaged more than a thousand horses for each mission, more than could be usefully employed to handle the farm work and herd the cattle. The comparatively small population in this large area of good pasture land produced an oddity—a pastoral people living off their flocks and herds without becoming even seminomadic.

The missions and the settlers were wholly dependent on their herds to furnish commodities for export. In the 1820's some cattle and horses were shipped to the Hawaiian Islands and cattle were sent by ship to both Tahiti and Fort George on the Columbia, but the staple products were the hides and tallow from the cattle. These were traded illegally to the Yankee ships for smuggled manufactured goods. "

After Mexico broke away from Spanish rule, the Mexican officials in the province of California permitted the trade to continue with few restrictions. Records are now scarce for the details of this early trade, but conservative estimates put the number of hides shipped out each year during the 1830's at over 100,000.

When the missions were turned into parish churches and the surrounding land was allotted to new settlers, the stock raising was taken over by the rancheros. The colorful way of life of these ranch owners was based on the produce of large herds of range cattle handled by vaqueros, who spent many of their waking hours in the saddle. They raised and trained horses for games and fiestas as well as for transportation and range work.

The great grizzly bears that roamed the hills furnished thrilling, dangerous sport for the expert ropers. The roping had to be done by a team of two or more men, since a single roper had no way of subduing a bear that would charge his horse as soon as the rope tightened. At this point, unless the second man caught the bear's hind feet in another noose, the roper had to drop his lasso in a mad dash for safety. With both ropes in place the bear could be stretched out and choked into submission. Then he was securely tied and hauled away to the nearest bullring, a stout corral with elevated perches for the spectators. Only the bravest horses could be used to make such a capture.

Once the spectators gathered at the bullring, the bear was tied securely to a wild bull by a thirty-foot rope and the two animals then fought to the death. Usually the grizzly won, but the bull conquered often enough to make the show interesting.

An important job for the vaqueros each year was the killing of thousands of cattle. The men carried long, heavy knives, similar to bolos, and rode alongside the running animals; with one skillful blow they severed the vertebrae of the neck. Some of the vaqueros preferred to use a lance shaft with a crescent-shaped blade instead of a point. A quick thrust of this blade against the hamstring brought the crippled animal to earth to be dispatched.

Each year the cattle were rounded up on a large plain, and those chosen for slaughter were cut out. After the first year the ground was strewn with vast quantities of weathered bones, which were then piled up to form a corral containing a hundred acres or more. Year by year, as the new bones were added, the fence grew wider and higher until it might be ten feet high and a hundred feet wide.

As the range horses increased, some of them escaped into the remote hills or into the swamplands of the central valley and became truly wild. Finally the bands were so large they were destroying grass needed for the cattle. Then they were attacked and several thousand were slaughtered. Usually there was no effort to salvage even the hides of these animals. Old accounts estimate as many as 40,000 being killed in a single year.

From the opening of the nineteenth century until the gold rush in 1849 the California stockmen consistently raised more horses than they could use, even though there was no ready market for the surplus. The Indians to the east in the Sierras liked horses to eat, but they preferred stealing to buying their meat. These Indians had nothing to trade even if they had wanted to buy anything.

Much farther to the east, at Santa Fe, an active market for livestock developed with the opening of the Santa Fe Trail to Missouri, but that market was across a thousand miles of rough mountain and desert trail, with bands of hostile Indians scattered along the way as an added hazard. No one from California was interested in driving stock to market over that route.

At Santa Fe, however, there were several adventurous Americans who considered such a venture feasible. One of them, Ewing Young, went out to California in 1830, planning to bring back a large drove of mules to sell to the sugar plantations in Louisiana, only to find on his arrival that mules were in short supply that year and commanded high prices. He returned with 1,500 horses instead and sent them on to the Missouri market. They added a new strain of Spanish stock to the well-mixed blood of the horses then being raised in the Ohio Valley. Other adventurous traders followed Young's example, supplying the Santa Fe market with both horses and mules.

From the clamor raised by the California rancheros, it would appear that stolen horses on the trail east greatly outnumbered those procured by legal means. That several large herds were stolen is a matter of record, and among the many horse thieves raiding the herds in the central valley none outranked that versatile pair, Peg-leg Smith, the mountain man, and his partner, Walkara, chief of the Utes. In a spectacular, well-planned raid in 1840, they crossed the Tehachapi Pass into the central valley and levied toll on the horse herds of every rancher from the Santa Ana River to San Juan Capistrano. Their greatest haul was at the mission San Luis Obispo, where they sneaked up in the night to the strong corral holding the best horses, cut a hole in the barrier, and made off with two hundred head of the best stock before the startled guards, who had been carefully watching the gate, realized what was happening.

The Californians organized two strong posses and set out in hot pursuit along the broad trail pounded out by the hooves of three thousand horses. The pursuers moved much faster than the thieves with their unwieldy herd, so Peg-leg decided on a stratagem to slow down the posse. While some of the raiders drove the herd on down the trail, the rest hid in the willows beside the first stream at the end of a long, dry stretch of trail. When the hot, dusty posse reached the creek, the whole party dismounted and hurried down for a drink. The raiders then rushed out from hiding and made off with all the saddle horses, leaving the Californians afoot until their comrades came to the rescue.

Even with this delay, the posse caught up with the herd and recaptured about fifteen hundred of the slower animals. The raiders drove the rest on to the Ute country along the upper Colorado and later took most of them south to the market at Santa Fe.

Though these drives of stolen herds were spectacular, one conducted by Miles Goodyear with legally purchased horses covered more than twice the distance. In April 1848 he bought 231 horses around Los Angeles and drove them east all the way to Fort Leavenworth, Kansas, planning to sell them to the army for use in the Mexican War. When he reached the fort at the end of a two-thousand-mile drive he learned that the war was over and that the bottom had dropped out of the local horse market. News of the rich gold strike at Sutter's Mill near Sacramento induced Goodyear to drive his horses back to California to sell to the miners in the booming new camps. In all, his trail herd had covered four thousand miles, traveling the return two thousand miles from Independence, Missouri, back to Sacramento in fifty-four days—something of a record for a trail drive with loose stock across mountains and deserts.

The available rangeland for horses in the Columbia Basin country was much less than that in California, but the range conditions were about as favorable. As a result the Indians in the basin could raise all the horses they cared to own and did not need to raid the ranches to the south, as was the habit of the Plains tribes. While some of the tribes, such as the

Spokanes and Sanpoils, who lived in the scattered pines on the northern edge of the grasslands, lost many of their foals each year to the wolves infesting their lands, they could easily replenish their herds by securing horses at a low price from the Nez Percés and Yakimas. They dared not resort to stealing from such powerful neighbors when they had no place to hide to escape punishment. In the whole basin there were no reported thefts of horses until the wagon trains came in along the Oregon Trail. Then some of the white men caught a few horses from the range herds, professing to believe that they were wild horses. The only large losses incurred by the basin tribes were in the buffalo country, where the Blackfeet, Assiniboins, and Sioux sometimes ran off with the herd from a hunting camp.

When the fur traders came to the Northwest they purchased a large number of horses each year to use as pack animals, since most of the rivers were unsuitable for navigation even for canoes. Boats plied the Columbia from Fort Vancouver upstream to Fort Nez Percé at the mouth of the Walla Walla, but beyond that point furs and supplies moved on the backs of packhorses. The Snake expedition, which made a great loop each year from Fort Nez Percé into southwestern Montana and Idaho, needed from three hundred to four hundred horses. While many of them returned in the spring, they were tired and worn, and most of them were replaced for the next trip.

For several years the men at Fort Nez Percé were too lazy to hunt deer and elk in the mountains or to fish for salmon in the river. Instead they bought cheap horses to eat, at the rate of about one horse each day. At Spokane House, a trading post below Spokane Falls, horses were seldom used for food, but the traders kept a number of riding horses, which they raced frequently in organized meets.

The Columbia Basin tribes never regarded their surplus horses as a desirable supplement to their food supply, although they would eat horse meat in time of dire need, or when the white men were paying for and butchering the animals. Along the Columbia, where the tribes had little use for horses, an occasional animal was killed for food. Meriwether Lewis wrote in his journal that he found an Indian who traded him several pounds of good dried horse meat for a trinket. He said that the Indians of the various tribes would eat horse meat cooked in the explorers' camp, so it was not considered taboo, nor was its flavor distasteful to them.

The Columbia Basin tribes were disturbed by some side effects of the

California gold rush. The large influx of gold hunters brought California into the Union in 1850 and underlined the pressing need for a railroad connecting the booming Pacific Coast with the Midwest. Such a road, traversing about two thousand miles of plains, deserts, and mountains, could not hope for enough revenue from the scattered Indian tribes to pay even a small fraction of the operating expense. Private capital had no interest in such a project. The road had to be handled by the federal government, which showed its interest by instituting the preliminary planning and sent five survey parties along parallel routes from the Mississippi River to the Pacific Coast in search of the best routes.

Along the northern route just south of the Canadian border the Indian tribes were powerful, warlike, and engaged in constant fighting among themselves. The situation was aggravated by the large bands of buffalo hunters who rode a few hundred miles across the mountains each year to the Montana Plains, the disturbed area. They, too, were good fighters, and they joined with the Crows in intertribal wars. Any route, even for a wagon road, through the Dakotas and Montana would be of little value unless the warring tribes were pacified first. The federal officials had had some success in 1851 at Fort Laramie in getting the tribes along the Oregon Trail to be more peaceful and to allow the wagon trains to pass. Now the same pattern was recommended for the northern tribes.

Isaac I. Stevens, an army officer and newly appointed governor of Washington Territory, in addition to conducting the northern survey had the task of arranging some peaceful agreement among the hostile tribes. He also wanted the treaties to include a grant to the government of the right to open roads across Indian lands. At a great council held in the Valley of the Walla Walla in 1855, the major tribes of the Columbia Basin signed such treaties, and forty Nez Percé leaders rode east across the mountains with Stevens to parley with the Blackfeet over the buffalo-country problem.

The Montana council was held at Cow Island on the Missouri, about a hundred miles below Fort Benton, in early October. Indians assembled from the far places. The Blackfeet came south 250 miles from their Alberta home, the Flatheads rode 400 miles from the Bitterroot Valley, the Nez Percés 600 miles from the Clearwater, and the scattered hunting bands left their buffalo grounds 100 miles to the south. This assemblage of diverse tribes from such a wide area on such short notice illustrates the great mobility of the mounted Indians of the West.

The council at Cow Island made peace between the hostile groups, and Stevens returned to the West Coast satisfied with his summer's work, but his peace program soon collapsed when Congress delayed approval of the treaties and the promised treaty payments. While the tribes grew impatient with the delay, restless white prospectors insisted that the treaties were in full force and that they had a right to travel freely through Indian lands. Soon there were clashes between these foolhardy prospectors and the Indians, and a few deaths resulted.

The crisis came to a head in May 1858, when Colonel Edward J. Steptoe led a force of 150 dragoons on a march across the rolling hills of the Palouse country toward Spokane Falls. He hoped to overawe the restless Indians and thus put a stop to the troublesome incidents. A large force of mounted Indians barred his way, outfought him in a day-long battle, and sent him scurrying to safety, abandoning wounded soldiers along the way.

In August Colonel George M. Wright was sent with a force of more than four hundred men to chastise the hostile tribes for their attack on Steptoe. In two engagements, at Four Lakes and Spokane Plains, Wright's well-drilled men with their new long-range rifled muskets easily defeated the Indian horsemen. Then Wright, in a sweep along the Spokane River, captured 850 horses from the Spokane tribe. He could not use the animals and would not turn them loose for the Indians to use against him, so he had them all shot. Their whitened bones were a visible reminder to the Indians for many years of their defeat. Wright's method of handling a captured Indian horse herd was later used on the plains against the Cheyennes.

While all this military activity in the Northwest finally brought peace to that region, the problem of regular mail service to the West Coast remained unsolved. Then, in 1858, the post office awarded a mail contract to the Butterfield Overland Mail Company, which planned to establish a stage line from St. Louis to San Francisco and agreed to make the run of 2,800 miles in twenty-five days. The company bought up a hundred Concord coaches, a thousand horses, and five hundred mules and set up a string of stage stations across the Southwest via El Paso, Tucson, Yuma Crossing, and Tehachapi Pass to the San Joaquin Valley and finally to San Francisco. This longer southern route was chosen over the central route to avoid the high mountains and heavy snows.

To maintain an average speed of five miles an hour across the rough country, fresh teams had to be ready at each station when the stage rolled in. It stopped just long enough to change horses, and a passenger had to be hardy indeed to endure such a ride twenty-four hours a day for twenty-five days, but some of them managed. Others stopped off every few days and rested until the next stage came along.

The stage lines needed good horses, heavier than the average range stock in the Southwest, if the teams were to stand up under the heavy work. Indians and whites alike found the herds pasturing near the stations tempting indeed, for the carefully chosen stage horses were larger and faster than the ordinary riding horses. In spite of constant trouble from horse thieves, bad weather, and the like, the mail went through on time and month by month the loads increased. Then, in 1861, the stage line was moved to the central route to keep it away from the Confederate states of Arkansas and Texas. On the central route Ben Holladay, the stagecoach king, made the fastest long-distance run on record when he drove from Folsom, California, to Atchison, Kansas, in twelve days and two hours—a distance of just over two thousand miles.

The twenty-five-day mail service of the Butterfield line was still considered slow, but any faster service would have had to depend on couriers on horseback, a system occasionally used in the West for special events. It was considered too costly for regular service. Such a service was finally set up at great expense by a private firm to carry mail between St. Joseph, Missouri, and Sacramento, California, in ten days. The first run began on April 3, 1860. The 1,966 miles of trail required 190 stations at intervals of about ten miles, with a stationmaster and an assistant at each. Four hundred and twenty good horses, above average for speed and stamina, were distributed along the route, with at least two at each station. Because easterners, particularly reporters, liked to call all western horses "ponies," this service was popularly known as the Pony Express. To make it function, eighty hardy riders were hired, each scheduled to ride a stretch of seventy-five miles at a time, using six or seven horses for the task.

At each station there were two exciting moments each week—one when the rider dashed in from the east, the other at the arrival of the rider from the west. Each time a fresh horse had to be saddled and waiting, while the stationmaster held a piece of bread and a cup of hot coffee ready to refresh the rider, who had no more than two minutes to make his change of mounts, munch his bread, swallow his coffee, and dash away to the next station. If he did not want the bread and coffee, his change of horses might be accomplished in two seconds rather than two minutes.

The tired horse that had just finished a ten-mile stint at a steady gallop was unsaddled, rubbed down, and walked around to cool off, then was fed and watered. It was allowed about ten days of rest before making the next run. Such speedy, hardy animals were valuable and warranted the best of care.

The mail was carried in a large, square leather pad called a mochila. With charges at $5.00 a half-ounce, letters were written in a fine hand on thin tissue paper. To cut down on the weight the horse had to carry, and to allow for more mail on each run, the horses wore the lightest bridles and small saddles. The riders wore light foot gear, and usually carried no weapons of any kind, trusting to the speed and stamina of their mounts to rescue them from danger in the form of hostile Indians or an occasional western-type "bad man."

The best known of the riders was "Pony Bob" Haslam, who had a regular run across the Sierras to Fort Churchill in Nevada. Once, when the Paiutes were out raiding, Haslam reached his change station near Virginia City only to find his mount gone. His tired horse carried him to the end of his run, but his relief rider was too frightened and ill to take the mail. On a fresh horse Haslam was off to Carson Sink, 35 miles away, where he secured another fresh horse for the 37-mile stint to Cold Springs and another fresh horse for the last 30 miles to Smith's Creek —a total of 190 miles without a rest. After resting nine hours, Haslam started back with the westbound mail, only to find the Cold Springs station destroyed. On he rode, finding a fresh horse at the next stop, and he finally crossed the Sierras to the end of his regular run—another 190 miles. His grateful boss paid him an extra $100 for his two extra stages.

The Pony Express continued its service at a heavy loss, the runs getting shorter week by week through the summer of 1861 as the new telegraph line was built from both the west and east ends. Finally the line was finished in October, and the Pony Express ended. In later years many riders who served as couriers for the northwestern gold camps or for the army claimed to have been Pony Express riders.

General J. E. B. Stuart narrowly escapes Union forces. Stuart's propensity for dashing about like a junior officer instead of directing his troops from the rear led him into many tight spots, gained him much publicity, and finally resulted in his death at Yellow Tavern in 1864. (New York Public Library Picture Collection)

9

Horses in the Civil War

ALTHOUGH THE CAVALRY with its color and dash loomed large in Civil War news and the public imagination, all the cavalry horses combined were but a small fraction of the vast numbers of those animals used in the war, in addition to a few hundred thousand mules. With the average service life of a horse in any of the military units set at about seven and a half months, the number in service at any given time should be multiplied by at least six to get an approximate total for the war, and a large majority of all the horses were of draft stock whenever such animals were available, for their chief duties were hauling anything that needed transporting—guns, ammunition, supplies, food, clothing, camp gear, wounded men. The northern armies had a much larger supply of draft animals available than did the South. This numerical superiority was more marked than ever during the latter part of the war, after the northern armies had cut the supply line from Texas that ran through Vicksburg, and had occupied the important horse-raising centers in West Virginia, Kentucky, Tennessee, and northern Mississippi. The wastage of war used up the horses in the South faster than they could be replaced to the point that the Confederate forces lacked teams even to haul the abundant food supplies from the farms to the underfed armies in the field.

The United States census for 1860 listed the total number of horses and mules combined for each state, but gave no total for horses alone. In the following figures, the percentage of mules in the total is higher for the states in the lower South.

In 1860 the southern states, including Arkansas and Texas, had about 1,947,000 horses and mules. The middle states—Kentucky, Tennessee, West Virginia, and Missouri—had about 1,800,000, which during the first two years of the war were divided about equally between the North and South, and the northern states had about 3,595,000. This gave the South in 1861 about 2,877,000 horses and mules, while the North had about 4,523,000, an advantage that increased greatly with the fall of Vicksburg on July 4, 1863, when the horses from Texas, Arkansas, and Missouri were cut off from the southern armies, while those horses were available to the northern armies occupying Missouri, Kentucky, and northern Mississippi. When it is remembered that a great many of the 2,000,000 animals still available in the South were mules, it is easy to understand why the North had such marked superiority in both cavalry and draft horses during the last year of the war.

At the outset of the war a large majority of the people in the entire country lived on the farms and in the small villages. This rural population supplied the bulk of the troops, which for the Union armies toward the end of the conflict totaled more than 1,000,000 men. The removal of this number of workers from the farming areas caused a serious shortage of workers, but the output of the farms continued to increase, particularly in the Midwest. New farms by the thousands in the prairie states stepped up grain production to the point where the armies and the urban population were amply supplied, while the export of wheat rose from 100,000 bushels in 1859 to 40,000,000 bushels in 1862.

Such an expansion of farming, even with the young men off to war, was possible for a number of reasons. Of great importance was the large immigration from northern Europe—about 800,000 people in all during the war years. Many of them moved directly onto new farmlands. Equally important was the rapid improvement in farm machinery that enabled one person, such as an older boy, a young woman, or a middle-aged man, to take a machine and a team and do the work formerly done by five to ten able-bodied field hands.

During the 1850's the farmers had sought new machines to replace men who flocked to the western gold fields. The resulting shortage of labor raised wages to the point that an expensive laborsaving machine was a profitable investment. Such machines worked better on the broad, smooth fields carved from the prairies, and on such crops as grain and hay. They were of little value on the small fields in the rocky New

England hills, where the farmers kept their old-style implements long after the West had adopted the new ways.

When the pioneers had reached the prairies covered with heavy sod they needed new kinds of plows to break the virgin ground. By the 1850's there were plows of steel with mold boards to cut through the sod and turn it over neatly. They worked better when drawn by horses, for the slow gait of the oxen did not produce a good scouring effect on the mold board or turn the sod so neatly. Following the steel plows in the fields came the double-width harrows, a saving on manpower but not on horses.

New seed drills planted the grain evenly and the grain then ripened more uniformly than when planted by hand. Drills for corn were slower to develop, for the corn had to be planted in hills, but by 1860 two men with a corn planter and a team could seed twenty acres a day, compared to the one half to one acre a day by a man with a hoe.

A successful reaper for cutting wheat and other small grains had been patented in 1834 by Cyrus McCormick. It needed many improvements and numerous demonstrations at fairs and other farm gatherings before it gained general acceptance among the grain growers. The reaper cut the stalks of grain and kept them on a platform, to be removed by a man with a rake in piles suitable for tying into sheaves, which then were shocked and left to stand in the fields while the grain finished ripening. The binder that cut, bundled, and tied the sheaves was not developed until after the war. The reaper with its driver and raker did the work of five men with cradles and five more with rakes.

At first the farmers tried to use the same machine to reap grain and cut hay, but this was not satisfactory, even with special attachments. Finally a mower was built exclusively for cutting hay. On both the mower and reaper the cutting bar worked better with the steady, faster gait of the horses than with the slower, uneven pace of the oxen. Also, all these expensive machines could farm more acres in a day with the horse teams. Each mower replaced five or more men with scythes, while the horse-drawn hay rake following the mower did the work of ten to twenty hand rakers.

For hundreds of years the best method of handling small grains had been to cut and bundle them for storage until winter weather put an end to field work. Then the farmhands, who otherwise would have been idle, beat out the grain with flails on the threshing floor and winnowed it in the breeze. This method was slow but it produced good clean grain with whole kernels, much in demand by the gristmills. Grain threshed out by animals was sometimes cracked and always contained excessive dirt.

Finally inventors developed a machine that would thresh the grain, separate it from the straw, and blow away the chaff. This was commonly known as a threshing machine, but in the trade and among farmers it was called a separator. The best of these could be moved from farm to farm, with horses furnishing the power from a treadmill. Separators turned out clean grain and left a pile of usable straw.

Corn was still picked and husked by hand, but new machines run by horses on treadmills shelled the grain from the cob, while other machines ground up the large, hard grains for stock feed. Hay presses formed the loose, cured hay into compact bales for easy storage and shipping, using horse power to operate.

Although all of these machines were in widespread use by 1860, fewer than half the farmers were progressive enough to adopt them and use them to advantage. Especially in the South the introduction of machines lagged. The South still had slaves for field labor, and the staple crops of tobacco, rice, sugar, and cotton did not lend themselves to the new machines.

For a century before the Civil War, range-raised horses of Spanish stock moved from the Southwest across the Mississippi at Natchez and St. Louis to help supply the animals needed by the rapidly growing farm and urban population. These horses were strong, tough, and hardy, but because of their small size they were considered too light to be draft horses or even good riding horses. The mares were healthy and sound, and when they were crossed with larger stallions they produced good foals that grew much larger than their dams, partly because of the heritage of their sires, partly because they had good pastures and supplemental feed during the growing period and were not subjected to the harsher environment of the open range.

Only mares and geldings were wanted in the eastern markets, for the mature range stallions were difficult to tame and dangerous to have on a farm. Also, such stallions were not considered desirable for breeding purposes when workhorses were wanted. Hence even the young stallions were gelded before they were offered for sale. This almost total absence of western stallions on eastern farms insured that the foals from the range mares would carry only half-Spanish blood, and those from the second generation only one fourth. The rapid decrease in the percentage of western blood under such a breeding program tended to obscure the amount of that heritage present in the eastern United States. But the cross breeding had to be carefully supervised, or a large number of horses with half-western blood would be mated with each other. Such random pasture breeding was common and produced mediocre horses.

The rapid change in the type of foals that can be produced under a carefully supervised breeding program stems directly from the ability of a stallion properly handled to serve twenty to thirty mares in a season. A little care and planning on the part of the individual breeder and some trading of stallion service with the neighbors could soon build up a supply of several hundred stallions with blood of some established breed that was at least seven eighths pure, even though the program had started with all the mares of range stock. This multiplying influence of a single stallion is graphically illustrated in the rapid establishment of the Morgan breed from a single horse, Justin Morgan.

Although a strain of horses can be kept at a high level by good stallion selection and good management, there are always many horse raisers too ignorant or indifferent to maintain such a program. Especially in the thinly settled areas, scrub stallions were allowed to produce scrub offspring in large numbers. These animals were about as small as the western horses but of poorer quality. Too often, in evaluating the horses of a certain region, the observer tends to stress all the fine animals he sees and ignores the many scrubs in the background. This was often true of the pine-covered hill country in the South.

An important factor in keeping down the infusion of western blood into farm stock was the practice of using the mares to produce mule colts for the small farms and plantations. There was a superstition prevalent among breeders of pure strains that once a mare had produced a mule colt, her next offspring would be adversely affected. Hence any mare once bred to a jack was seldom bred after that to a stallion. The breeding of mules in Missouri and in the hill country of the South was important business, since the animals were in great demand for field work on the cotton and sugar plantations. They were hardier than either horses or oxen and could be worked by Negroes, who seldom were permitted to ride or drive horses.

In the South the upper class owned a large number of fine horses for pleasure riding and driving, fox hunting, and racing. They paid little attention to draft horses. On this account the proportion of fine riding horses in the total horse population was high, especially in the towns and around the larger plantations. In sharp contrast, the northern cities and towns were crowded with draft horses, and on the northern farms draft horses were the counterparts of mules on the plantations.

The many fine pleasure horses owned in the North by the upper class often received scant attention from the visitor, for many of them were kept for harness use. They carried the businessmen and their families about the towns, but they did not appear numerous among the many draft teams hauling their loads along the city streets. When they were ridden in the parks and on the bridle paths they might go unnoticed by the visitor, even when they were present in large numbers. Not evident either was the fact that almost all the harness horses could easily be broken to ride if necessary, for they were of the same type used as saddle horses, and since the upper class in the more populous North greatly outnumbered that class in the South, the total number of good potential cavalry horses was at least equal to that of the South.

A vivid illustration of the number of pleasure horses available, particularly those used in harness, is offered by the picnic parties held by the people of Washington near the Bull Run battlefield on July 21, 1861—a bright, warm Sunday and just the day for an outing. By the hundreds the carriage folk in Washington, including six senators and ten congressmen, ordered their lunches packed and their carriages brought around early. Then they drove off to the west, hoping to see something of the great battle that was predicted for the day.

They crossed the small stone bridge on Cub Run and took their places on the next rise overlooking Bull Run and the country beyond, where the battle was already in progress about a mile away. They ate and visited, discussing all the rumors flying around, and wondered what was really happening under the great clouds of smoke rising from the cannon and small arms busily firing off their black powder charges.

No one seemed aware that war is not the safest of spectator sports, and, in fact, the holiday crowd did not get in the way until late afternoon, when the Federal soldiers began an orderly retreat across the small stone bridge, with a rear guard to keep the Confederate cavalry at a distance. As the retreating columns grew in numbers, some of the picnickers packed up their things and started for home, their carriages mingling with the marching soldiers. Then a Confederate shell burst just above the stone bridge, wrecking a wagon and completely blocking the road, and the panic began.

Cannon, supply wagons, ambulances, carriages, horsemen, and foot soldiers all dashed for the blocked bridge and jammed together there in a struggling mass. The ranks of retreating soldiers soon dissolved into a screaming mob. Teamsters cut their horses loose and rode off, leaving masses of vehicles blocking the road. Soldiers dropped muskets, ammunition, canteens, blankets, haversacks—anything that might impede their flight—and scurried away across the fields. And the frantic picnickers, the cause of much of the panic and confusion, ran too, until they collapsed from exhaustion, and all the while the people too poor to afford carriages for a Sunday outing remained safe at home.

At the beginning of the Civil War, when the South organized cavalry from its large number of volunteers, each man brought along his own horse, while some officers had two or more. Almost every young man who had a horse wanted to serve in the cavalry—the glamor arm—and ride into battle, not slog along on foot. These men were good riders, accustomed to outdoor life, and they quickly became effective raiders.

Each man who furnished his own horse was allowed forty cents a day to pay for its use, and if the animal was killed or disabled in battle the owner was given the appraised value and a thirty-day furlough to find a replacement. The average military life of a cavalry horse was estimated at less than six months, and finding suitable remounts became a serious problem after two years of war. The number of men on furlough from an active cavalry unit seriously depleted the ranks in a campaign when the fighting was heavy.

In the northern army during the first year of the war the cavalry was given scant consideration. Units were slow in getting organized, in securing equipment, and in finding horses. Often months went by before the men had horses for their drills. It was this lack of official appreciation and help more than anything else that hindered the development of an effective northern cavalry arm. Another factor was the difficulty in securing horses. Careless procurement officers and tricky horse dealers combined to foist off on the troops a sorry collection of low-grade nags, while the large supply of superior animals in the hands of influential private citizens in the Middle Atlantic and New England states went untapped. Once the procurement service was improved, an ample supply of good cavalry horses was found.

Much has been written of the lack of riding skill among the northern rank and file. This was true of the regiments raised along the seaboard, where the men were clerks, artisans, and factory workers who required about two years of training to become good cavalrymen. However, in the Ohio Valley the young men had handled and ridden horses from childhood, but they had spent so much of their time caring for work-horses every morning and night—harnessing, feeding, stabling, and watering them—in addition to spending long hours with them in the fields, that they wanted to get away from horses for a while. The southern horsemen, by contrast, had slaves to handle all the stable work while the masters did the riding.

Once the brilliant, dashing cavalry officers of the South had led their eager commands on a series of spectacular raids, demonstrating the effectiveness and worth of the cavalry in active service, some of the northern generals were greatly impressed and turned more attention to raising an effective cavalry of their own if only to protect their armies in the field, especially the supply lines and supply depots. And the newspaper publicity in the northern newspapers about such brilliant cavalry officers as J. E. B. Stuart and Nathan Bedford Forrest made the cavalry service seem more glamorous than before, thus encouraging the young northerners to volunteer for it.

In European wars the generals had used their massed cavalry in thunderous charges against the enemy infantry formations. The southern generals who had read their histories considered this was the most important function of the horsemen, although such use had come to disaster at Waterloo half a century earlier. The best northern generals preferred to use their cavalry as dragoons, with horses to transport the men into combat position quickly. Then the men dismounted and became infantry for the actual fighting, for infantrymen had superior firepower, both in volume and accuracy. Both sides depended on their cavalry for scouting and for raids on supply lines, especially the railroads.

James Ewell Brown Stuart, formally listed as J. E. B. Stuart but usually called Jeb, was the best known of the southern cavalry leaders. A dashing, bold, brilliant, flamboyant leader, he traced his ancestry to the royal house of Scotland. At West Point he was called "Beauty" Stuart for his lack of chin, a defect he covered with a beard once he graduated. In combat he liked to gallop along at the head of his men, who followed him in blind devotion into any danger. His propensity to dash about like a junior officer when he should have been directing his division of troops as commanding general led him into many a tight spot, and finally led to his death at Yellow Tavern in 1864.

A lieutenant in the United States Army when war broke out, Stuart resigned at once and joined the Confederate cavalry. He rose rapidly in rank as he demonstrated his qualities of leadership, and by October 1861 he was a brigadier general in command of all the cavalry of the Army of Virginia.

A reconnaissance in force by the cavalry in June 1862 displayed the effective use of cavalry and the special qualities of Stuart as a daring leader who took needless risks. Union General George B. McClellan, commanding the Army of the Potomac, had come ashore with his forces near Yorktown and was advancing toward the Confederate capital at Richmond. General Robert E. Lee interposed his Army of Virginia between the Union forces and their goal and by June 10 was planning an attack on McClellan, but first he needed exact information about McClellan's right flank on the low ridge north of the Chickahominy River. Stuart was chosen to lead a picked body of his cavalry on the scouting assignment.

Before dawn on June 12, Stuart left Richmond with twelve hundred men and two artillery pieces and moved north, ostensibly bound for the Valley of Virginia. After a march of twenty-two miles he camped for the night near the South Anna River. At dawn he put his column on the road again, marching southeast toward Old Church twenty miles away, only to encounter a small Union force at Hanover Court House. Stuart tried to catch them in a trap but they fled to safety in time, dashing off to spread news of the raid.

About noon the column flushed another small Union force and put it to flight. That afternoon Stuart luckily found the bridge across Totopotomay Creek undamaged and unguarded, furnishing him an easy crossing. The streams all along his route were difficult to ford or swim at any time of the year and in early June were running bank-full from recent rains, making sound, unguarded bridges a necessity for rapid travel. One bridge strongly guarded, or one burned one, would have been a serious obstacle to the cavalry column.

Two and a half miles beyond the bridge at Old Church, Union forces blocked the road but scattered before a cavalry charge. They also abandoned their camp and all their supplies, which were then burned except for an ambulance and a keg of whiskey, both of which were taken as booty.

At this point Stuart had finished his assignment and had acquired accurate knowledge that McClellan had no important forces along the ridge. His duty was to get both the information and his men back to headquarters as rapidly as possible, a ride of only forty-two miles by the route he had come, but Stuart was hoping for excitement and headlines. He soon convinced himself that to retrace his route would expose the column to great danger, for the Union troops might have destroyed one of the bridges and they might be waiting in force to attack him.

He reasoned that if he moved rapidly to the south behind the rear of McClellan's army, he might cut the railroad that was McClellan's main line of supply. Then he could rush on south to the James River before an adequate force could block his way. From that point he could return to Richmond by keeping to the south of McClellan's left flank, especially if Lee would create some small diversion on the enemy's front. Thus Stuart could ride completely around a large enemy force, a dangerous, exciting feat seldom tried and then almost never successful. If he returned safely, all the newspapers would praise his deed. His dubious colonels promised to follow him whichever way he chose to go, so he led his column southward at once to utilize the few remaining hours of daylight.

At Tunstall's on the railroad Stuart expected a fight, and he ordered his cannon to the front of the column only to have it bog down in knee-deep mud and remain there, in spite of the combined efforts of the teams and gun crews. Then a sergeant had a brilliant idea—place the captured keg of whiskey on the gun carriage as a reward for the men as soon as they had freed the gun. With good teamwork and one mighty heave they lifted cannon, carriage, keg, and all onto dry ground and enjoyed their well-earned treat, but the delay kept them out of the action at the railroad station.

There the small Union guard scattered before the charging horsemen. A train approached; the engineer became alarmed and sped off in a shower of bullets that did little damage. The cannon needed to disable the engine was still stuck in the mud.

As soon as the weary troopers had torn up a stretch of track, cut the telegraph line, and set fire to the stores, they were again on the long road south toward a ford near Forge Bridge on the lower Chickahominy

River. They rode all night under a full moon, reaching the ford at day-light only to find the crossing too dangerous because of the swirling flood waters. A mile downstream they found the remains of the bridge, the abutments still intact. Timbers from an adjacent abandoned ware-house furnished beams that just reached across the gap. Boards torn from the walls supplied the flooring. As the last troops crossed, the bridge was set on fire to hamper any pursuers, and just in time. A troop of Union cavalry rode up and opened fire on the rearguard until it was out of range.

Still thirty miles from Richmond, Stuart had to push on with his weary men and jaded horses. The entire command, except for one offi-cer killed in a skirmish, reached safety within Lee's lines on June 16 after four days and two nights of grueling work. They were well pleased with their success, and with the resulting press notices.

Glamorous and thrilling as it was, the ride from Old Church on was of dubious military value, and it had placed an important segment of the army's cavalry in extreme danger. Stuart escaped with little loss and brought back the important information in time, but on another such mission his disregard for the prime military objective resulted in disaster for Lee's army.

Through two years of anxiety and frustration the northern people had read of successful exploits of the Confederate cavalry, including brilliant raids in Kentucky by General Nathan Bedford Forrest, while they had nothing exemplary to admire in their own men. Then, in the spring of 1863, the improving northern cavalry staged a raid equal in brilliance, daring, and execution to anything the southerners had done, and the northern people responded with a great outburst of applause and appreciation.

Early that spring General U. S. Grant decided to capture the southern stronghold of Vicksburg on the east bank of the Mississippi by attacking from the south. He would have to march his troops down the west bank and ferry them across several miles downstream. His flotilla of boats would have to run the heavy fire of the Vicksburg shore batteries by night. Grant's immediate problem was how to turn the attention of the Confederate commander, General John C. Pemberton, to another area for the few critical days needed for the operation and thus keep him from concentrating the Confederate reserves to oppose the landing.

Grant planned three simultaneous diversions for Pemberton, one of them being a cavalry raid through the heart of the state of Mississippi, which at that time was swarming with southern soldiers. If Grant's cavalry could dash south and threaten the railroad supply line to Vicksburg, Pemberton would be forced to deploy some of his reserves to guard the line.

Chosen to command the raid was Colonel Benjamin Henry Grierson of the Illinois cavalry, in peacetime a music teacher who disliked horses. When he was eight years old, a pony had kicked him in the face, breaking his cheekbone and scarring him for life. But when he volunteered for war service and showed his potential as an officer, General Henry W. Halleck assigned him, against his strong protests, as a major in the cavalry, for to the general he looked like a good cavalry type. In a year's time Grierson had made a favorable impression on Grant for the good work of his command in action. He was promoted to colonel and was given command of a brigade of three regiments of cavalry, numbering at the time about seventeen hundred men. Grant asked him to take his forces out and cut the line to Vicksburg about two hundred miles south of Grierson's post at La Grange, all but ten miles of the raid through enemy-held territory. Grierson planned to strike the railroad line about thirty miles east of the state capital at Jackson, destroy the station, cut the telegraph lines, tear up some track, burn bridges and culverts, destroy any military stores he could find, and when he had finished those chores he was to make his escape as best he could with several thousand irate Confederates closing in on him from all sides.

Grierson's men were well mounted, having been given the pick of all the horses captured in Mississippi and western Tennessee or brought in from the big remount depot at St. Louis. He also had six light field pieces with picked crews. At dawn on April 17, 1863, he led his men out of La Grange and marched them south for thirty miles before halting for the night. On the eighteenth they were on their way again at dawn and soon began encountering stray scouts but no real resistance. That night his men found a good camp on a large plantation that furnished them with food, forage, horses, and mules, although all of these were given up rather reluctantly. Early the next day they moved on, slowed by a driving rain that muddied the roads.

On the fourth morning the command turned out in the wet at 2:30 to stand inspection. Every man who was sick, and every horse showing signs of lameness or saddle sores, was taken from the ranks. The sick men, the "Quinine Brigade," were given the ailing horses and were sent back to La Grange. With Major Hiram Love in command, and one field piece for added protection, they marched off up the track made the day before, while the main force slipped off through the woods to return to the road further along. This left only the tracks of the retreating men on the road and confused enemy scouts, who thought the whole command had turned back and was headed for Oxford, off to the northwest.

Once the southern commanders in northern Mississippi received word from their scouts that Grierson was moving south they were sure his objective was the Mobile and Ohio Railroad paralleling his route some thirty miles to the east. They quickly gathered troops to guard the stations and sent some of their cavalry to intercept the raiders.

To increase southern anxiety about their railroad, Grierson sent one regiment under Colonel Edward Hatch to attack it at any spot he was able to reach, then retreat northward to the home base. Hopefully the Confederate cavalry would follow him. To further confuse the enemy, in the morning when the main column moved south Hatch was to follow for a short distance, then reverse his march to blot out the southbound tracks. As Grierson moved off into the woods again, Hatch retraced his route for a mile or so before turning east toward the railroad.

This deception worked so well that all the pursuing cavalry followed Hatch and caught him right after lunch, but Hatch had time to dismount his men and place them behind good cover to receive the charge. He beat the enemy off and went on to the north, burning bridges, capturing horses and mules, and beating off several attacks against his rearguard. With this burst of activity he held the attention of his pursuers for five critical days.

The day after Hatch left, Grierson sent out one company of cavalry under Captain Henry Forbes to move southeast and attack the Mobile and Ohio at Macon, then march cross-country and rejoin the main column if possible. Forbes found Macon too well guarded, so he turned and rode away with his thirty-five men, while the alarmed Confederates moved up two thousand troops by train to reinforce the place.

On April 24, after one week on the road, Grierson reached his goal, Newton Station on the railroad to Vicksburg. His men captured a westbound train loaded with timber and supplies for the forces at Vicksburg, and an eastbound one with ammunition and goods from the factories at Jackson. Then two battalions moved eastward along the tracks and two moved west, tearing up the rails and heating them over fires made by the crossties until they were warped beyond all use.

This surprise attack so close to his headquarters in Jackson greatly alarmed General Pemberton. He hastily sent troops to the east along the railroad to block any advance Grierson might attempt against the capital and ordered cavalry to block the roads of escape to the northwest and northeast. He also recalled the cavalry from Port Hudson on the Mississippi and moved them east. All this furor and assembling of troops drew attention away from General Grant and allowed him to complete his preparations for the river crossing almost unobserved.

Meanwhile, Captain Forbes with his thirty-five men had approached the Mobile and Ohio Railroad again, this time south of Macon at Enterprise, where he expected to find Grierson. Instead he found a strong enemy guard. He rode forward with a handkerchief on his saber for a flag of truce and convinced the officers who rode out to meet him that Grierson's whole command was just behind him. He called for the immediate surrender of Enterprise and the entire garrison. The officers replied that they needed an hour to discuss the matter. Dee Alexander Brown in *Grierson's Raid* quotes Forbes on the sequel:

> We never officially knew what the Confederates' reply was, as for reasons best known to themselves they failed to make it reach us. Perhaps it was lack of speed. We fell back, very cheerfully, four miles, and fed, and resumed our retreat, which was diligently continued all night. We learned afterwards from the Southern papers that our reply was forwarded six miles on our track that evening with an escort of 2,000 infantry, under the impression that we were at least 1,500 strong.

Forbes and his men then hurried along to overtake their comrades, but this proved to be a difficult task. Colonel Grierson was hurrying to reach the Pearl River ferry before it could be destroyed. To slow his pursuers, he had his men burn each bridge after they crossed it. Forbes and his men followed the trail of ruins and were forced to swim five rain-swollen rivers. They despaired of ever catching up and sent three men with the freshest horses ahead to let Grierson know they were still following. The three caught Grierson just as he was crossing the bridge over Strong River in the night. With a clatter of hooves they dashed up and saluted. "Captain Forbes presents his compliments, and begs to be allowed to burn his bridges for himself."

Grierson's luck still held at Pearl River. The ferry was unguarded and the Negro ferryman was persuaded to come across in the dark, being convinced that the force was an Alabama regiment. The ferrying was a long, slow process over the wide, flooding stream. Once across, the column moved on west to Union Church, hoping to turn north there and join Grant at Grand Gulf. On the way they captured Hazelhurst Station on the New Orleans and Jackson Railroad and wreaked their usual destruction. Then at Union Church they had a brush with some enemy cavalry. That night a clever, alert scout discovered the Confederates had plans for an ambush on the road west. Grierson made a strong feint in that direction, then dashed back to the southeast to Brookhaven Station, wrecking the installations there.

With large enemy forces closing in on him from four sides, Grierson ran for Wall's Bridge, where he had his sharpest fight of the raid—losing one man killed, three wounded, and five captured—but he seized the bridge, crossed the stream, and raced on all that afternoon and late into the night. The Williams Bridge lay ahead and a force from Port Hudson was approaching it from the west to close it, but the officers stopped for the evening at a dance. When they reached the bridge in the morning they were too late. Grierson's men had crossed at midnight.

The column did not even pause for breath. The refuge at Baton Rouge was still thirty miles away, and they had several large detachments of angry Confederates on their trail. By this time some of the men were so tired they slept soundly in the saddle, or fell off and continued sleeping on the ground until roughly awakened. At Sandy Creek crossing they captured the guard of about forty men, and another forty-two at the Comite crossing.

Three miles west of Comite River they felt safe and stopped to rest at a plantation, but one of the colonel's orderlies, sound asleep in the saddle, rode on down the road until he awoke at a picket's challenge. It is difficult to say who was the more confused of the two. Finally two companies of Union cavalry were sent out to determine if the approaching troops were really Yanks. They escorted the tired men back to Baton Rouge and the great raid was over.

Dee Alexander Brown quotes Colonel Grierson's summation of the historic raid:

During the expedition we killed and wounded about one hundred of the enemy, captured and paroled over 500 prisoners, many of them officers, destroyed between fifty and sixty miles of railroad and telegraph, captured and destroyed over 3,000 stands of arms, and other army stores and Government property to an immense amount; we also captured 1,000 horses and mules.

Our losses during the entire journey was 3 killed, 7 wounded, 5 left on the route sick; the sergeant-major and surgeon of the Seventh Illinois left with Lieutenant Colonel Blackburn, and 9 men missing, supposed to have straggled. We marched over 600 miles in less than sixteen days. The last twenty-eight hours we marched 76 miles, had four engagements with the enemy, and forded the Comite River, which was deep enough to swim many of the horses. During this time the men and horses were without food and rest.

Major General J. E. B. Stuart was in his glory, staging a grand review of his five brigades of cavalry, 9,536 men in all. When plans were made in the spring of 1863 for Lee's invasion of Pennsylvania that summer, Stuart assembled all his cavalry units near Brandy Station to prepare them for the coming campaign. As a final touch he determined to put on a great pageant near his camp, where a wide field, a convenient smooth hillock, and the Orange and Alexander Railroad combined to offer room for the cavalry to maneuver and grandstand seats for the guests who had been invited from the whole area. A great ball was held on the evening of June 4 and the review followed the next day. It ended with a wild cavalry charge with drawn sabers against the massed artillery of twenty-four guns firing blank cartridges.

To the men in the ranks this was all a great bore, and they were really disturbed when they learned they were to repeat the whole performance, except for the sham battle, for General Lee on June 8. After the second review they all made final preparations for an early start the next morning, when the entire Army of Virginia was to begin its fateful march along the road that led to Gettysburg three weeks later.

That night Stuart slept in the open under a tree on the hillock that had served as a grandstand. He was awakened at dawn by the sound of gunfire to the east at the fords of the Rappahannock River. A large body of Union cavalrymen was on the march, seeking information on the significance of Lee's increased activity. They came across the fords and boldly attacked Stuart's forces, catching them by surprise and driving them back. Then Stuart rallied his men and brought up new units, including some infantry support. The fighting was long and fierce, the greatest cavalry battle of the entire war. When the Union cavalry finally withdrew at sundown it was proud that it had proved it could hold its own in a pitched battle against an equal number of Stuart's men, something it had never done before. The Union cavalry had come of age.

Stuart was impressed with the strength of the Union cavalry, while he was chagrined and humiliated at the realization that it had caught him by surprise when he was in charge of the entire scouting force of Lee's army. Southern editors commented rather acidly on the fight, stressing the surprise element. Stuart's determination to redeem himself in the eyes of his public on the forthcoming northern march explains some of his difficulties during the next three weeks.

After a few preliminary maneuvers Lee led his army across the Blue Ridge and down the Shenandoah Valley, while Stuart with three brigades of cavalry marched north on the east side of the hills. To keep his columns compact and to speed the pace, Stuart took a minimum of wheeled vehicles—just six field pieces, their caissons, and the ambulances. At this point, with the march just starting, the men and horses showed some effects from the two reviews, the battle at Brandy Station, and the subsequent march into position for the northward movement.

Stuart soon found his chosen route occupied by long, solid columns of blue-clad infantry of the II Corps of Major General Winfield Scott Hancock, and had to veer to the east. Hampered by this detour and the necessity of avoiding the Union troops, Stuart was unable to proceed as rapidly as he had planned. In two days his cavalry had covered only thirty-four miles, a performance the southern infantry usually bettered under such circumstances. Even so, the slow pace was tiring to the horses, since they had to be under saddle for long hours and they had already been on scanty forage for several days.

A long march on June 28 finally brought the cavalry to the deep, difficult Rowser's Ford on the Potomac two days late. It managed the crossing without any losses and was on Maryland soil ready to perform the two important duties that Lee had assigned. First, it was to keep close to the right flank of the corps of Confederate troops led by Lieutenant General Richard Stoddert Ewell, who was moving toward York, Pennsylvania. Second, it was to gather important information about the movements and troop dispositions of the Union forces and transmit it promptly to General Lee.

Stuart and his men did neither of these assigned tasks and so nullified Lee's plans. Instead he allowed himself to be diverted from his duty by the easy spoils of the rich farming country. His greatest temptation came when he reached Rockville on the main supply road from Washington to the Union army, and he succumbed.

Rockville was peopled by southern sympathizers, who informed Stuart that a big wagon train of supplies was approaching from the east. He immediately set his men at the edge of town and waited. Up the road from Washington came 150 brand-new wagons, piled with army supplies and drawn by teams of sleek mules in shining new harnesses. The small detachment of Union guards riding in advance turned and galloped back at the first sign of the raiders. They ordered the wagons to turn at once and make a run for it. About half of the wagons were gathered in by the raiders in one swoop before they could get turned around. The rest had a good chance of escaping as their teams swung down the road at a brisk trot. Then one of the wagons overturned, blocking the road. Only twenty-five wagons ahead of the accident escaped, their trotting mules outdistancing the weary cavalry horses vainly pursuing them.

The eager troopers swarmed over their prizes. They had taken 400 teamsters, 900 mules, and 125 wagons loaded with hams, bacon, sugar, hardtack, bottled whiskey, and enough oats to feed 5,000 hungry horses for a week. Several hours elapsed while the troopers reorganized their ranks and lined up their wagons. By the time they were ready to proceed the bottles of whiskey had vanished.

Those shiny new wagons with their sleek teams were too much for Stuart. He decided to take them along, although they would seriously lengthen his column and would slow the march. One of the three cavalry brigades had to follow behind the wagon train as a rear guard, too far away to be of help if an emergency arose on the road ahead. Stuart realized that he was behind schedule and that his march would be slowed, so he kept his men on the road for twenty miles that night to make up for some of the lost time.

On June 29 he reached the Baltimore and Ohio Railroad, the main line from tidewater to the Union army. His men pulled up some of the track, putting the line out of commission for several hours, but the alert engineers on approaching trains saw the break in time to avoid wrecks. They stopped short and backed out of danger. Stuart then moved on north at noon, reaching Westminster about five o'clock, where he found enough forage for all his horses. Many of the tired men were kept busy all night distributing the forage and feeding the animals.

On the morning of June 30, while Stuart was escorting his precious wagons along the road to Hanover, Lee was asking his aides again, "Where is Stuart?" Without his cavalry to scout for the army, Lee was fumbling along as best he could, trying to keep in touch with his various units and at the same time searching for information about the movements of the Union armies converging on him. The absence of cavalry also added to his supply problem. All foraging for the army had to be done by soldiers mounted on horses taken from the wagon trains and the artillery.

All through this part of Pennsylvania the soldiers were busy capturing a large number of horses from the prosperous farms. Most of these were sleek, well-fed draft animals of Percheron, Clydesdale, or Conestoga stock. On first sight these huge animals aroused the enthusiasm of the southern teamsters, but after a few days of service the same men complained that the big horses ate twice as much as the others and then only of the best fodder and grain. They were too slow, clumsy, and heavy to drag a field piece into position over open country at a sharp gallop. Where the pasture was poor and the going rough, as it was most of the time in the army, the smaller, compact southern stock with a strong heritage of the old Chickasaw blood was much better.

Near Hanover, Stuart's men found a squadron of cavalry on the road, drove them back through the town with a brisk charge, and returned from the action with a few prisoners and some ambulances, only to be attacked by Brigadier General Elon J. Farnsworth, who put the Confederate van to flight and almost captured Jeb Stuart at the same time. The main body of Stuart's forces stopped the attack, but the whole command was so scattered by then, with the reserve brigade still far down the road behind the wagons, that Stuart was late in mounting a counterattack. When he had cleared the road he led his men on another grueling night march.

With the safety of the wagons still seemingly his chief concern, Stuart detoured miles to the east, then turned northwest again toward Carlisle. So on the morning of July 1, with the battle of Gettysburg opening in full fury, and Lee hampered by the absence of the cavalry, Stuart was at Dover, twenty-five miles away, with his tired men and worn-out horses. He was headed for Carlisle, away from the fighting, but he still had his wagons.

Jeb Stuart approached Carlisle toward evening on July 1, only to find that General Ewell had left and the town was being held by militia.

Stuart thought he could browbeat them into surrendering, and when that failed he tried to frighten them away with cannon fire, but their commander, Brigadier General William F. "Baldy" Smith, was more than willing to fight, and he held his men steady under the galling cannonade.

The action was abruptly broken off when word came up the road from Gettysburg that Lee was engaged in a major battle there and wanted Stuart to bring his cavalry at once. The exhausted troopers mounted their staggering horses and again rode all night. On the afternoon of July 2 the worn-out horsemen rode into Lee's lines. Stuart then proposed keeping his men in the saddle all night in case they might be needed in a hurry, and he had to be reminded of their complete fatigue before he would allow them to break ranks and get some sleep. Although Lee had his cavalry back with the army again, it was of little use until it had rested two days, but Stuart was still happy with his new wagons, whose shiny paint and sleek teams had done more to render impotent the entire cavalry of Lee's invasion army than all the Union soldiers combined.

After ten more months of hard fighting, on May 9, 1864, Jeb Stuart led his men for the last time. A strong cavalry force under General Philip H. Sheridan came south in a raid against Richmond, first capturing the advance base of Major General Fitzhugh Lee, Stuart's right-hand man, at Beaver Dam. The alarmed guards had fled after setting fire to the storehouses, burning up about 915,000 rations of meat and 504,000 of bread, food desperately needed by the underfed southern soldiers. Sheridan's men freed 378 prisoners and destroyed the reserve medical supplies, 100 railway cars, and 2 locomotives. Then they moved on rapidly toward Richmond, which was lightly guarded at the time.

Jeb Stuart pursued Sheridan, hoping that the Richmond garrison could check the Union advance and that he could strike in the rear at the same time. Stuart's horses were weak from lack of forage and rest, and his men badly needed sleep and rest, but Jeb pushed on. After allowing his men four hours' sleep, at 1:00 A.M. on May 9 he was again on the move, and by 8:00 A.M. he had his men in position on Sheridan's left flank at Yellow Tavern, a few miles north of Richmond.

Sheridan quickly closed with Stuart and placed his men in position to attack. He used his cavalry as dragoons, dismounting them to fight as infantry as soon as they had ridden to their posts. His reserves he kept mounted. In this kind of fighting the blue-coats were highly effective, being rated by Jeb Stuart as superior to the regular Union infantry. Soon the battle was joined, with Sheridan sending probing attacks all along the southern line, searching for a weak spot to exploit.

Then came a lull of an hour or so. At 4:00 P.M. a stir in the woods and fields held by the Union line was the first sign of a determined advance. Jeb Stuart watched from the crest of a hill as the action developed, sitting at ease in his saddle with bullets whistling all around him, scoffing at the thought of danger. Then he rode toward the left with Major Andrew Reid Venable and left him there, while he moved on to the extreme left.

The assault came with a roar—three regiments of Michigan cavalry that broke the southern line and drove the men back in confusion. Stuart, instead of returning to his duties as general, drew his service revolver and shot at the blue-coats as they passed. Soon they returned, some of them on foot. One of these shot Stuart with a pistol, inflicting a mortal wound.

And so passed the greatest cavalry leader of them all, his life thrown away by his careless action. At the very last he was the dashing leader instead of the responsible commander, and without his inspiring leadership the dwindling Confederate cavalry lost much of its effectiveness.

Another flamboyant southern cavalry leader operated in the West— General John Hunt Morgan, who timed his great raid into Ohio to match Jeb Stuart's work in Pennsylvania. In that hectic summer of 1863 General Braxton Bragg, commander of the Confederate Army of Tennessee, was an unhappy man. About six thousand of his troops had been sent down to Mississippi to fight against Grant just when Bragg was expecting an attack against his own forces by General William S. Rosecrans and a drive by General Ambrose E. Burnside against Knoxville to the east. General Morgan proposed that he take the cavalry and make a raid in force into Kentucky and thus draw off Burnside's cavalry. This should stall any advance for a few weeks.

Morgan, after some brilliant early successes, had suffered defeats in March and April and was eager for a chance to wipe out the sting of those failures by a ride through enemy territory like the one recently completed by Colonel Grierson in Mississippi. Morgan also wanted permission to cross the Ohio River and raid the rich farmlands to the north. In that hotbed of southern sympathizers, Copperheads led by Congressman Clement L. Vallandigham, perhaps the people would be friendly and turn out to help the southern raiders. Bragg refused permission and directed Morgan to stay south of the river, where he would be available to help Bragg's army at once if Rosecrans started south.

About the middle of June Morgan left his camps with 2,460 mounted men in eleven regiments, and two field pieces. By the time Bragg tried to recall him on June 24, Morgan was out of reach. He crossed the Cumberland River on July 2, easily evading the Union guard stationed there to stop him, and reached Green River on July 4. There he found the bridge guarded by five companies of Michigan infantry, whose colonel refused to surrender at Morgan's demand, saying, "On any other day I might, but on the Fourth of July I must have a little brush first." The "little brush" resulted in the repulse of the six hundred attackers with a loss of eighty dead and wounded. Morgan was forced to seek an easier crossing downstream. The next day Morgan encountered another small Union force, which he overwhelmed with an all-out attack, again losing eighty men, including his brother Tom, one of his officers.

Then, ignoring General Bragg's orders, Morgan sent an advance force to capture two steamers on the Ohio and used them to ferry his command across on July 8. His advance into southern Indiana badly frightened the inhabitants. Basil W. Duke, Morgan's brother-in-law and commander of a brigade, has this account in his *History of Morgan's Cavalry*:

> A "great fear" had fallen upon the inhabitants of that part of the State of Indiana. They had left their houses, with open doors and unlocked larders, and had fled to the thickets and "caves in the hills." At the house at which I stopped, everything was just in the condition in which the fugitive owners had left it, an hour or two before. A bright fire was blazing upon the kitchen hearth, bread half made up was in the tray, and many indications convinced us that we had interrupted preparations for supper. The chickens were strolling before the door with a confidence that was touching, but misplaced. General Morgan rode by soon afterward, and was induced to "stop all night." We completed the preparations, so suddenly abandoned, and made the best show for Indiana hospitality that was possible under the circumstances.

Morgan had a skirmish with the militia at Croyden, Indiana, that cost him another thirty-one men. There he learned of Lee's defeat at Gettysburg and had to give up a tentative plan of driving eastward into Pennsylvania to join up with Lee's army there. He also learned in short order that he could expect no aid from the Copperheads, who turned out by the thousands for noisy anti-Union demonstrations but wanted all the fighting and the armies to stay far away from their homes, and were as bitter about losing horses and supplies to the raiders as were staunch Union supporters.

By this time the Union troopers and the Indiana militia were gathering. Morgan had covered four hundred miles, crossed three major rivers, and suffered a loss of five hundred men, some of them stragglers. Bragg was in full retreat in Tennessee, Vicksburg had fallen to Grant, and Morgan's raid could no longer help by attempting to divert troops from those areas. Morgan had to move quickly if he wanted to escape being surrounded, but his men and horses were breaking under the strain and exertion of forced marches.

Traveling at his best speed Morgan crossed into Ohio and bypassed Cincinnati in the night, covering ninety miles in a day and a half. A reporter on a Cincinnati newspaper wrote this story of the raiders' passing:

> East Sycamore, Hamilton County, Ohio. . . . On Tuesday the 14th instant, at early dawn, the inhabitants hereabout were aroused from slumber by the clattering of hoofs on the stony pike, and the clanking of *stirrups* (I suppose, as I didn't see any sabers or the like). On peeping through the window, I recognized them immediately as sesch, from their hard looks, their clothes of many colors and fashions, and their manner of riding. They did not ride in any kind of order, unless it was *disorder*. As many as could, rode abreast. Some galloped, some trotted, and others allowed their horses to walk slowly while they slept in the saddles. They were not uniformly dressed. Some wore a whole suit of the well known blue which designates our soldiers; others had part of a suit, but most of them were arrayed in citizens' garb. Some were barefooted, some bareheaded, and one, I noticed, wore a huge green veil. . . . Some wore jackets outside their coats, as though they had dressed in a hurry. . . . Some had ladies' gaiters, dress patterns, and the like protruding from their pockets; and one bootless, hatless, shirtless being held his *suspenderless* pants with one hand while he held the

bridle with the other, and heeled his horse into a gallop. . . . Generally they made no distinction between the property of the Copperheads and that of the "Abolitionists," as they call all unconditional Union men. 'Cause why? They either did not *know* their friends, or else they considered the Northern Butternuts beneath the respect of Southern rebels, horse-thieves, free-booters, guerillas, or whatever else they may call themselves.

Morgan expected to reach the shoals of the Ohio River above Buffington in three days. There he planned to cross back into Kentucky and run for home. But when he reached the ford after 130 miles of hard riding he found the river booming along bank-full from heavy rains, and three hundred soldiers with two cannon entrenched on the north bank.

Morgan decided to give his men four hours' sleep, then attack at dawn. When two regiments finally advanced, they found that the guard had departed hastily in the night. Before the cavalry could attempt the crossing, two gunboats came up the river and blocked their passage, and a large force of Union cavalry attacked from the rear. In the ensuing fight Morgan lost about 120 men killed and wounded and 700 captured. He fled north with the rest, away from the river.

That afternoon he regained the river bank at Blennerhassett Island, and 300 of the cavalry crossed before the gunboats came around the bend and opened fire on the crossing. Morgan now had fewer than 700 of the 2,460 men who had started on the raid. He ran north near the river, dodging and twisting for six more days, losing men all along the way as the horses gave out. Finally on July 26 he gave up, surrendering 364 men. In the thirty days since the raiders had left Sparta they had covered 700 miles, and during the last eighteen days they had had about four hours' rest out of each twenty-four. Their total accomplishment was that they delayed Burnside's advance for a time and did some small damage along the way—a rather meager return for the sacrifice of eleven regiments of cavalry.

Morgan's raid was a great sensation at the time. Day after day, for nearly three weeks, the newspapers played up the story as the raiders evaded many traps and outrode their pursuers, and since this was Ohio's only taste of war on her own soil, the inhabitants made the most of it.

Contrary to customary military usage in war, Morgan and his chief officers were locked up in the Ohio penitentiary, where they were treated like common criminals instead of prisoners of war. Their flowing locks were sheared, their beards shaved. After four months of confinement, Morgan and six comrades made a sensational escape, and five of them returned south in time to celebrate Christmas.

The Civil War marked the end of the effective use of large bodies of cavalry in a major war. Although cavalry units were still kept by all the armies, they were really more for show than use. In scouting and in patrolling large areas of rough country the cavalry was still very useful for another half a century.

Roping California style. In southern Texas and in the central valley and coast ranges of California, cowboys worked in pairs, one lassoing the calf by the neck, the other by the hind feet. This way the calf was thrown without either rider having to dismount. (Pen and ink by Charles M. Russell, Courtesy, Amon Carter Museum, Forth Worth, Texas)

Plummer's men at work. Henry Plummer's holdup gang had one thing in common with the inspectors, or road agents, of the stage lines they robbed: They took the best saddle horses, too. Soon, all holdup men in the West were known as road agents, and the original meaning of the term was forgotten. (Pen and ink by Charles M. Russell, Courtesy, Amon Carter Museum, Forth Worth, Texas)

10

Horses in the Developing West

HORSES FROM THE TEXAS RANGES were trailed across to New Orleans even before Philip Nolan's day, but there was little demand for Texas cattle in the East until the Civil War. Then the fighting men needed large quantities of meat and the quartermaster service especially liked good beef that could walk up to the cook wagons and even wait around a few weeks before being used. Out on the plains of Texas the cattle roamed almost untended after the men went off to war, and the herds grew larger each year. Many small herds were gathered up and driven cross-country to the Mississippi River, with a group of young Texans staging the top trail drive of them all.

In the fall of 1862 these devil-may-care youths from the San Antonio area were organized by seventeen-year-old W. H. D. Saunders to round up some big longhorn steers and drive them to New Orleans for the Confederate garrison. Thus they could combine fun, patriotism, and profit. They had not heard that Admiral David Farragut had captured the river port in April.

Soon Saunders and his pals rounded up eight hundred head of prime steers and started north on a wide arc that would take them around the bayous and marshes of the coast to approach New Orleans from the northwest. Across the country they went—swimming the Guadaloupe,

Colorado, Brazos, Trinity, Naches, and Sabine rivers—and so reached Louisiana, where trouble appeared in the form of a troop of Confederate cavalry on guard to prevent any supplies from the West reaching the Union forces.

The earnest young men finally convinced the guard of their patriotism and the purity of their intentions and were allowed to proceed when they promised to keep well to the north of the Union army. They decided to strike the Mississippi near Port Hudson and take their herd across to Mobile, Alabama. When they finally came out on a bluff overlooking the river, a mile wide and forty feet deep, they found no ferry within reach.

Too young and brash to appreciate the dangers involved, they put the steers down the slope in a wild rush that carried all but about a hundred into the current. The laggards were sold to contractors on the west bank, while riders guided the swimming steers to the far shore. The rangy steers, raised in the Texas brush and toughened by several hundred miles of trail with six major river crossings, swam the Mississippi just as they had crossed the smaller rivers.

A cavalry patrol from Port Hudson arrived and took the whole herd and the riders in charge, holding them for several days near the fort under the suspicion that they might be trying to take their beef to the Union forces at Baton Rouge. Finally the quartermaster bought the steers for the army and young Saunders enlisted. This reckless exploit of the young Texans ranks as one of the greatest cattle drives in range history.

Even before the war a few Texas cattle had been trailed to faraway places such as Quincy, Illinois, and mining camps in the Colorado goldfields, although it staggers the imagination to try to visualize those longhorns moving through the farming areas of central Missouri and southern Illinois.

The demand for all sorts of military supplies brought a great increase in manufacturing plants in the northern states. They continued to pour out goods for the growing country after peace came. New mines and mills and miles of new railroads all needed gangs of men who demanded and could afford to buy meat as a regular food. The price of beef cattle rose to thirty or forty dollars a head in the Midwest, while large range steers could be had by the thousands in Texas for two or three dollars. The possible gross profit of $30,000 in cash for a thousand head delivered to market looked like fortunes in the making for many war veterans living in a state desperately needing an inflow of ready cash.

The obvious course was for men to drive these steers to market, which by 1866 was the nearest railhead of the new lines inching their way west and southwest from Kansas City. In spite of many hardships and individual disasters, the whole drive pattern was profitable and continued for twenty years on a large scale, with an estimated 5,700,000 Texas cattle moving north in that period.

Although the herds might vary in size from 500 to 3,000 head, stockmen soon found that the optimum number was from 1,500 to 2,000 animals, handled by a crew consisting of a trail boss, a foreman, a cook, a horse wrangler, and enough cowboys to average one to each 150 cattle in the herd. The cook drove the chuck wagon carrying the cooking gear, the food supply, and the bedding rolls for all. He usually had a team of four mules, with the cowboys using their ropes to help the rig through the worst spots. The men each had a riding string of ten horses, with an extra horse for the trail boss, who rode farther each day than the rest, scouting ahead for watering places, good bedding grounds, stream crossings, and possible danger from buffalo. Thus the horse wrangler had a remuda of about 150 horses to handle along the way, usually well to the rear of the herd.

On the trail there was little need for a highly trained cutting horse or roping horse. Each man did need a good swimmer for crossing the rivers. While all range horses could swim, not all of them took willingly to water, nor could they all carry a man in the saddle in a deep stream. This swimmer also had to be gentle and cool when it got into a tight place, such as the middle of a bunch of swimming cattle that started milling in the deep water.

Another carefully picked mount was the night horse. It had to be gentle, dependable, and sure-footed, and have keen eyesight in the dark and a good sense of direction. It was ridden only on night herd. When the cattle were restless or a storm was brewing, all the night horses were saddled in the evening and picketed near camp for emergency use. The rest of the saddle string were ordinary horses, many of them only green-broke at the start of the drive. Most of them were apt to be sold with the cattle at the shipping point. With 300,000 or more cattle moving north most years, this brought about 8,000 horses to market each year.

All the horses on the trail drive and for most of the range work were geldings. Stallions fought too much, and mares were notorious bunch-quitters and addicted to stirring up trouble in the herd. Both the stallions and mares were left on the home range to raise more foals, while the geldings did the work. Such geldings liked to follow a mare, so in some remudas one old bell mare was taken along, her only duty that of furnishing something for the geldings to follow.

When the trail drive started each man was allocated his saddle string, which he then controlled absolutely. Not even the trail boss could use one of his horses without the rider's consent. The rider also had to keep his horses in condition and work them in proper rotation. Each morning and each noon he saddled a fresh mount, working each horse in turn a half-day and putting it back in the remuda for three days. As some careless riders learned the hard way, a man might have a string of ten horses and still be afoot if he did not handle them wisely.

Some of the trail herds were bought from Mexican stockmen, who delivered them at the Rio Grande. The rest were gathered in southern Texas. When the first spring grass appeared in late February the cattle started moving north, keeping pace with the advancing spring. The object was not to make a quick trip to the shipping pens but to reach that point with fat stock.

Each day a herd would move steadily northward, grazing along from daylight till dusk, scattered over a broad front and strung out for a quarter of a mile or so. One man rode "point" on each side of the herd, even with the leaders but a hundred yards or more off to the side. Another rider followed about halfway back on each side, while the rest of the men brought up the rear, keeping well back so the cattle would not feel crowded or driven. They thought they were moving of their own volition, following some of the strong older steers who were natural leaders. The only time the herd was bunched and driven was at a river crossing or some other obstacle on the trail. When evening came the leaders were gently halted, and the herd slowly collected around them.

In trail work, even for a short distance, the cow horses needed to be easygoing, ambling along with head drooping, never making a quick move to disturb the feeding animals unless one of them lagged badly or started away from the herd. On pleasant days the trail was long and dull, with a stop for lunch and a change of mounts at the noon break, yet the herd would cover fifteen to twenty miles with no effort and would reach the bedding ground with full stomachs, content to lie down, drowse, and chew their cuds until morning.

As the railroads pushed farther west and the cattlemen had a choice of shipping points, the herds might be held on pasture for a few extra days or weeks. Some herds were trailed north into Nebraska and eventually to the Canadian line, to be brought back to the shipping pens in September. These herds moving through all the plains country had an influence on the development of western range culture out of proportion to the number of cattle, horses, and men involved.

Through all the turmoil and disruption that the Civil War brought to the eastern United States, the mining frontiers from the eastern foothills of the Rockies on west to the Pacific coast continued their development almost unchecked. The long series of gold rushes began at Sutter's Mill in the central valley of California and moved north in a series of leaps into British Columbia, then south into Idaho and northeastern Oregon and finally into Montana, ending in 1865 at a rich strike appropriately named Last Chance Gulch. Each new camp drew many men from the older ones and brought in a swarm of outsiders, newcomers to the West, many of them evading military service in either the northern or southern army. As each new camp sprang up out in the wilds, it had the same basic needs as other communities—food, supplies, and transportation. From the first the miners wanted mail brought in and stages to carry out the gold and passengers ready to leave.

Throughout the entire West the new mining camps depended on horses in large numbers. The rich placer deposits were never on navigable streams, and the rich lodes of ore were always found on the ridges and steep slopes in rough country where erosion had removed the loose overburden to expose the minerals. Extending railroads into new mining districts was always a slow process, especially when the finds were made several hundred miles out in the unsettled country. People, mail, and freight came in on horses or mules, or in vehicles drawn by horses, mules, or oxen from the nearest rail station or boat landing as far as five hundred miles away. An important factor in the rapid development of each new camp was the presence of a large supply of Indian horses in the vicinity. This was especially evident in the strikes in the Columbia Basin and western Montana.

When gold was discovered on the Clearwater drainage in Idaho in 1860, the Nez Percés, who had been trading for years with the wagon trains on the Oregon Trail, turned to supplying the miners with meat, fish, and some vegetables. When the rich diggings at Florence were opened late in the summer of 1862, high above the Salmon River on a wooded plateau, the newcomers were surprised at the amount of snow piling up around them early in the winter. The camp was soon isolated, and the miners faced possible starvation until some Nez Percés with a string of hardy packhorses broke a trail across the high ridges and brought in an ample supply of flour.

A new gold camp might have supply centers on two or three sides and still be far from any of them. A case in point is the Grasshopper Diggings, later called Bannock, in the extreme southwestern corner of Montana. It was three hundred miles away from the nearest source of supplies at Lewiston, Idaho, across a trail that held to the high, timbered ridges of the Bitterroots for over a hundred miles. Off to the northeast, four hundred miles away, was Fort Benton at the head of steamboat navigation on the Missouri, and to the south an equal distance was Salt Lake City. In 1863 an Idaho merchant, Lloyd McGruder, loaded up a pack string with assorted merchandise and went east along the old Nez Percé Trail, then up the Bitterroot Valley and across the Continental Divide and on to Bannock, only to find that his prospective customers had rushed off to the rich new strike at Alder Gulch. He followed them and sold out his goods at a nice profit in Virginia City. On his way home in November, in a heavy snowstorm high along the trail, he was murdered by members of his party who were part of the Plummer gang. His horses and mules were driven into a side canyon and killed. All the horse gear was burned and the metal parts shoveled off a cliff into a deep snowdrift. Then the robbers with their loot rode out through Lewiston on the stage and traveled via Portland to San Francisco, where they were arrested on suspicion and returned to Lewiston. One of the gang talked at the trial and the rest were found guilty and hanged. Months later, when the snow melted, the law officers went up the trail and found enough evidence to support the informer's story.

As soon as rich diggings opened up, a stage line was established with stage stations all along the way, with about fifteen horses and two or three men at each station. In 1863 a new stage line went north from Salt Lake City on the Overland Stage route. At Fort Hall it branched, the left-hand fork going west to the Boise Basin diggings, then along the old Oregon Trail to Walla Walla. The right-hand fork went on north to Virginia City and later was extended to Helena and Fort Benton. Several short feeder lines branched from both of these major lines.

To keep the whole network of stage lines in the West operating at a profit, they were organized into divisions, each under a tough superintendent who had great responsibility and power. Joseph A. Slade, the terror of the Overland, was among the toughest of these. To check on the superintendents, the company hired inspectors known as road agents to travel the stage routes, riding in the coaches or requisitioning saddle horses at the stations. They often posed as ordinary travelers, but they carried credentials to support their demands and recommendations.

The road agent's practice of selecting the pick of the saddle horses from the station herd was also the practice of the tightly knit gang of robbers organized by Henry Plummer to steal horses and gold and hold up stages. Members of the gang were sometimes known as the "Innocents," from their coded call for help in a tight spot, "I am innocent." Plummer had several of the stage line employees either as gang members or bribed to help his men by furnishing fresh horses on demand. This practice soon led to the gang's being called a bunch of road agents, a name that soon spread to include all holdup men in the West, and the original meaning was forgotten. Plummer's gang terrorized the whole region from Fort Benton to Salt Lake City until one summer a fever tick bit a miner and set off a chain of events that ended in the hanging of Plummer and several of his gang in Bannock and Virginia City in the winter of 1863–64.

All the great gold strikes in the West were of placer gold that could be extracted from the gravel by rather primitive equipment and a good flow of water. About the time the placer strikes ended, there came a new series of strikes. Large amounts of precious minerals were found in ores imbedded in rock seams. To dig out these ores required mines sunk into the hard rock and required drilling and blasting to loosen the rock. A hard-rock mine usually had seepage water, requiring pumps. Heavy machinery run by steam power was needed for the pumps and for the hoist that lifted out the ore. Such a mine required a large crew of hired miners, a large amount of invested capital, and a large organization for proper development. A mine of this type had a much longer life than a placer mine. Some that were opened in the 1870's are still producing.

A good hard-rock mine made heavy, continuing demands on the transportation system. The combination of ingenuity and sheer muscle power used to get some of the necessary masses of steel into place high on a mountainside are fascinating and inspiring. On the last steep slope, with a grade of 10 percent or more, a favorite gambit was a "dead man," a length of log eighteen inches or more in diameter sunk into the hillside to a depth of perhaps six feet. Such logs were spaced up the slope about two hundred feet apart. A huge pulley block was secured to the post, and a long steel cable hitched to the front of a wagon passed through the pulley. A team hitched to this cable could then pull downhill and exert an effective force at least equal to the combined weight of the six or eight horses used, and the mass of steel moved up the slope and into place near the mine pit. The machinery included a steam boiler, a hoisting engine and a large hoisting drum, and a good steam pump. As soon as the mine started producing ore, the great wagons brought in two or three tons of coal at a load for the boiler, again using the dead man. On the return trip the wagons were loaded with ore. A roughlock on both rear wheels might hold this load on the downgrade, or in the snow the cable might be used again, this time as a brake.

In the early strikes some of the rich silver ores from the mines required special smelting. Then a crew of men high-graded the ore at the sorting tables, discarding every trace of waste rock and rubbing off the loose dirt. The hand-picked ore then went into heavy canvas sacks to be hauled away to the steamboat landing at Fort Benton, being shipped via New Orleans to smelters near Liverpool, England, that extracted the silver from the Liverpool mine high in the Montana mountains.

After several mines were opened up in a district it was profitable to build a smelter nearby on a good stream to supply the necessary water. The vast quantities of charcoal required for the smelting process were procured locally. For miles around the hills were stripped of their great gnarled yellow pines and mountain firs except for a few tough old specimens on a cliff. Teams hauled the logs to a level spot, where they were carefully stacked, covered with dirt, and burned into charcoal to be hauled to the smelter in the valley below.

When the railroad reached the district it brought coke for the smelter and the charcoal burning stopped. The bare hills were covered in a few years with knee-high bunch grass that offered free forage for the livestock from the small farms along the creeks. Bands of range horses from the hills came down each evening to drink, each band identified by its range, such as Lava Mountain, Rattlesnake, or McCauley Flats. Family horses turned out on the range to rest for a few weeks could always be found easily, for each one went back to its own band until rounded up again.

Each year the gnarled old trees among the rocks scattered their seeds across the hills. Heavy stands of seedlings appeared, first in the sheltered draws, then on the hills, smothering the grass under ever-deepening layers of needles. A century after the charcoal burners finished their destruction, mature pines and firs furnish saw logs from the second-growth forest, and there is no more open range in the hills.

The occupation of the Great Plains by the stockmen awaited two closely related major changes—the slaughter of the buffalo and the penning of the Plains Indians on the reservations. The buffalo not only ate grass that otherwise might nourish livestock, but they were a bad influence on both horses and cattle. Given the least opportunity, these animals dashed off to join the buffalo herds and were extremely difficult to recapture. Any kind of farming in buffalo country also suffered from the passing herds that could break down the fences and destroy the crops in their ordinary progress from one feeding ground to another.

The Plains Indians were a menace to both the stockmen and the farmer. They resented intruders in the hunting grounds that they had held for centuries, and often resorted to drastic means to rid their lands of the unwelcome strangers. Congress set aside reservations for the various tribes with little result. The Indians still roamed the plains on horseback, subsisting well wherever they found buffalo. Soldiers sent to guard the tribes could not keep them penned up, and on their slower horses they had a difficult time catching the Indians when they did leave the reservations. Obviously, if the buffalo were destroyed, the Indians could be controlled.

Until the railroads reached the edge of the buffalo country there was little profit for the white men in killing the animals for market. Only a limited number of robes could be produced each year by the Indian women—a task none of the whites seemed to relish. Untanned hides and meat were expensive to transport and so were difficult to sell at a profit.

When the westward-extending railroad lines reached the buffalo country in Kansas the whole picture was changed. With cheap transportation, the hides could be sent east to commercial tanners, who developed new processes to improve the leather and make it more desirable. They also could process robes cheaply. Suddenly the buffalo herds presented to the adventurous an opportunity for profitable Wild West excursions, and in a short time the plains were overrun by eager hunters.

Once they reached the herds, the hunters' big guns boomed from dawn till dusk, while freight wagons hauled by three or four spans of horses or mules hauled away great piles of dried hides, and barrels of pickled tongues and cured hams, to be loaded onto the boxcars waiting at the nearest siding. Under this heavy, sustained onslaught the buffalo herds dwindled from twenty million to a few thousand in two decades. By 1885 the ranges had been freed of both buffalo and Indians.

Even before the buffalo were killed off, the army had developed new tactics to use against the elusive Indian bands. The soldiers learned that Indian war parties could roam the plains with impunity during the summer, playing hide-and-seek with the cavalry, or they could vanish entirely. In the winter the same Indians were less mobile. Once they had established winter quarters for their families, with reserves of food and all their belongings gathered in some sheltered spot, they were highly vulnerable to surprise attacks during storms. Also the practice of slaughtering captured horses instituted by Colonel George M. Wright against the Spokanes in 1858 proved equally effective on the plains. Even so the Indians resisted fiercely and often effectively for about fifteen years from 1865 to 1880.

The general plan for policing the western lands was to build army posts at strategic spots, each one with a detachment of cavalry ready to ride out on short notice and settle any Indian trouble in the surrounding country. Even though this was a sound plan, in practice several difficulties prevented its successful application. One of these was the problem of adequate personnel. Army life at a frontier post was boring, living conditions for enlisted men were often deplorable, and the starting pay was $13 a month. Volunteers for the cavalry usually came from the big cities during the winter months, when it was difficult for a homeless, jobless man to stay alive. Many of the recruits had no previous experience with horses and were lacking both in stamina and the adventurous spirit so desirable in a cavalryman on the frontier. Several of these green recruits in a cavalry troop lowered its effectiveness considerably when Indian warriors were at hand.

Army officers liked each soldier on active duty to carry along enough items to be ready for a variety of contingencies—a worthy concept in theory, but one which in practice burdened the individual with many pounds of equipment that seldom was needed. With such a load of extras, the cavalryman needed a large, strong horse to carry him and all his gear on the march. Then he set out to chase the elusive red man— his horse carrying saddle, bridle, weapons, ammunition, mess kit, canteen, overcoat, blanket, bed sheet, halter, hobbles, picket rope, rations, and a feed bag with perhaps a few pounds of oats. A cavalry unit with each horse so encumbered did well to cover twenty miles a day over an extended period, no faster than a well-conditioned infantry unit moved. If a field piece was taken along, and an ambulance or two plus wagons for the cooking gear, extra food, and grain, the whole column was further slowed and its field of operations restricted to the smoother ground. A cavalry column could travel forty or fifty miles a day on a forced march by leaving much of the gear behind.

To secure the large horses the officers considered best for the cavalry, ordinary saddle-stock mares were crossed with draft stallions to increase the size; then these in turn were bred to thoroughbred stallions to increase the speed. Such horses measured about sixteen hands and weighed from eleven to twelve hundred pounds. They required more forage and a supplement of grain to keep up with a western saddle-type animal subsisting on grass.

In contrast a war party of Indians traveled light. Each man had his lightweight horse gear—usually a bridle and a pad saddle, weapons, a small robe, and a parcel of dried meat—the whole load weighing not more than the trooper's saddle. The Indian's horse was smaller and tougher, and it subsisted well on natural forage. Such a war party could loaf along, kill a buffalo now and then, pasture their horses a few times each day, and still keep well ahead of the cavalry.

Even when the Indians moved with their families and all their gear, they just loaded up the pack string and took off across country at a good pace, going where no wagons could follow, and covering twenty, thirty, forty, or even fifty miles a day until the emergency had passed. If one of the horses they were using started to lag, they had plenty of horses in the loose herd to change to.

From their Civil War experiences, some of the officers were addicted to the use of the saber in a charge. Sabers could be effective against a cornered Indian, or in a crowd trapped among the tipis—situations that were rare indeed. A dismounted cavalryman firing his carbine from a steady rest was much more effective against a mounted Indian than one charging about on his large horse futilely waving a saber at a will-o'-the-wisp enemy, and a good service revolver was a more effective weapon for a mounted man than a saber.

The basis for the Indian wars was the friction between red man and white stemming from different basic concepts about man and his place in the universe, and from difficulties in communicating with one another. A few simple examples serve to illustate this situation.

A white man's concept of home was a house, cabin, shack, earth lodge, or cave in which a person lived much of the year. If a person did not have a fixed abode he was a homeless wanderer and could not claim to own any land, nor could a group of people claim to own land jointly. To a Plains Indian home was a large expanse of buffalo country in which he pitched his tipi wherever he chose, moving about frequently but always keeping within certain boundaries. The white man insisted that if the Indian did not stay in one place and farm the land he had no right to it, and the white man felt he had a moral obligation to take the land and farm it. The Indian believed that all the land was created for man and the animals to live on, and no single individual could ever own any of it. Also the Indian considered it his duty to steal horses from anyone who was not an avowed friend.

When white settlers moved in and tried to impose their concepts of land use on an area that had been held for many decades by Indian tribes, the differences, especially concerning land ownership, soon built up into open conflict. Although the white man was the invader and had instigated the fighting in the Indian's homeland, he insisted that the Indian should carry on his fighting under the white man's rules of war developed by the European countries, even though the Indian had never heard of those rules, and the white invader seldom followed his own rules consistently. As a result, when the Indian used his customary defense methods against the invader, the white man accused him of committing atrocities and used the incidents to justify his own atrocious conduct toward the Indian. In the end the more numerous and better-organized whites wore down the Indians with whiskey, disease, and fighting until the surviving remnants of the fighting tribes could be controlled on reservations.

A number of violent clashes between the mounted warriors and the soldiers, usually the cavalry, highlight the course of the long struggle. Three of these were with the Cheyennes, a proud, warlike people who had been driven from their villages and cornfields in northern Iowa. They moved out onto the plains, acquired horses, and became true nomads. They had no serious trouble with the whites until the gold rush to the Pikes Peak area in 1859 resulted in the occupation of some of their best hunting grounds.

In 1864 a small band of Cheyennes, driving a herd of their own horses, were stopped by an officious cavalry lieutenant who was trying to find some stolen cattle for a settler. When he found the Indians had no cattle, the settler claimed some of their horses, which the braves would not surrender. The lieutenant then tried to take the horses and provoked an argument that ended in a skirmish with light losses on both sides.

In retaliation for this armed resistance, a body of cavalry rode north to a friendly Cheyenne village 130 miles away. Catching the people by surprise, the troopers killed about sixty women and children and destroyed the tipis. Enraged by this senseless slaughter, the Cheyennes and their neighbors, the Kiowas and Arapahoes, rode far and wide across the plains attacking settlers, stage stations, and travelers. For a time they entirely disrupted communications between the mining camps and the East.

The cavalry turned out in fruitless pursuit and was roundly criticized by the citizenry for its lack of results. During the disorder the Cheyenne chief, Black Kettle, remained peaceful. At the specific request of Colorado's governor he camped his band on Sand Creek near Fort Lyons. Here he suffered a surprise attack by Colonel John Chivington and a thousand Colorado volunteers. In that peaceful Indian village of seven hundred, two thirds died in the massacre.

Chief Black Kettle survived and still remained peaceful. Four years later he was camped on the Washita with another village of friendly Cheyennes. Lieutenant Colonel George A. Custer rode out with his Seventh Cavalry, hoping to find just such a village, peaceful and unsuspecting, that could be wiped out with little danger to the troops. Approaching under cover of a driving snowstorm, Custer achieved complete surprise in a dawn attack. The cavalry galloped through the camp cutting down everyone it could reach, killing more than a hundred men and a much larger number of women and children. The winter food supplies were destroyed, the tipis burned, and 850 captured horses shot. For this massacre Custer became an object of Indian hatred throughout the plains country.

While the Cheyennes were having their troubles in Colorado the Sioux were on the rampage in the Powder River country of Wyoming. The army decided in 1866 to build two new posts to guard the newly opened Bozeman Trail to the Montana goldfields. While the Sioux chiefs were at a council at Fort Laramie protesting the plans, one wagon train passed safely through the disputed area. Then when Colonel H. B. Carrington led his men out to build the posts, Fort Phil Kearney on Big Piney Creek and Fort C. F. Smith at the Bighorn crossing, the Sioux turned out in impressive numbers. They rode about the building sites shooting at the sentries, chasing the horse herds, and attacking supply trains—a constant threat to any white they could find.

The fall buffalo hunt brought a brief interlude in the harassment. Nelson Storey luckily arrived at Fort Kearney during the lull and against orders of Carrington slipped away one night with his herd of eight hundred Texas longhorns. He reached the gold camps without a single loss. His determined, alert herders with their new type of repeating rifles discouraged any attacks by the small hostile bands they met along the trail.

With the end of the fall hunt the Sioux returned. In December they shot up a woodcutting detail a few miles from the fort. A rescue party of eighty mounted men led by Captain W. J. Fetterman went to the rescue. Then Fetterman, disobeying orders, chased the retreating Indians over a ridge and rode into a clever ambush. He and his entire command were wiped out in a few minutes.

The next summer the Sioux staged two coordinated attacks, one against each post. On Big Piney Creek a work detail took the precautionary measure of placing their heavy wagon boxes on the ground in a defensive pattern before starting to work. When the Sioux charged, the men dropped their tools, grabbed their new breech-loading guns, and took refuge in the wagon boxes. With rapid, accurate fire from the new rifles they beat back the Sioux until the red warriors broke off the fight, discouraged by their heavy losses. On the Big Horn the haying crew took shelter along a fence of heavy logs and beat off the charging horsemen, proving to the Sioux that it was foolhardy for mounted men to charge against sheltered troops armed with the new rifles.

Far to the south in the Texas Panhandle in the summer of 1874 the Comanches learned the same bitter lesson when they sent seven hundred horsemen charging against thirty buffalo hunters holed up at Adobe Walls, and were beaten off with heavy losses. A year and a half later in a winter campaign the cavalry columns of General Phil Sheridan harried and chivvied the Comanches into submission, finally penning them up on their reservation. This put an end to the great horse-stealing tradition of the tribe and brought relief to the border settlements of Texas and the rancheros in northern Mexico after a hundred years of terror.

In the north the Sioux were having further troubles. Surveyors for the proposed Northern Pacific Railroad came through the Yellowstone Valley with a large military escort. Then gold was discovered in the Black Hills and the whites moved in by the thousands. Just before the gold rush the Sioux called a council of war chiefs of the surrounding tribes to meet with them in the Yellowstone Valley and organize a concerted drive against all the whites. They believed that a force of several thousand warriors could easily rid the entire buffalo country of the enemy.

Although several of the invited tribes did not join, large war parties were out in the spring of 1876. The army saw the gathering storm and attempted to forestall the hostilities by striking first. Three separate columns of troops were marched toward the center of Indian strength. General George Crook came north from New Fort Fetterman on Powder River with about eleven hundred men. Crazy Horse of the Sioux led a thousand red horsemen south to stop him. After a day-long fight Crazy Horse forced Crook to retreat; then he returned with his warriors to the main Indian camp on the Little Big Horn.

There, under the towering cottonwoods, the tipis filled the valley floor and several thousand horses grazed in little bands on the hills to the west. It was an imposing demonstration of the ability of these nomadic bands to assemble two or three thousand horsemen in a short time, but they could not stay together for an extended campaign. After a few days they had to scatter to hunt buffalo meat for the cooking fires and to find fresh pastures for the horses.

Lieutenant Colonel George A. Custer, scouting the area with a strong force of cavalry, discovered the Indian camp. His superiors expected him to hold the Indians at bay until the supporting columns could come up, but Custer, eager for glory, divided his forces, sending his left wing to attack from the south while he led 225 men of the Seventh Cavalry around the bluffs to charge from the north. Custer had boasted that with his Seventh Cavalry he could cut his way through the entire Sioux nation. On this summer afternoon he was stopped only halfway through. There his entire command went down before the charging Sioux warriors, perishing on the sun-baked slopes before they could reach even the first tipis. The jubilant warriors rode back to camp for a victory dance, scattering the next day to their separate hunting grounds.

After the Custer defeat the army was more determined than ever to place all the Indians on reservations. In the Columbia Basin the officers first focused their attention on the Wallowa and Salmon River bands of the Nez Percés, whose livestock grazed on a million acres of rough rangeland coveted by the white stockmen. When these bands were forced from their ranges in June 1877, fighting broke out before they could be penned up and their horses taken from them. The Nez Percé War, involving 140 fighting men against more than 2,000 soldiers, was really a chase across 1,100 miles of wild, rough country. The hostile segment of the tribe, about 700 people in all, rounded up most of their horses, put their camp gear and other belongings on several hundred pack animals, and rode off eastward across the mountains pursued by General Oliver O. Howard and beset by three other armies Howard called out to attempt to block the Nez Percés' path.

The war was more a contest between horses than men—range-raised Nez Percé horses of old Spanish stock against cavalry mounts. The Nez Percés started with about 2,000 head, which they augumented along the way, their largest accession being 173 mules from Howard's pack string at Camas Meadows. Most of the Nez Percés' losses were of tenderfooted animals whose unshod hooves wore down to the quick on the rocky trails. They also lost a few hundred to Crow raiders and saved a hundred or so when some of the fugitive Nez Percés escaped into Canada. Even with all these losses, the herd captured by Colonel Nelson A. Miles at Bear Paw battlefield numbered more than 1,100 animals, a remarkable record for horses carrying loads every day for two and a half months over rough country while subsisting on natural forage. Howard and his men had most of their mounts replaced twice, and Colonel Samuel Sturgis, who joined the chase in Wyoming, wore out his horses in just a few days.

A great deal has been written about the military genius of Chief Joseph, one of the Nez Percé leaders, who was indeed a very fine man of exceptional ability, but he had no talent for war. The success of the Nez Percés was achieved by the ability of the individual fighter to ride well and shoot straight, the efficiency of the Nez Percé family unit in handling its own horses and packs, and the superior performance of the Nez Percé horses.

In the Nez Percé War General Howard used forty Bannock scouts under Chief Buffalo Horn for the pursuit in western Montana and southeastern Idaho. Buffalo Horn formed a poor opinion of the ability of the officers and men he served with. He reasoned that if 140 Nez Percé warriors, burdened with several hundred noncombatants, mostly women and children, could do so well against Howard's superior forces, a war party of several hundred with no such encumbrances should be able to defeat any number of soldiers that could be sent against it in the desert plateau of southern Idaho. His sentiments were shared by other Bannocks and by many restless Indians scattered throughout the Northwest.

The conflict known as the Bannock War was precipitated in the spring of 1878 by a quarrel in Camas Valley, when the Indians objected to settlers' hogs destroying the tribal camas meadows. In a short time Buffalo Horn's successful raids with a force of about 150 men attracted recruits until he had more than 800 to lead across the sparsely settled ranges of southern Idaho, killing ranchers and travelers and burning buildings.

General Howard, wanting to bring this outbreak to a quick conclusion, assembled his forces, but before he could reach the scene of the fighting Chief Buffalo Horn was killed by a lucky long-range shot fired by a volunteer civilian at the chief's scouting party near Silver City. Without a leader the war party was ineffective. Howard soon chased it out of Idaho and into Oregon, where its members scattered among the ridges and narrow valleys and soon were lost in the wilds. Once the men had stashed their war gear they were just ordinary Indians out looking for stock or going visiting. In a short time they had all unobtrusively rejoined their villages and the big war was over.

In the Sioux country of southeastern Montana the army posts still had trouble with raiding parties of young men out to steal horses. Orders went out to the posts that such thieves should be pursued until the horses were recovered, even though this wore out both the stolen horses and the cavalry mounts used in the pursuit. Late in March 1880 a band of about forty Sioux stole a herd of horses from Fort Custer on the Yellowstone. Captain Eli Huggins, with a troop of cavalry, chased them. Here is an extract from a letter of the captain to his sister reporting the chase, furnished by Dorothy Huggins, a grandniece.

Fort Keogh
April 5, 1880

Dear Hattie:

I have just got back from what people are kind enough to call the most successful Indian scout ever sent out from Keogh. I was out 12 days, and rode more than I did all last summer. Used up the horses of my company completely but got back all the stolen horses 44 in number, and took 5 prisoners. Killed one indian and had a sergeant killed. Lived almost upon buffalo meat for 4 days. I will write some of the particulars soon. . . .

According to Captain Huggins' daily estimates, his command traveled more than 390 miles in twelve days across the gently rolling hills and open plains. This type of determined, successful pursuit soon cut down the number of horses stolen.

After 1880 the Great Plains were free from Indian wars and roving bands of buffalo hunters. The continuing influx of stockmen soon occupied all the desirable range country.

The basic pattern for the range cattle industry in the American West was developed on the Mexican Plateau, and it moved north with the moving herds to the limits of the open grasslands. This pattern of cattle management was so sound that it was adopted with little change by the westward-moving Americans. As the stockmen moved north they followed two lines of travel—one across the Rio Grande into Texas and on north through the length of the Great Plains into Canada, the other across the Colorado at Yuma into California, then north and east into the Columbia Basin. High mountain ranges interspersed with plateaus covered with desert scrub separated these two routes, and the northward-moving herds did not mingle again until they reached southeastern Idaho and Montana. Along the way, both in southern Texas and in the central valley and coast ranges of California, the local people developed some variations in saddles and how to use them in roping stock. These differences were soon apparent to even the casual visitor, but they had little effect on the efficiency of the working cowboy.

The Californian liked a saddle with a high fork and horn, and a single wide cinch called a center rig. In his roping he used a reata of braided rawhide sixty to a hundred feet long and three-eighths of an inch in diameter. In action he carried the coils in his left hand. He swung a wide loop and could rope an animal forty or fifty feet away. Once the loop settled on its mark, the roper took his dally, one or two turns of the reata around the saddle horn, and the horse braced to tighten the rope and throw the catch. When roping calves for branding, one Californian caught a calf by the neck while another threw a loop on the two hind feet, and the calf was stretched out near the branding fire without either rider needing to dismount. When the man with the iron finished, his helper cast off the ropes.

The Texan used a saddle with a low horn and two cinches, a double rig. His rope was shorter, usually a "grass" rope about forty feet long, tied firmly to the saddle horn. He rode close to the animal and swung a small loop. When the calf went down the Texan jumped off his horse and held his catch on the ground with his hands on its muzzle and his knee on its neck. As soon as the brand was done, he cast off the rope and remounted. Two Texans working in this fashion could catch more calves than two Californians could. They also worked much harder and got dirtier.

Cowboys from the two sections still argue over the merits of each type of saddle and rope. For speed roping in the rodeo arenas, the short rope with the hard-and-fast tie is superior, but in the open the reata man can make fancy catches the short-rope man cannot even attempt. When these two schools of roping and of making saddles met in Montana the result was some crossing: a saddle was produced that has a single cinch, but it is farther forward than the California cinch. This is the three-quarter rig. This saddle has a high horn. Some of the northern cowboys used the wide loop and the dally, while others, usually around Miles City, often used the double rig, the short rope, and the hard-and-fast tie.

Cattle from California were taken by ship to the Hudson's Bay Company post at Fort Vancouver in 1826. The factor, Dr. John McLaughlin, conserved his stock and steadily increased his herds. In 1839 Ewing Young trailed a herd of cattle across the mountains from California to the Willamette Valley. The Great Migration of 1843 brought in about five thousand more cattle, and each succeeding summer the covered-wagon trains arrived with more stock.

Cattle moving on the long journey along the Oregon Trail sometimes became worn and footsore. All along the way from Fort Laramie to Fort Hall old mountain men set up little shacks stocked with a few supplies for the travelers. They also had fresh horses to trade for the tired stock that recovered quickly with a little rest and good feed and were then ready to be traded off, one fresh animal for two weary ones, many of them cows.

When the Mormons had their argument with the federal government in 1857, many of the traders, wanting to avoid any trouble, packed up and moved their herds north into the Beaverhead and Deer Lodge valleys of Montana. These cattle were generally larger and were better animals than either the California or Texas cattle, for they had come from the Midwest, where good bulls from England helped produce heavier stock than the slim Spanish type. During the gold rushes in the 1860's the Montana stockmen prospered by supplying beef to the miners, but when the rush ended the Montana ranges produced more beef than the local market could use. Some of the mature beeves were trailed south to the Green River station on the new Union Pacific, although the freight rates to Chicago were about $10 a head.

In the mountain valleys of western Montana, owing to the ample supply of fence poles on the hills, the stockmen could modify the open range methods and so cut down on the amount of labor needed from the range riders. *The Rocky Mountain Husbandman* in 1875 carried this description of such a ranch.

This ranch contains 500 acres of land, under fence, mostly meadows with a good dwelling surrounded by a vigorous growth of young cottonwoods. . . . [The owners] have about 3,000 head of cattle and about 3,000 head of sheep, besides a herd of forty short-horns. . . . Their home ranch (seven miles distant) is well improved. . . . Fences are all good and pastures immense. A fence, six miles long running across the valley, connects the steep, rocky ranges on either side. Five miles above this, is another fence from mountain to mountain, forming an enclosure of thirty square miles of 19,200 acres. Through this, there is a dividing fence along the creek about midway of the valley, thus dividing the pastures of fifteen square miles, one for summer and one for winter range. The one for winter use contains a warm spring. . . . Above this enclosure, is a vast tract of country, to which they enjoy the undisputed right, a range that is so hemmed in that the stock cannot get out in winter and seldom in summer.

A few years later, when the buffalo country east of the mountains was opened and the stockmen moved out of their valleys, they had to go back to the old open range methods that had come up from Texas with the trail herds. By the time the cattle were well established in central Montana the Sioux Indian menace was gone from the Yellowstone Valley and herds could be driven east to the railhead at Bismarck, North Dakota. As the Northern Pacific was built westward, these drives shortened until Miles City, Montana, became the chief shipping point for Montana cattle and horses.

For many years the Sioux had blocked any intrusion by the stockmen into northeastern Wyoming, the Powder River country, and central Montana, the Judith Basin country, both ideal ranges for stock. Once this tribe had been confined to reservations in the 1870's a vast new area was ready for cattle. The buffalo were slaughtered rapidly and cattle from both western Montana and southern Wyoming moved in. They were soon followed by trail herds from Texas, then by trainloads of breeding stock and feeders from the Midwest that met trainloads of beef cattle on their way east to the markets. Investors began buying ranches for the potentially great profits. They were followed by cattle companies formed in Europe, particularly in Scotland and England, that brought in much foreign capital and with it the disadvantages of absentee ownership.

In this new rush the ranges were soon filled to capacity, and a struggle began over water rights and the control of pasture on public land. Cattlemen were faced not only with heavy competition from fellow cattlemen but with a new menace, the sheepmen, who moved in with large flocks. Soon came another troublesome group, the homesteaders, also called nesters, who filed claims on public land even when it was on the stockmen's ranges. To protect their ranges the cattlemen began stringing the new barbed wire around their claimed boundaries, and the old open range quickly vanished except for a few isolated small areas. With the new fences came the end of the old pattern of stock raising, for the new landholdings demanded new management methods.

The barbed wire fence marked an end to the West of the cowboys, roundups, trail herds, and wide-open cow towns—the Wild West so glamorized by later generations. This romantic period lasted about twenty-five years, from the close of the Civil War to the end of the open range. While some small out-of-the-way areas in the West still carried on in the old style for another twenty years, cattle raising and horse raising generally settled into a more prosaic routine.

In the days of the open range a cattleman first secured by one means or another a narrow strip of land along a good stream. His control of the water for the stock gave him control of the pasture on public lands on both sides of the stream as far back from the water as a cow could walk for a drink, not more than five miles. Thus for each quarter section of land he owned the stockman controlled sixteen hundred acres of pasture. He located the buildings of his home ranch on the bottom land near the creek and built his ranch house, bunkhouse, barn, corrals, and blacksmith shop. This was the headquarters for all operations and home for the cowboys when they were not on roundups or trail drives.

An old Texas account speaks of the cowboy:

> The cowboy is a man attached to a gigantic pair of spurs. He inhabits the plains of Texas, and is successfully raised as far north as the thirtieth degree of latitude. He is in season the year round, and is generally found on the back of a small mustang pony. . . . This fact has given rise to a widely diffused belief that the cowboy cannot walk. . . . Some scientists however, dispute this as several specimens have been seen—under the influence of excitement and while suffering from intense thirst—to detach themselves from their mustangs and disappear into business houses where their wants were attended to by a man wearing a diamond breastpin and a white apron.

This description is from *On a Mexican Mustang Through Texas* by Sweet and Knox, and contains a large portion of truth. A cowboy—also known as a cowhand, cow puncher, cowpoke, waddie, or vaquero—was, with his horse, a basic ingredient in western range life. He could be a cowboy without a cow, but not without a horse.

On a cattle ranch the spring work began when the ranch horses from the winter pasture were brought in, a few hundred head. They were corraled, examined, and sorted out. The brood mares, stallions, yearlings, two-year-old fillies, and all the three-year-olds were turned out again. The two-year-old stallions were gelded and turned out; the four-year-old geldings were put into a smaller corral and turned over to the buster, who rode each of them three times before they were assigned to the riders, two or three to each man.

The older geldings were the saddle stock from the previous year. Each cowboy who had worked on the ranch the last season was given all the horses left from his last year's string, while a new man was assigned all his horses by the boss. Under this system each man had his good horses in addition to the two or three green-broke broncs, although in some outfits most of the used horses were sold each fall and each rider might have four or five broncs to work with all summer.

Any of these showing real cow sense were kept, and the rest went to the eastern market as gentle saddle horses. Cowboys did not like to work for an outfit that practiced this system.

The cowboy always rested his cutting horse, roping horse, and night horse as much as possible. If he went to see a girl he usually had a very gentle "girlin" horse that would walk peacefully alongside the girl's mount so the two riders could hold hands, but if the cowboy was just going to town or on an errand he rode one of his broncs to give it more training. Thus in town he usually referred to his mount as his bronc, until townspeople and easterners began calling any western horse a bronc, using the word equivalent to cayuse, but to the range man any unbroken horse from Percheron to Shetland pony was a bronc until gentled.

In addition to the cowboys, each roundup camp needed a cook with his chuck wagon and a horse wrangler to handle the remuda of about 150 horses. A cowboy was really a grown man with a tough job, but the wrangler could be a callow youth just getting his start in range work or a ranch-raised boy in his early teens. His herding job was tedious but it required much less skill and muscle and was less dangerous than working with cattle.

By the time the new calf crop was on the ground, the cowboy and his horses were ready and the roundup started. Each draw and coulee was carefully combed and all stock was driven to an open, flat space, the holding ground. Each calf was roped and branded and the bull calves were altered; then the herd was put back on its range and the roundup moved on to another area. In range work each man took a fresh horse every morning and noon, using his broncs a great deal and saving his cutting and roping horses for the work at the branding fire.

Each year a number of cows strayed off the home range and ended up in a neighbor's roundup. A large ranch would send one of its men —known as the "rep"—to represent it at the neighbor's branding. The rep was a dependable top hand who helped with the regular work until the branding was over; then he took his owner's cows with their freshly branded calves back to the home place. Small ranchers who could not afford full time reps often combined to hire one to represent four or five outfits.

In the fall another roundup was staged to gather up the beef animals ready for market. These were chiefly four- and five-year-old steers and the older, dry cows. They were driven to the nearest shipping point and loaded into cattle cars usually bound for Chicago, although stock-yards were later built at several other cities. Often a cowboy or two would ride east with the cattle and return in due time, flat broke but with all sorts of tales of the odd doings of city folks.

Then, in 1874 came the barbed wire fence—"bob-wire" to range people—and the poor cowboy was in a bind. If he stayed on the ranch he blistered his hands digging postholes and stringing wire, and once the fences were up several of the crew were out of jobs anyway, for fenced ranges needed few riders.

Windmills for the plains country were greatly improved during the 1870's and were installed on the ranges away from the creeks so the stock could use the grass that had previously gone to waste for lack of drinking water. To keep the cattle near their own watering troughs, cross fences were run, dividing the ranch lands into several fields. Herds were moved from field to field to prevent overgrazing of any area. The cross fences again cut down on the amount of riding needed, although one man working full time was now needed to ride out each day to grease and oil each windmill and pump and to make sure the cattle were getting enough water. This job involved as much climbing up and down the towers as it did riding, but it was considered a step above digging postholes.

A few bad winter storms that caused stock losses when snow lay deep on the hills for several days convinced the ranchers that some hay to carry the cattle through the worst blizzards would be a means to increased profits. So they fenced the hay meadows; bought mowing machines, hay rakes, and stacking equipment; and broke more teams to harness. For this work they wanted larger horses of the draft type and brought in some draft stallions to put with the brood mares. All of these changes came together—fences, windmills, haying machinery, draft horses—and ranching became more of a business as it lost much of its old romantic aura.

The great stamina of the western range horses as shown in the Nez Percé War raised some question about the desirability of crossing range horses with draft stallions to produce large mounts for the cavalry and teams for the field artillery. Perhaps the western horses could do cavalry work without needing to be any larger. In 1897 the Bureau of Animal Husbandry conducted a road test with horses taken directly from a range band and used with no special conditioning.

[166]

Two young Wyoming cowboys, Bill and Bert Gabriel, were hired for the ride. They caught two unbroken horses and gentled them, but did not shoe them or give them any feed except pasture grass. They left Sheridan, Wyoming, on June 5, 1897, and rode by easy stages of about twenty-six miles a day, allowing their horses to graze by the roadside for their entire subsistence. On the ninety-third day, September 6, they reached Galena, Illinois, with their horses in as good condition as when they had left Sheridan. This impressive record helped sell thousands of range horses to the British army for use in the Boer War, and a large number for polo ponies, but it did not impress the army officers, who still preferred the larger, less durable horses for their cavalry.

About the time the Gabriel brothers reached Illinois, three other Wyoming cowboys from just across the Big Horn Range to the west of Sheridan were riding north with a band of horses, hopeful of reaching the new Yukon gold camps. They planned to follow the trail opened by the Northwest Mounted Police across the foothills and mountains from Edmonton. Transportation in the Yukon was a serious problem, and the few horses at Skagway Beach sold for three or four hundred dollars each. To tap this rich market the men started with seventy-five five- and six-year-olds carefully chosen from a large herd. They believed that horses raised in Wyoming could live and work in the Yukon.

With a chuck wagon to carry their camping gear and food, and a few friends to help haze the band along for the first few days, they started north late in the summer of 1897, crossing into Canada at Sweet Grass and paying duty of $2 a head. They planned to wait until the rivers froze, then cross on the ice, but continued chinook winds spoiled this plan, so they shipped the horses to Edmonton, where they spent two months breaking them for use as pack animals, and then with a bobsled went on to Peace River in February, after selling off about twenty of the more stubborn animals.

On this winter trip the range horses proved that when handled by experienced men they could manage through the winter on grass, except for a little grain fed to the team pulling the sled. At Peace River the men left the sled and put all their supplies on pack animals. At Dease Lake they worked most of the summer packing supplies from the head of navigation on the Stikine River to posts in the back country. After the trip of two thousand miles and two months of heavy packing, the horses were still in good condition.

During the winter of 1898–99 most of these horses were lost. They were turned out to pasture in the open glades, and the local Indians killed them for food. In the spring, with only eight horses and seven mules left, the men pressed on across the range to the Pelly River, a tributary of the Yukon. There they built a large raft, loaded their entire outfit, and started downstream, only to have their ungainly craft capsize in the rapids. The men escaped the wreck with one horse and two mules. In this wild northern country the horses had proved that they could live well on forage, even though they could not evade the weapons of the Indians or the white water of the rivers.

During the hard times throughout the country in the 1890's the cattle and horse business suffered. Saddle horses were hard to sell at any price, and the ranges filled up with unbroken, often unbranded, animals. The Boer War relieved the situation. The British government had men in ten western states buying horses by the thousands to ship to South Africa. Large buying stations were opened at Miles City, Cheyenne, Sheridan, and Denver, and word went out that sound animals five to nine years old were worth $40 a head, cash. Horses were shipped to the stations from all over the West, and the resulting cash sales brought instant prosperity to the ranch country. Since many of these horses had never been ridden and buyers wanted only broken horses, cowboys gathered around the corrals ready to gentle any mount for three to five dollars. Even so, some of the horses crowhopped a little when they were galloped up to the waiting inspector, who usually took them anyway. One observed that he didn't mind a horse that galloped a little high. Any real bucker was turned back. This good market lasted through the summers of 1900 and 1901. By that time the range bands had been reduced and the country was recovering from the hard times, so many horses could again be sold to the eastern markets.

The Moncreiffe brothers, Malcolm and William, had ranches in Wyoming. When the Boer War came they were given the contract for buying all the horses for the British army. Two of the Moncreiffes were interested in polo and tried out western horses as polo ponies. Many of them were excellent mounts, for any horse with the potential to be a good cutting horse could easily learn to follow the ball and to handle itself in a scrimmage. This market, although small, held up well until about 1920. Some of the cowboys who helped train these ponies on the Moncreiffe ranches became good enough players to compete on regular teams with the best.

Horse thieves played an important part in the West before the Civil War, but in the latter part of the nineteenth century cattle rustlers were more of a problem to the stockmen. Only along the Mexican border were large losses of horses in a single raid common. John Chisum, ranching in southern New Mexico, lost twelve hundred horses in one swoop to a small party of Mexican bandits from south of the border. He and his men gave chase and had to shoot three of the thieves before they could reclaim their herd.

Throughout the Northwest horse rustling was widespread and many small bands were driven off. These could be run across the line into Canada rather easily. When they were sold the rustlers tried to find some loose Canadian horses to bring back for sale at Miles City. In southeastern Idaho a frontier character, Shoshoni Bob, had a good working pattern. His place served as a way station for horses taken in the Beaverhead Valley to be sold later in Nevada. Horses rustled in Nevada were taken back along the same route to be sold in Montana. While these losses were aggravating to the ranchers, their total value was much less than that of the stolen cattle.

Wild horses on the plains disappeared with the buffalo. As the cattlemen moved in they trapped or shot the mustangs to protect their own range horses and to conserve the pasture. In the rough country and in the mountains and on the desert plateaus of Arizona, Nevada, and Oregon wild herds flourished from about 1885 on. At the start these wild ones came from the regular ranch stock that was neglected for years when the price of horses was low. In Arizona in 1898 a stockman shipped a trainload of choice geldings to Kansas City and netted twenty-five cents a head on them. Ordinary horses did not sell for enough to pay transportation costs. As a result young stock ran wild, often unbranded, and in time their progeny became truly feral. They were a headache to the stockmen, for they cropped the grass so closely they destroyed its roots, thus ruining the range. In good market years, 1900–1901, many of them were trapped and sold, but when the Boer War was over wild horses were worthless, and their quality had deteriorated badly because the best of them had been captured. Soon the ranchers started shooting the wild scrub animals. From 1903 to 1914, when a good two-year-old could be purchased from a tame band for five or ten dollars, no one wanted a captured wild horse even as a gift.

On the large, fairly level fields of the Midwest horses were preferred to oxen for most farm work and all road work. As new farm machinery was developed the farmers soon realized that the work in the fields could be done much faster with larger machines and fewer men. The larger machines cultivated more acres a day, speeding up the whole process so that each man could farm more land. It was necessary to cultivate more acres a day rather than work more days, since the season for each farming operation is strictly limited by the weather and the rhythm of growth. Especially in plowing and seeding, any work not done at the right time was scarcely worth doing, since the cost was too high compared to the results.

The larger machines required either more or bigger horses. Soon the farmers were favoring the draft-type animals when they could be found. To meet this demand larger animals with some Shire blood were brought in from Ontario, where the English settlers raised them. These horses were about sixteen hands high and weighed from twelve to fourteen hundred pounds, a size most popular on the farms for the next half century.

In spite of the immediate popularity of these grade Shires, little effort was made to import Shire stallions from England for the breeding program. Instead, several of the midwestern horsemen became interested in the new draft-type Percherons being developed in France. In 1801 the Percheron was celebrated as a saddler and a hunter, with many of them being bought for the cavalry and to haul the diligence, the French equivalent of the stagecoach. The French government, through the military program of breeding and procurement, fostered the lighter type, but the farmers in the Perche area demanded larger horses of the draft type.

The breeders, in meeting this demand, developed the modern blocky, heavily muscled gray animal, with the stallions weighing about two thousand pounds each, the mares two or three hundred pounds lighter. This large new draft type is the horse the Americans imported in the 1850's, beginning with three stallions. The blocky Percherons were not readily accepted by the horse breeders of the Midwest until the first two or three crops of colts grew up. The demand for these grade Percherons was so strong, especially during the Civil War, that the stallions were used a great deal. Their colts, bringing from fifty to a hundred and twenty-five dollars more in the market, immediately interested all the breeders. The popularity of the Percheron that started at that time lasted until the demand for draft horses died out in the 1920's. Census figures showed the Percherons outnumbering the combined Shire,

Clydesdale, and Belgian registrations seventy thousand to twenty thousand in 1920.

Evidently because it had been a good cavalry type, the Percheron crossed well with mares of nondescript saddle stock from the western ranges. A half Percheron from an average range matured at twelve to fourteen hundred pounds. A second cross, Percheron to half Percheron, produced a fine draft animal of about sixteen hundred pounds in weight, suitable for heavy hauling. A half Percheron bred back to a stallion of good saddle stock raised a horse of about eleven hundred pounds, a size desired for teams hauling carriages, light wagons, and stagecoaches. These lighter horses were more active and agile than the crosses from the other draft breeds.

The farmers in general seldom owned purebred draft animals. They were too large, ungainly, and costly and required more care. The beautiful, huge purebreds, weighing about a ton each, were used in matched teams for showy work about the cities, especially on brewery wagons and, in circuses, to haul wagons and cages in the parade or to furnish a broad platform for the bareback riders in the ring.

In the 1870's the open plains of the West beckoned to the adventurous farmer. Encouraged by the new railroads and the new machinery, he moved west into a region of scant rainfall that required new farming patterns to produce profitable crops. Summer fallowing, the process of cultivating a field each year but cropping it every other year, doubled the farmer's plowing and harrowing. To break even on such land each man had to cultivate large fields, finishing each operation quickly. He managed this by using even larger machines and more big horses to each machine. The limit on a set of harrows and drills was reached with one man driving thirty-six horses. The very large combined harvester-separator with forty-two horses needed a crew of about six men, one to drive and the others to handle the grain as it spewed forth. Such large hitches were not common. On most fields teams of four to eight horses were the custom.

While the large machines and the large teams cut drastically the number of men needed, they kept the number of horses at a maximum. The census reported that the average wheat farm had ten horses, with about twenty-six acres cultivated for each horse used. These horses worked long hours when plowing, harrowing, cultivating, and harvesting, but they had long rests between these tasks. The Bureau of Animal Husbandry figured that each horse worked about six hundred hours a year.

Most of this work was concentrated in the spring and fall periods of two months each.

High on the list of machines that directly replaced men was the binder, put on the market in 1867. It cut the grain, bound it into sheaves or bundles, and dumped six or seven at a time for the men to put into shocks. The grain could finish ripening in the shocks while it was waiting for threshing time. The binder was of special value in two ways. It gave the farmer more working days during the harvest, since he could start cutting partially ripe grain, and it saved the straw in a stack for winter use.

The threshing machine, also called the grain separator, had been improved too. Until the development of the steam tractor the larger models were run by horse power, eight to twelve horses walking around in a circle and turning a set of gears to operate the machine. When the large steam tractor was introduced into the grainfields in the 1880's, the threshing machines were made much larger to handle more grain per hour.

With the threshing rig came a large crew of men and several teams. Four- or five-bundle wagons brought the sheaves from the field to be pitched directly into the maw of the monster. The straw was blown out onto a stack while the clean grain was delivered from a spout at the side, either into sacks or into a bin that could be dumped into a wagon. A string of wagons hauled the wheat to the granary or to the railroad siding.

Few farms were large enough to supply all their own teams and the threshing crew. Usually the farmers of an area joined forces and traded work, each furnishing a specified number of teams and drivers at each farm. A little simple bookkeeping evened up the accounts at the end of the season. With this system the threshing machines could operate every day from when the grain first ripened until the fall snows came, except for rainy days. This schedule allowed one machine to handle the grain from a large acreage.

In an effort to eliminate labor, the header was developed to cut off just the ripened heads, leaving the stalks standing. This eliminated both the shocking and the pitching of bundles onto the wagons, for the header delivered directly into the wagon box. Grain cut by a header had to be ripe and was usually hauled directly to the threshing machine. The straw could not be saved and was something of a nuisance when plowing time came.

The ultimate harvesting machine was one that combined the cutting and threshing operations and so was called a combine, with the accent on the first syllable. The combine, in one operation, cut, threshed, and delivered the cleaned grain into a hopper, spewing the straw all over the field. It grew so large it had to be pulled by as many as forty-two horses, with the power to run the machinery delivered by a great cleated bullwheel. These unwieldy monsters gave way to "baby" combines using eighteen horses that could maneuver better in the fields. To turn the forty-two-horse team and the machine around a square corner required a great deal of skill on the part of the driver, and the large machine could not cope with small irregularities of the land surface.

After the grain was threshed and sacked it had to be hauled to the nearest railroad siding for shipment to market. Twenty miles was considered the extreme distance a farmer could haul grain over dirt roads and still recover his costs. Beyond that distance he could grow grain profitably only if he fed it to stock.

The census of farm animals throughout the wheat belt showed very few colts compared to the number of adult horses. This is a sharp contrast to the range country of the West, where the colt crop ran very heavy each year. These mountain states supplied a steady stream of range-raised stock to the farm markets in the central states. The mares went to the corn belt farmers who raised some stock, perhaps only one or two colts a year, but the aggregate number was very large. These breeders furnished workhorses for both the wheat farms and for the towns and cities. Many of these range mares, besides raising foals, pulled the family buggy or took the children for rides.

The western-raised geldings also were used a great deal for light harness work, pulling buggies and light wagons. Many of them were used under saddle too, for each of the large farms kept one or two for all sorts of errands. Some men used saddle horses to ride behind the harrows, guiding the teams with extra long lines, instead of plodding along in the dust.

The use of horses and horse-drawn machinery on the farms reached its peak about 1900, to be rapidly supplanted in the next three decades by the new gasoline motors.

In order to break even on the large farms of the western plains, the farmer had to finish each operation quickly. He managed this by using larger machines, drawn by larger numbers of horses. Since few farms had enough horses, usually the farmers of an area joined forces and traded work. *Above, team hauling a combine* (Oregon State University Archives). *Below, teams hauling wheat* (Sherman County Historical Society)

11

Horses for Work and Play

UNTIL THE EARLY TWENTIETH CENTURY the streets of
America's cities and towns were crammed from early morning until
about midafternoon with a multiplicity of horse-drawn vehicles of
every description, from the huge brewery wagons piled high with barrels and drawn by massive matched teams, groomed and polished, to the
dusty, rickety little wagons of the old-clothes men, each drawn by a
small, decrepit nag. By midafternoon many of the delivery wagons had
finished their rounds, leaving more room on the streets for the carriage
trade. Although the total number of vehicles was not very large, the
congestion was great and the traffic moved in confusing, irregular patterns. The vehicles moved slowly; they were difficult to maneuver and
halts were frequent. A loaded dray needed two minutes or more to
cover one city block, and when it backed into the curb to unload merchandise it often blocked half the street as well as inconveniencing the
pedestrians on the sidewalk.

Mingled with the large drays were the horse-drawn buses, horsecars,
cabs, hacks, and light delivery wagons of all sorts, as well as a few carriages, buggies, and carts, and some people on horseback. Many small
collisions occurred, usually causing only minor damage while producing
a great deal of sound and fury from the drivers. Any such accident
left the teams and rigs in something of a tangle that required a great deal
of time and patience to unsnarl, while impatient drivers crowded their
teams in from all sides. An occasional runaway furnished excitement,

added to the confusion, and injured or killed some of the people, while a fire in the business district could block traffic for hours.

In a large city all of these horses had to be stabled near the congested business district where they were used, occupying blocks of valuable real estate. The large draft teams, and the horses for the horsecars, cabs, fire engines, and police work all received good treatment and good food, since their sleek shiny coats were good advertisements for their owners, and with good treatment they could work better and for a greater number of years. Even so they were confined to their stalls from fifteen to twenty hours a day. They had light, airy stables with comfortable clean stalls and plenty of food and water. They were brushed and curried and kept well shod for the hard work on the cobbled streets.

Buyers for the car lines and buses had a strong preference for roans from five to nine years old. The lineback buckskin, with his black dorsal stripe and black points, also rated highly. Any horse with a white foot was considered undesirable, since the hoof on that foot might give trouble. This same dislike for white feet was common in the northwest stock country and was noted by a fur trader in 1801, at a time when the Indians were the only stockmen there.

One serious problem for all the stablemen was the storage and disposal of the large quantities of manure cleaned from the stalls each day. Deep storage pits were hard to empty and damaged the manure, while outside storage at ground level brought strong protests from the neighbors in spite of the efforts of the stablemen to convince them the piles were actually beneficial to their health. This was in the days before flies had been identified as disease carriers. The accumulated manure was sold as fertilizer at a nice profit to the stablemen, but no regular system of daily or even weekly haulage was ever instituted to keep the area comparatively clean. Manure dropped on the city streets was cleaned up by the street sweepers, but on the unpaved streets it just became a permanent part of the surface. On dusty days the fine, dry particles were blown about to lodge on peoples' clothes, skin, and lips.

A dramatic addition to city traffic came with the construction of the fire engine—a combination of steam boiler with its furnace, and engine and pump, all mounted on a single chassis drawn by three large horses of the heavy carriage type, able to gallop briskly through the city streets with their load. Before the development of this portable power plant, all pumping at fires had to be done by the large crews of men who also pulled their pumper into position.

Each fire station combined the enginehouse with the stable for the horses. They stood in their stalls behind spring doors which opened when the alarm rang. The horses moved at once into position, their harnesses descended onto their backs from overhead frames, firemen fastened a few buckles and snapped the yoke to the collars, and the whole rig was ready to roll in three to five minutes from the first alarm, with the brass bell clanging and black smoke pouring from the stack. A wagon carrying more firemen, lengths of hose, and several ladders followed close behind.

In all cities where horsecars were used the car tracks were often blocked by the fire hoses whenever the blaze occurred in the business district and the firemen had to run their hoses from hydrants across the street. To keep this interruption of car service at a minimum, the car company had emergency wagons that answered every fire call along the streets carrying car tracks. By the time the firemen were laying their hoses, the emergency crew was on hand to span them with jumpers, long iron frames that furnished temporary tracks for the cars right across the hose lines. Some of the emergency wagons had towers built on the wagon bed, rising several feet into the air. With one of these wagons on each side of the tracks, the hose lines could be suspended from one to the other, allowing traffic to pass unhindered beneath.

A city police force used many horses in routine work. In addition to those for the mounted police, who often had jobs of directing traffic, controlling crowds, and dispersing mobs, teams were needed on the paddy wagons and ambulances. Horses for the mounted police were carefully chosen for their calm dispositions and were of the light saddle type, beautifully colored, well groomed and well trained geldings.

Light delivery wagons for milk, bread, and groceries were each drawn by a single horse in the heavily populated areas, although two horses were often used for delivery wagons in the residential areas and the suburbs. Often the small delivery vehicles were enclosed, with a sliding door on each side. The driver stood in the middle, with the lines being passed through a slot in the front. Peddler wagons were the open box type, with a seat up front, but when at work the driver usually stood on a low step hanging down at the rear. These peddlers called their wares as they drove along. Small ice wagons handled by one man were also of this type, with a heavy canvas cover to pull over the blocks of ice. Larger ice wagons with two or three men had a driver on the seat up front, with the others on the step behind.

Although there were hitching posts or rails along the streets, most delivery wagons carried iron hitching weights—circular discs each weighing about five pounds—on the footboard. They were fastened by a leather strap to the horse's bit. When the driver stopped for a delivery, he placed the weight on the parking strip as a temporary hitching post. Such weights were seldom used on any pleasure vehicle.

Especially in a small town the livery stable was an important business establishment and social center. The stable rented out driving rigs and saddle horses, and often took care of the doctor's horse and buggy. The animal was fed, watered, groomed, harnessed, and hitched to the buggy whenever the doctor needed to make a house call, especially to a farmhouse. Traveling salesmen used livery rigs a great deal, arriving by train and driving to outlying towns and villages. Livery rigs formed an important segment of every funeral procession. Young men in town often hired livery rigs to take girls to dances, picnics, or just for a buggy ride on Sunday afternoon.

The well-to-do town or city dweller usually had a combined carriage house and stable near the family dwelling with a handyman to look after the horse and to work on the lawn and shrubs in his spare time. Larger establishments, with perhaps a carriage, a cart, the carriage horses, a child's pony, and a riding horse or two, might require a full-time coachman with a helper.

The head of the family frequently rode his saddle horse to the office each day, turning it over to the office boy, who took it to the nearest livery stable and went after it again when it was needed. On Sundays this saddle horse was ridden on the bridle paths in the parks or even out of town along a country road. If the head of the house was not out riding, he drove the carriage and took the family out for a Sunday drive; otherwise this duty was handled by the coachman. Most men considered it a sign of masculinity to ride and drive well.

Cab service in the towns and villages was handled by the four-wheeled hack with two horses. This hack was considered a necessity for formal occasions for any family not owning a carriage. It was used at weddings and funerals and to carry people to important social functions. In large towns and cities the two-wheeled hansom cab was used a great deal. It was drawn by one horse, the driver sitting outside at the back on a raised seat.

On the bottom rung of the city horse ranks were the sorry animals that handled the odd jobs and hauled the wagons to gather up the old clothes, old bones, empty bottles, and general junk. These poor creatures were kept in dark, damp, smelly quarters and were usually underfed and ill-treated. They worked as long as they could walk and died in harness, collapsing on the street, their misery ended by a policeman's bullet. The carcass was then hauled off to a glue factory.

These horses were so obviously and publicly mistreated that they aroused the sympathies of many of the upper-class women and so helped build up the sentiment that led to the Society for the Prevention of Cruelty to Animals. They also inspired many pathetic stories, of which *Black Beauty* is a widely known example. Some of the stories had a contrived happy ending in which the abused car horse was rescued, restored to health, and finally became a great racer.

The number of horses needed in towns and cities increased with the increasing population, even though many of the families with large establishments moved out to the suburbs to get more room for their animals. In 1910 about three million horses were listed for nonfarm use, with an estimated three hundred thousand in New York City. It was during this period of heavy urban use that the term "one-horse town" was commonly used to describe a small, backward place.

While horsemen in the United States had always been interested in raising fast running and trotting horses and quite early in the eighteenth century began importing stallions from England to improve the speed of their colts, they lagged far behind the English in registering their animals and in keeping detailed breeding records. Most of them made a written record of the sires of their better foals, but there was seldom mention of the dams.

As interest in racing continued to grow in the larger cities, more racetracks were built close by, with railroads to haul the spectators who arrived in large numbers. Betting on the races was the great attraction and the bettors were interested in the pedigrees of the various contenders. All of this led to the formation in 1873 of the American Jockey Club, which assumed control of all registration records of Thoroughbreds in the United States and certified those eligible to enter approved races. To be accepted for registration a horse had to prove fifteen-sixteenths Thoroughbred ancestry. Even then it would be turned down if it showed some unusual color pattern carried by a recessive gene which cropped up to the embarrassment of the breeder.

In the United States, Kentucky was considered then—as it has been ever since—the best area for raising running horses. The excellent grass on soil of weathered limestone produced horses with good bone structure, while the mild climate permitted the young animals to run about outside in all but the worst winter storms. This gave them plenty of exercise and made them more nimble than they would have been with supervised exercise on a track or a smooth field. Good horses were raised in many other localities, too, in a program to meet the growing demand for more animals to fill the racing cards at the new tracks.

Large-scale horse racing, well publicized in the daily press, attracted public attention and drew overflow crowds to the big special races, such as the Kentucky Derby at Louisville, patterned after the original Derby at Epsom Downs. In addition to the heavy betting at the tracks, large amounts were wagered on each race at a big meet by hundreds of thousands of people scattered throughout the cities who had little desire to see horses run but did like to bet on them. This widespread public interest gave many people, through the press reports, many new words and expressions, enriching our common speech with "dark horse," "left at the post," "sleeper," "won by a nose," and more recently, "photo finish."

Only a small proportion of each year's colt crop was good enough for the racing meets. Those that showed no gift for speed had to be sold for other uses, but since they had been bred up for this highly specialized activity, it was difficult to adapt them to other uses. Their nervous energy and strong desire to run unfitted them for family riding or driving. Even when handled by a highly skilled rider they were of little use around stock, especially for open-range work. The Thoroughbreds found it difficult to pick their way over rough country and had a strong tendency to stumble in the hills. But worst of all, in the cowman's opinion, they were too excitable around the stock. Whereas the good cow horse could slog along, content to follow at a distance the slowly moving herd and conserve his energy for needful bursts of speed when a critter tried to break away, the Thoroughbred wanted to be right up there pushing the stragglers. It champed at the bit, fretted, tossed its head, and pranced along sideways when held on a tight rein. In a quarter of a mile or so this behavior started the animal frothing a little on the bit and sweating heavily on the neck and flanks. This strong tendency to fidget and sweat earned in range country the derogatory term "hot blooded," although in many other circles of stockmen the same term is used to describe quality breeding.

In all the racing programs the promoters emphasized their interest in developing the breed. The breeding program was highly successful, their horses were the fastest in the world (this refers to all the Thorough-breds throughout the world as a breed) on a smooth track at middle distances from about three quarters of a mile to three miles. Some of the breed that grew too tall for the racetrack were trained as hunters. They were taught to jump fences, hedges, ditches, and streams as they followed a pack of hounds across the landscape in pursuit of a fox. In this sort of running their long legs gave them an advantage in clearing the obstacles along the way.

Horse racing had appeared especially sinful to the Puritans of England because it was closely associated in their minds with the Stuart kings and their Cavalier followers. This same evaluation was carried to New England by the early Puritan settlers, and was another irritating difference between them and the slaveholding, fox-hunting plantation owners of the South. Large-scale betting at the many racetracks helped keep this disapproval alive.

The northern rural population was much less opposed to harness racing than to racing under saddle. A trotting horse hitched to a buggy or cart was still to them a working horse, quite different from a horse kept only for pleasure riding, and they took a great deal of pride in driving fast trotters. Also a shiny buggy drawn by a fast trotter was a desirable rig to carry a doctor speedily on his errands of mercy. Prosperous businessmen and lawyers often drove such a turnout, since it was an asset to their businesses.

During the colonial period a few natural pacers were brought into New York by the Dutch. This was probably the source of the strain known as the Narragansett pacers that was remembered in tradition and legend, although there has never been a specimen positively identified as such after 1800. Some trotting horses were imported too, without any positive identification of the individual animals. Not until well into the nineteenth century did these trotters and pacers command enough attention to insure a permanent registry of their own.

In 1818 a trotting horse, Boston Blue, attracted attention by covering a timed mile in less than three minutes. Later the same horse trotted from New York City to Philadelphia, a distance of eighty miles, in a day. After a few days of rest he trotted back again, seemingly none the worse for the trip. At about the same period some of the Morgans were listed as good trotters, but the modern trotter was developed from a cross between imported English Thoroughbred stock and one of the American mares.

Abdallah, grandson of the imported English stallion Messenger, was mated to a trotting mare and sired Rysdyk's Hambletonian. Foaled in 1849, this potent sire produced 1,333 foals of record. From this crop 150 of his better sons sired 1,487 trotters and 220 pacers, while 80 select daughters foaled 110 trotters and 7 pacers, all of whom were fast enough to appear in the record books. Thus from the offspring of this one sire the American Standard Bred horse registry was established. These horses are widely known as Hambletonians.

Harness races for both trotters and pacers were popular at all the county and state fairs where the farm folk gathered. Less formal meets also enlivened the programs of many special occasions and local celebrations. In trotting races, instead of determining the winner in a single race, three heats are run and the horse making the best showing in the three heats is declared the winner. Also trotting races are usually limited to three or four horses, since the sulkies take up more room than a running horse under saddle. Another interesting difference is that horses in a running race start from rest, while in a harness race all the entries are going nearly full speed when they pass the starting post.

Impromptu harness races were difficult to stage in most places. Not many rural roads were wide enough for two vehicles abreast, and people frowned on the staging of such activities in the streets. Any good straight stretch of country road could be used if it had broad, grassy shoulders on each side. Many a brush was staged on a Sunday morning as the people were on their way to church.

Pacers have always been scarcer than trotters, but the best of them have been very fast. At the opening of the twentieth century Dan Patch, a coal-black pacer, claimed a world record of 1:55 for the mile. This was not set in a match but under special conditions, with a fleet-running horse "breaking the wind" for him (running a few yards in advance), and so is not too highly regarded among harness men. Dan Patch earned a great deal of money for his owner by appearing at fairs for exhibition heats, but he was carefully kept out of match races.

At harness racing meets today the crowds are immense and enthusiastic. Most of them have some knowledge of trotting horses and take a keen interest in the individual animals. The trotters attract very little attention from the betting public or from the sportswriters, so they do not race for as large stakes except in two or three of the greatest races. The breeders of trotters do have a steady market for their slower animals, since they make excellent carriage and buggy horses. The pacers have always been known as smooth-traveling saddle horses and so are prized for pleasure riding.

Another form of entertainment utilizing horses, Buffalo Bill's Wild West Show, was the physical embodiment of one of those scintillating ideas that sometimes comes to a fortunate individual. The show was an immediate success because it appeared at an opportune time and was presented by a well-known, picturesque character with the right background. By striking the right note, the show was a financial success and was the basic inspiration to many western towns to develop local shows along the same lines for the tourist trade. It furnished the general pattern for many frontier-day celebrations that have had an enduring popularity throughout the West and have encouraged the riders of today to practice many of the skills so widely used on the open range in the 1880's.

William Frederick Cody, after an adventurous life in the untamed West, had turned to the stage in order to cash in on the reputation he had earned by his exploits. The gross exaggerations that appeared in the dime novels of the time also helped bring in the crowds. He toured the country for several years, appearing in different melodramas based somewhat loosely on his real-life adventures.

It began in June 1882, when he returned to his home in the small new town of North Platte, Nebraska, and expressed his surprise that the community was making no plans for a Fourth of July celebration. At once his friend, the mayor, made Bill chairman in charge of producing something suitable. Bill laid plans to use the local fenced-in racetrack for contests in shooting, riding, and bronco busting, with prizes for the events donated by the local merchants. He decided that a suitable last act would be an exhibition, using a wild steer and a gun loaded with blanks, of how he killed buffalo. Five thousand handbills advertising the event brought in about a thousand contestants together with most of the people within 150 miles as spectators. The outstanding success of this impromptu show convinced Cody that a traveling show organized along the same lines would attract cash customers in large numbers throughout the country.

The following spring, 1883, Cody started out with his Buffalo Bill's Wild West Show, which endured until 1912 when it was absorbed by the Sells-Floto circus. In the intervening period of twenty-nine years the show toured the United States, England, France, and Germany, attracting great crowds, enjoying enthusiastic applause from the crowned monarchs of Europe, and bringing some understanding of the Old West to millions of people.

At first Cody tried for strict realism in everything, but soon had to modify some of the scenes. He realized it was dangerous to use actual broncos after a team of six ran away with a stagecoach loaded with dignitaries. He learned that for the show ring and the arena slower, gentle horses did very well when they all milled around at about the same rate of speed.

After years of successful operation Cody took his show to the Columbian Exposition, the Chicago World's Fair of 1893. By then his program had settled into a definite pattern, its scope shown by this program as presented at the fair.

Overture, "STAR SPANGLED BANNER" COWBOY BAND, WM. SWEENEY, LEADER.

1. *Grand Review* INTRODUCING THE ROUGH RIDERS OF THE WORLD AND FULLY EQUIPPED REGULAR SOLDIERS OF THE ARMIES OF AMERICA, ENGLAND, FRANCE, GERMANY AND RUSSIA.
2. *Miss Annie Oakley*, CELEBRATED SHOT, WHO WILL ILLUSTRATE HER DEXTERITY IN THE USE OF FIRE-ARMS.
3. *Horse Race* BETWEEN A COWBOY, A COSSACK, A MEXICAN, AN ARAB, AND AN INDIAN, ON SPANISH-MEXICAN, BRONCHO, RUSSIAN, INDIAN AND ARABIAN HORSES.
4. *Pony Express*, THE FORMER PONY EXPRESS RIDER WILL SHOW HOW THE LETTERS AND TELEGRAMS OF THE REPUBLIC WERE DISTRIBUTED ACROSS THE IMMENSE CONTINENT PREVIOUS TO THE RAILWAYS AND THE TELEGRAPH.
5. *Illustrating a Prairie Emigrant Train Crossing the Plains*. ATTACK BY MARAUDING INDIANS REPULSED BY "BUFFALO BILL" WITH SCOUTS AND COWBOYS. N.B. THE WAGONS ARE THE SAME USED 35 YEARS AGO.
6. *Group of Syrian and Arabian Horsemen* WILL ILLUSTRATE THEIR STYLE OF HORSEMANSHIP, WITH NATIVE SPORTS AND PASTIMES.
7. *Cossacks*, OF THE CAUCASUS OF RUSSIA, IN FEATS OF HORSEMANSHIP, NATIVE DANCES, ETC.
8. *Johnny Baker*, CELEBRATED YOUNG AMERICAN MARKSMAN.

9. *A Group of Mexicans* FROM OLD MEXICO, WILL ILLUSTRATE THE USE OF THE LASSO, AND PERFORM VARIOUS FEATS OF HORSE-MANSHIP.

10. *Racing Between Prairie, Spanish and Indian Girls.*

11. *Cowboy Fun.* PICKING UP OBJECTS FROM THE GROUND, LASSO-ING WILD HORSES, RIDING THE BUCKERS.

12. *Military Evolutions* BY A COMPANY OF THE SIXTH CAVALRY OF THE UNITED STATES ARMY; A COMPANY OF THE FIRST GUARD UHLAN REGIMENT OF HIS MAJESTY KING WILLIAM II, GERMAN EMPEROR, POPULARLY KNOWN AS THE "POTSDAMER REDS"; A COMPANY OF FRENCH CHASSEURS (CHASSEURS A CHEVAL DE LA GARDE REPUBLIQUE FRANCAIS); AND A COMPANY OF THE 12TH LANCERS (PRINCE OF WALES' REGIMENT) OF THE BRITISH ARMY.

13. *Capture of the Deadwood Mail Coach by the Indians,* WHICH WILL BE RESCUED BY "BUFFALO BILL" AND HIS ATTENDANT COWBOYS. N.B. THIS IS THE IDENTICAL OLD DEADWOOD COACH, CALLED THE MAIL COACH, WHICH IS FAMOUS ON ACCOUNT OF HAVING CARRIED THE GREAT NUMBER OF PEOPLE WHO LOST THEIR LIVES ON THE ROAD BETWEEN DEADWOOD AND CHEYENNE 18 YEARS AGO. NOW THE MOST FAMOUS VEHICLE EXTANT.

14. *Racing Between Indian Boys on Bareback Horses.*

15. *Life Customs of the Indians.* INDIAN SETTLEMENT ON THE FIELD AND "PATH."

16. *Col. W. F. Cody* ("BUFFALO BILL"), IN HIS UNIQUE FEATS OF SHARPSHOOTING.

17. *Buffalo Hunt,* AS IT IS IN THE FAR WEST OF NORTH AMERICA —"BUFFALO BILL" AND INDIANS. THE LAST OF THE ONLY KNOWN NATIVE HERD.

18. *The Battle of the Little Big Horn,* SHOWING WITH HISTORICAL ACCURACY THE SCENE OF CUSTER'S LAST CHARGE.

19. *Salute.*

Cody's success brought a host of imitators until at least forty had tried their luck at the Wild West game. Some of them, such as Pawnee Bill Lillie, were fairly successful over a period of years, while others faded after a short run. Their combined efforts presented the American people with the highlights of western life and gave the term "cowboy" respectability. No longer was it equated with rustler and badman.

All of these shows used a large number of western horses purchased in the markets of Miles City, Sheridan, Cheyenne, Denver, and many smaller places. Easterners of all classes could see for themselves how attractive, active, and intelligent western saddle horses were, obviously larger and better stock than the Indian ponies of the plains. They also learned that all the odd extras on the western saddles were put there to aid in specific tasks.

Cow towns of the West saw the advantage of giving eastern visitors a closeup look at the old range activities. They began giving shows each summer featuring bronco riding, steer and calf roping, and bulldogging. At each show a band of Indians in costume and with their tipis were on hand to add an important touch of color. For a large, successful event that would attract tourists, the town staging the show had to be on one of the new railroads and near an Indian reservation. Some earlier publicity as an army post during the Indian wars or as a shipping point for range horses and cattle also helped. It was the happy combination of these factors that was so important to Cheyenne, Sheridan, Miles City, Pendleton, and Calgary as they staged their spectaculars variously known as Frontier Days, Stampedes, and Roundups. Many of the people who came from the East on their vacations included stopovers for one or more of these celebrations on their way to Pacific Coast points.

Then came the first truly Western novel, Owen Wister's *The Virginian*, with a cowboy hero and most of the action out in the open spaces. Although he had very little to do with cattle in the various scenes and incidents, the Virginian appealed to a large and varied audience as a genuine cowboy. This book added to the romantic aura surrounding the old rangeland and its people. Also one of its saddle horses was introduced by name and played a strong role on several occasions, while another horse was the key figure in an important dramatic sequence.

When the Northern Pacific Railroad reached Livingston, Montana, in 1883, it provided easy access to the wonders of Yellowstone Park, for many years our only national park. Passenger service through the park was furnished by real western stagecoaches drawn by four- or six-horse teams. At various stations along the way through the park, guides with saddle horses and pack strings were ready to conduct visitors to more remote sections in an unspoiled, readily accessible wilderness. The use of horses on the coaches continued until after World War I. Private automobiles and motor vehicles of all kinds were also barred from the park to keep it unspoiled.

In the same period that Wild West shows were having such a vogue, traveling circuses multiplied rapidly, until in 1885 they reached their maximum number with more than fifty shows on the road at one time. With their menageries and sideshow freaks they combined a horse show and hippodrome races. In the smaller shows the prize horses were the grade Percherons, plump and broad backed, used in bareback riding events. These horses cantered around the ring, live action in slow motion, moving at about the speed of a brisk walk. Light riding horses supplied plenty of action in the races. In the larger shows beautiful riding horses were used in drills and spectaculars.

In the small towns along the way circuses were always trading for new horses. Some of the animals they palmed off on the farmers had fictitious pedigrees and hurt the local breeding programs. One year P. T. Barnum on a swing through the central states disposed of a number of pinto stallions, assuring the purchasers that the animals were pure-bred Arabians and that the pinto coloration was a characteristic of one of the best strains of that breed, when in fact no recognized Arabian has ever been a pinto. In later years American breeders of the beautiful, authentic blood bay and iron gray Arabians had to work very hard to root out this misconception.

One trained horse from Cody's show was presented to Sitting Bull when he had completed his tours with Buffalo Bill. This horse was loose outside the Sioux chief's cabin when he was shot to death by Indian police in 1890. Something in the action, possibly the sound of the shots, gave the horse its cue for a trick and it sat down and slowly raised its right hoof in a salute, badly frightening the Indians, who were sure this was a spirit horse of some kind.

After 1885 the number of circuses declined rapidly, some of the smaller shows going broke and being disbanded or being absorbed by the larger competitors. Finally the field was dominated for about a decade by the Ringling Brothers' "Greatest Show on Earth." Far behind in second place came Barnum and Bailey, which finally sold out to Ringling. Sells-Floto was a poor third, even after it took over Buffalo Bill's Wild West Show and Pawnee Bill's Far East Show.

Above, a horse-drawn ambulance preparing to leave the yard of New York's Bellevue Hospital, 1896. Already horses were beginning to disappear from city streets. Note the trolley cars in the lower Broadway scene of the same period, below. By 1907 New York had no more horse-drawn buses. Soon all the carriages and dray wagons were replaced by cars and trucks. (Photographs by Byron, The Byron Collection, Museum of the City of New York)

12

Draft Horses
Lose Their Jobs

THE RAPID GROWTH OF THE CITIES from 1890 on was not matched by a corresponding increase in the number of horses used in the urban areas. Year by year new machines took over many of the tasks formerly done by horse muscle, first in carrying people, then in transporting goods. Cable cars, trolley cars, elevated railroads, and subways furnished mass transportation. Horsecars were the first victims of the change, then the horse-drawn buses, which were driven from the streets of New York by 1907. The peak of the nonfarm use of horses was reached in 1910, with more than three million animals listed in this category. After 1910 the total number of horses in urban use diminished rapidly, while the number of people was increasing by about a million a year in the cities and towns.

Three major factors contributed to this drastic change: new interest in public health, rising real estate values, and adequate substitutes for horses in the form of gasoline motors for cars and trucks. As the general public became better informed about contagious and infectious diseases and how they were spread, the undesirability of filthy stables scattered throughout the community became evident. Widely read articles spread information, and fictional stories built up strong emotional reactions against the prevailing conditions. Once the public health officials began to set up stricter regulations and then to enforce them, first on the cow barns and the milk suppliers and then on the stables, the cost of keeping animals in the city increased rapidly.

During the same period real estate values in the business districts soared under the pressure of increased population; land suitably located for multistoried office buildings and stores cost too much to be used to stable horses. The well-to-do packed up and took their horses and carriages to the suburbs, commuting to the office by train. Draft teams were moved too, but it was not economically feasible to stable them very far from their work areas, and the many bulky loads of hay for feed and straw for bedding created additional congestion in the crowded streets.

When a few scattered vehicles propelled by gasoline motors first appeared on the city streets in the 1890's they were regarded as interesting novelties, but the rapid improvements in their construction soon made them practical for many city chores. The new cars had strong appeal to two groups, the cab drivers and the truck men. Enthusiastic acceptance of taxicabs by the upper classes made them an instant success. It soon became fashionable to use taxis for afternoon shopping, for making social calls, and for attending evening functions. With taxis on call, many middle-class people could move into apartments while they sent their horses to the country or sold them. The increasingly difficult task of finding good servants at low wages was another factor in this change.

While the increasing use of taxis cut the number of horse-drawn hacks and carriages, the hansom cabs, which cost only half as much to operate, managed to survive for many years. In the losing contest with the horseless carriage, the last horse-drawn vehicle to succumb was the hearse. Until the middle 'thirties many people considered it indecent to use a motorized hearse to carry a corpse to the cemetery.

The heavy draft horses on the large drays and vans disappeared about as rapidly as did the carriage horses. The huge new trucks, with their wide tires of solid rubber and exposed chain drives, lumbered ponderously along the city streets at about ten miles an hour. Even so they moved at about triple the speed of the horse-drawn drays and took up much less street room. They caused no manure problems and could be parked in the corner of a dark basement.

The early popularity of both the autos and the trucks was confined to the cities where graded and paved streets furnished smooth all-weather surfaces with gentle grades. The dependence of the service vehicles on improved streets is illustrated by the practice common among taxi drivers of dumping a fare on a paved street nearest to his destination, leaving him to trudge a few blocks through the storm rather than chance being stuck in a mudhole or snowbank.

World War I speeded up the replacement of horses by machines. The armies' demands for horses far outstripped the supply, which was strictly limited to the number of animals that could be transported to Europe on the available ships. As the German U-boats took a heavy toll of shipping, the number of horses sent had to be reduced. In 1913, the year before the war, the export of horses to England and France was less than a thousand. By 1915 this had increased to 289,000, and by 1916 to 357,000. After that the ships were needed to transport American troops and supplies, so horse export fell to 278,000 in 1917 and to 84,000 in 1918.

Meanwhile the armies were paying high prices for all the motor vehicles they could secure, stimulating the manufacturers to improve models and increase production. Tractors with caterpillar treads were in great demand for making armored tanks, and four-wheel-drive trucks hauled heavy loads on poor roads, especially near the front lines. In 1918, instead of horse-drawn caissons supplying shells to the field pieces along the constantly moving front, these big trucks rolled right up to the batteries with the shells stacked up like cordwood. Light whippet tanks carried both the heavy machine guns and the ammunition for them, replacing the horse-and-cart system of the French army. Horses displaced by the machines were used to replace those killed in action, which in turn went into the soldiers' messes as a supply of fresh meat. Many a soldier realized the significance of a good stew of fresh meat the day after a German shell had killed an artillery horse or two close by.

The war also brought great demands on the American farmers to increase their crops of food grains, especially wheat, for the armies and the many millions of hungry civilians in the war-torn countries. For years western Europe had secured millions of bushels of wheat from Russia through the Black Sea ports that were now cut off by the Turkish troops holding the Straits. Although both Argentina and Australia had wheat, it took ships too long to haul it when a run to Montreal and back could be made so quickly.

The sudden heavy demands on the American grain supply brought new measures to increase production and to cut down domestic use. One way to achieve great savings was to stop feeding grain to the millions of horses in the cities, replacing them with trucks. Since the motor trucks and buses could be operated with fewer men, their use was considered profitable as well as patriotic.

After the war ended, the grain market slumped and the wheat growers were pinched. Many of them had been operating on money borrowed so they could increase their production of grain for the war effort. With the low market for wheat, they were broke. Those who managed to hang on had to turn to further mechanization to lower their production costs. By eliminating teams and working both the machines and themselves long hours they survived, while the number of draft horses on the farms shrank to a new low.

The depression of the 1930's brought a federal program for cutting farm production by paying farmers not to plant crops. Especially in the South the cash payments were used to buy tractors and other farm machinery. The owners drove their tenant farmers off the land and changed their holdings from small plots to large fields suitable for machine farming. Most of the plantation field work had been done by mules, with large herds of mares to breed the mules. As the mules were replaced by machines, the brood mares were shipped off to market and down went the horse population again.

At the same time an expanding market for food for dogs and foxes created a market for all the discarded horses. Many people had turned to fox farming to supply fur, and to provide cheap meat for their animals, the worn-out work teams, the aged cab horses, the culls from the breeding herds, and scrub wild horses from the western ranges all went to the canneries for the few dollars they would bring in ready cash. Although this meat was not inspected and the canneries were not held to high sanitary standards, many of the firms turned out a product of good quality, an edible meat with no waste, cooked and ready to serve at a retail cost of ten cents or less for a one-pound can. Through the tough depression years many a poverty-stricken family supplied its protein needs by eating horse meat, thus emulating their remote ancestors who had lived and hunted in western Europe forty thousand years ago. This strong demand for low-grade horses had a beneficial effect on the entire horse-raising program. It cleaned the scrubs from the pastures and freed the western ranges of herds of low-grade wild horses.

The general decline in demand for any kind of horses in the period 1920–45 was especially hard on the purebred draft animals. The 1920 census listed more than 95,000 registered horses in the draft breeds. In twenty-five years they had dwindled to a few thousand, most of them being retained for sentimental reasons.

Following World War I, the army high command, not yet realizing that cavalry as an effective fighting force had been obsolete for many years, decided to rebuild some of the cavalry regiments. At the same time it instituted the Army Remount Breeding Plan in 1921 to encourage stockmen to raise horses that would meet cavalry requirements. To accomplish this the army purchased stallions to stand at service in horse-raising areas. Once the program was well established, nearly seven hundred stallions were maintained, young animals being purchased each year to replace those that were retired. Annually these stallions sired about ten thousand colts.

The army officers had learned nothing from their predecessors' experience in chasing mounted Indians—especially the Nez Percés—which had shown that the Indian horses were much more durable and able to cover more miles a day than the best of the cavalry sent against them. The officers also ignored the Department of Agriculture experiment in which two range horses were ridden from Wyoming to Illinois in 1897 with good results. They stayed with their old specifications and encouraged the farmers to specialize in grade Thoroughbreds, supplying 644 Thoroughbred stallions, 18 Morgans, and 17 Arabians. World War II finally brought an end to this program and deprived the officers of their last excuse to wear spurs.

Out of the pages of history. In a furious evocation of the Old West, drivers jockey for position in the chuck wagon race at the Calgary Stampede. (Jack De Lorme Photography, Ltd.)

13

The Renaissance of the Light Riding Horse

THE COWBOY OF THE AMERICAN WEST was first introduced to the general public through the medium of the dime novel as a rough, boisterous young man, often an undersirable character, involved in all sorts of daring adventures and hair breadth escapes from hostile Indians, stampeding cattle, and outlaws. The romantic image thus established was made more admirable and was given depth and color by the many Wild West shows touring the country from 1883 to 1912. This new image was reinforced by the roundups, stampedes, and rodeos of the western Frontier Days celebrations. Owen Wister in his novel of Wyoming, *The Virginian,* made the cowboy a believable person in a western setting and gave him enough respectability to make him welcome in the homes of the middle class. Zane Grey, who followed soon after, also was accepted as suitable for living rooms and public libraries, to the delight of young people longing for good adventure stories.

Then came Eugene Manlove Rhodes, the first good writer with genuine range-country background. His stories, appearing in the *Saturday Evening Post* over a period of several years, attracted millions of readers. Beginning with "The Little Eohippus," these entertaining tales with their excellent illustrations presented genuine western characters who were just people, never simon-pure or entirely depraved, but an interesting mixture of good and bad, making them rather unpredictable. *The Trusty Knaves* is a good example. These stories, given such wide circulation, molded the cowboy concept for a whole generation of young Americans.

By the end of World War I motion picture industry was developing the westerns, sometimes called horse operas or oaters, as a large, profitable segment of its output. These westerns were filmed in scenic primitive spots, with cowboys, rustlers, outlaws, Indians, horses, and cattle furnishing the action. In the big chase scenes, when bands of mounted men galloped across the landscape at some distance from the camera, the hero wore a large white hat, a symbol of his purity and an easily recognized badge. Usually the hero rode a white horse, although later cowboy stars each had their own special horse that was as well known to the young movie fans as the hero himself. Two outstanding examples were Tony, the sorrel ridden by Tom Mix on many adventures, and Trigger, the palomino that carried Roy Rogers through peril after peril. In some of the pictures the hero and the good guys were Royal Northwest Mounted Policemen in colorful costume riding into action.

The bad guys, of course, wore black hats and dark clothes and rode black, dark brown, or dark bay horses, but all the horses in these movies, whether ridden by cowboys, outlaws, or Indians, were of the stock horse type and carried western gear. They dashed about over plains, hills, and mountains so different from the country lanes and bridle paths of the settled areas in the East. When the radio serials about the West began, the hero might be a cowboy turned sheriff but he still rode a western horse.

For the two decades between the wars, as the draft horse population of the United States dwindled steadily, the young people reveled in stories, and radio programs extolling the westerner, his horse, and his riding gear. When families went vacationing to the mountains or the seashore the children wanted to rent horses to ride even if for only an hour or so. On many western beaches along the ocean and by some of the lakes, while most members of the family played in the sand or splashed in the water, these youngsters rode bravely along the wide, safe beaches that were still in a wild setting away from highways and fences.

Middle-class people who could afford western vacations increasingly turned to the western dude ranches, where they could spend a week or more in a rather close approximation of western ranch life at the turn of the century. The guests wore cowboy hats, jeans, and boots, and helped with the ranch chores. Each one had his own saddle horse to ride about the ranch or across the hills. All of this was a far cry from the gaited horses, English saddles, and tailored riding habits of the East and satisfied a different want. As the popularity of the dude ranches increased, many new ones were established in the hill country throughout the East, with western-type housing, corrals, horses, and gear.

When a family, conditioned by a taste of western life, decided to buy a horse or two, the members were not looking for just an animal, but for something that would tie them to the whole culture complex of the romantic old Wild West. This reaching back for a romantic period, softened by the golden haze of time, carried with it social acceptance by friends and neighbors, even though they did not turn to horse owning. This is in contrast to the ridicule heaped on Don Quixote when he attempted a somewhat similar reconstruction of olden days.

The same influences of fiction, Wild West shows, and movies had a marked effect on people in western Europe. In Germany, France, and Italy western riding clubs were formed, with all the members dressing in western clothes and using western gear on their horses. Perhaps centuries of use and adaptation of horse gear to meet varying range conditions have achieved a pattern of such intrinsic utility that it can be put to advantage in many other places, thus making it easier for the western aficionados to justify their cult.

After World War II, two beautiful motion pictures in full color, "National Velvet" and "My Friend Flicka," added a new element to the old westerns—young people sharing the starring roles with beautiful horses. Television serials became regular features in millions of homes, with old cowboy movies supplementing the new series done especially for the video screen. In all of these pictures the horses, almost without exception, were of the stock-horse type—compact, agile, and well suited for fast work in the rough country so favored by the cameramen.

When American children matured to the point where they wanted riding horses of their own, they wanted western stock horses with western saddles. They wanted to wear identifiable western garb, especially hats and boots. There seems to have been little interest among the young in general for gaited American Saddlers with their pad saddles and their riders in tailored pants and jackets, topped by a derby hat. When the large American middle class began buying horses to satisfy their children, they had to get those of the stock-horse type and outfit them with western saddles and bridles.

When a family finally decided to buy its first horse, a common pattern was to find a placid, well-broken mare about ten years old, and over a period of a few years gradually work up to animals suitable for shows and parades. The gentle mare, about the same age as the child learning to ride, could be trusted to take good care of the inexperienced rider in most situations, and most families preferred such a horse to a pony. In a year or two, as the young horseman became more skillful, he might improve to the point where he could be trusted with the raising of a colt from the mare, or he might want quicker results and ask that his parents buy a younger, faster horse that could compete in the small horse shows and would look good in the parades.

Once the parents started taking their young people to horse shows of any kind, they soon learned the advantages of buying a horse of one of the accepted breeds for show work, both for halter and performance classes. The strong tendency of middle-class families to own pedigreed dogs inclined them to buy pedigreed horses, especially when they realized that the initial price was rather unimportant. The heavy expense was in the day-to-day upkeep and the first-class equipment. It cost about the same to maintain a scrub as a registered animal of which the whole family could be proud.

When these people began looking for horses registered in a breed of light riding stock, they found there were only two with strong connections with western history and the old days of the open ranges. These were the Quarter Horse that was developed largely in Texas, and the Appaloosa from the Pacific Northwest.

The Quarter Horse is by far the most numerous of all the light saddle horses, with an estimated total of about a million, but it is rather difficult to arrive at any accurate figure. A current list of horse associations devoted to the registration of breeds lists four different breed registries for the Quarter Horse. Of these the American Quarter Horse Association is the largest, with a total of about 600,000 animals and a current annual rate of 60,000 new registrations. Since the Quarter Horse was originally considered a type rather than a breed, the sponsors registered animals already registered in established breeds such as the Arabian, Morgan, and Thoroughbred.

The Quarter Horse appeals to a great many people interested in western horses, for most of the animals are of the stock-horse type and they are closely associated with several phases of American history in Virginia, Kentucky, and Texas.

The second breed with a western heritage is the Appaloosa, something of an oddity in the roster of established breeds because of the distinctive coat pattern which it shares with no other breed. The Appaloosa has symmetrical dark spots on a white background, with the most prominent on the rump. This type of marking is not to be confused with the pinto, which has splotches of white and dark.

The highly colored Appaloosa has appealed greatly to the younger generation of riders both on account of its appearance and its history. It was a favored horse in ancient Persia, China, and Egypt, and was used by people of rank throughout Europe. It is closely associated with the Nez Percé Indians of the Columbia Basin and their great retreat in the War of 1877. Starting with a total of 339 registered animals in 1946, the breed has grown to about 126,000 in 1970, the fastest rate of growth shown by any breed during the period, and is now firmly in second place among the light-horse breeds in the United States, although it is still far behind the Quarter Horse in numbers.

The great success of the Quarter Horse registry and the Appaloosa registry has inspired the formation of many other associations, each devoted to the perpetuation of a certain strain of horse and of developing it into an accepted breed. A new breed can be established in a decade or two if the original type is well chosen and the foundation stock is very carefully selected. Then, under a strictly supervised breeding program, a number of the animals can be bred true to the chosen pattern, but it is usually rather difficult to secure public acceptance for the new breed. Some of the new associations have not established themselves yet, but they are registering horses for public sale. This gives the prospective buyer a wide choice of registered horses as long as he does not insist on owning an animal of a recognized breed.

Two other fine breeds, the Morgan and the Arabian, were used in the western stock country, but in general people who knew of these breeds thought they really belonged elsewhere.

The Morgan blood lines had always produced fine saddle horses of the sturdy stock-horse type and were well suited to the activities that interested young riders. They were beautiful, intelligent, and easily trained, but in the popular mind they were horses closely associated with Vermont and were used primarily for light harness work. Many of the best stories about Justin Morgan stressed his ability to pull heavy loads. His progeny were often valued as good trotting horses. Purebred Morgans and part Morgans were scattered throughout the western states and some ranchers specialized in raising them for saddle stock, but they were not featured in western fiction and western movies, so they did not acquire the acceptance they merited as stock horses. Since 1950 the breed has gained wider acceptance and the registry has increased rapidly. In 1958 only 870 new foals were registered, compared to 2,280 in 1969, a very substantial growth.

Arabian horses were also raised on western ranches, the center of the early development being in Oregon, where the breed has been fostered since 1900, and the largest Arabian Horse Show in the world is still held annually in Salem. Just over 30 percent of the total number of Arabians registered in the United States are owned in the three Pacific Coast states, and another 24 percent are in the mountains and on the plains. In spite of this strong showing in the West since 1900, the general public is inclined to associate Arabians with the exotic Near East and the deserts of Arabia and Africa. This conception was built up by many works of fiction, especially by Lew Wallace's novel *Ben-Hur*, with its great chariot race won by a team of four matched Arabians. Desert movies such as "The Sheik" and "The Desert Song" added to this concept. Arabians used in circuses and in parades usually carried riders in eastern costumes, and Arabians were featured in many paintings of European generals and nobility. In addition, the ordinary prospective horse buyer considered the Arabian to be high priced and too refined and delicate for range work.

In spite of this image the Arabian has been gaining rapidly in popularity in the period since 1950. The breeders are raising the heavier, stockier horse rather than the delicate type featured in so many of the paintings. Total registration in the United States increased from 7,680 in 1952 to 44,952 in 1969, and at present is increasing at about 15 percent each year.

The horse population of the United States, after several decades of constant decline, is now on the increase, with most of this increase in the accepted breeds. Scrub horses, nags, and misfits are dwindling in numbers, thus raising the average quality of American horses. The horse industry, with about four million animals, is becoming of enough importance to again attract the attention of the Department of Agriculture.

Throughout history the man on horseback has been given a special rating, and horsemen have condescendingly looked down from their lofty heights at the plodding pedestrian. Although the man in the saddle is physically only two or three feet higher than the man on the ground, psychologically he occupies a much loftier station. Also he has a thrill and a sense of power that comes from controlling a strong, well trained, spirited horse that he cannot get elsewhere.

For most horsemen, American and European, their riding unites them in spirit with the bold horsemen of history—the Mongols and Cossacks, Bedouins and Moors, vaqueros and gauchos, Plains Indians and cowboys. Their kinship to these colorful horsemen of the past leads them to prefer the sturdy, agile steeds of the open ranges and the accompanying range equipment and costumes. A good riding horse, while definitely a luxury item to most of them, brings a sense of fulfillment far beyond the monetary cost. In spite of all the machines now available for recreational use, the saddle horse has a secure place in the affections of modern man. Even in a forty-acre field a rider can escape for a time from the crowded, mechanized world into a brief enjoyment of that sense of belonging with those wild, free bands of galloping adventurers who have filled so many pages of history and romance.

Selected Bibliography

FOR DETAILED BIBLIOGRAPHICAL material on the early spread of horses from central Asia consult Glenn R. Vernon, *Man on Horseback* (Harper & Row, New York, 1964), and Francis Haines, *Appaloosa: The Spotted Horse in Art and History* (University of Texas Press, Austin, 1963). Vernon also has much good material on the development of horse gear. An extensive bibliography on Indian horses is in Frank Gilbert Roe, *The Indian and the Horse* (University of Oklahoma Press, Norman, 1955).

For material on the early Spanish horses read Bernal Díaz del Castillo, *The Conquest of New Spain* (Pelican paperback, Penguin Books, Baltimore, 1963); and R. B. Cunninghame Graham, *Horses of the Conquest* (ed. Robert Denhardt, University of Oklahoma Press, Norman, 1949), which includes accounts of several of the conquests. Herbert E. Bolton, *Coronado: Knight of Pueblo and Plains* (Whittlesey House, New York, 1949) has many references to horses.

Stewart Holbrook, *The Old Post Road* (McGraw-Hill, New York, 1962), deals with the early stage lines in New England. For the American West, accounts by two early travelers are valuable. George Catlin, *Indian Tribes of North America* (London, 1847) relates his experiences on the Great Plains. Lewis Hector Garrard, as a youth of seventeen, observed closely and wrote well of his travels and his horses in *Wah-to-yah and the Taos Trail* (first published 1851; 1938 edition ed. Ralph P. Bieber, Arthur H. Clarke Company, Glendale, California).

A good account of cavalry operations is Dee Alexander Brown, *Grierson's Raid* (University of Illinois, Urbana, 1954). A firsthand account of range life is Floyd C. Bard, *Horse Wrangler* (University of Oklahoma Press, Norman, 1960). Many additional details on horses in the West can be found in J. Frank Dobie, *The Mustangs* (Little, Brown and Company, Boston, 1952) and in Walker D. Wyman, *The Wild Horse of the West* (Caxton Printers, Caldwell, Idaho, 1946).

Quotations were used from the following:

CATLIN, GEORGE, *Indian Tribes of North America*. London, 1847.

CORTES, HERNANDO, *Five Letters, 1518–1526*, trans. by J. Bayard Morris. New York, Robert McBride & Co., 1929.

DÍAZ DEL CASTILLO, BERNAL, *The Discovery and Conquest of Mexico, 1517–1521*, trans. by A. P. Maudsley. London, G. Routledge and Sons, 1928.

DUKE, BASIL W., *History of Morgan's Cavalry*. Cincinnati, 1867.

GREGG, JOSIAH, *Commerce of the Prairies, or the journal of a Santa Fe trader, during eight expeditions across the great western prairies, and a residence of nearly nine years in Northern Mexico*. New York, 1844.

MILLER, JOHN ANDERSON, *Fares Please*. New York, Dover Publications, 1960.

RUXTON, GEORGE FREDERICK AUGUSTUS, *Adventures in Mexico and the Rocky Mountains*. London, J. Murray, 1861.

SEABRIGHT, THOMAS B., *The Old Pike: A History of the National Road*. Uniontown, Pa., published by the author, 1894.

STEWART, DESMOND. *Early Islam*, in *Great Ages of Man, A History of the World's Culture*. New York, Time, Inc., 1967.

THOMPSON, DAVID, *David Thompson's Narrative of his Explorations in Western America, 1784–1812*, ed. by J. B. Tyrell. Toronto, 1916.

Index